ROUTLEDGE LIBRARY EDITIONS: LIBRARY AND INFORMATION SCIENCE

Volume 34

END USER SEARCHING IN THE HEALTH SCIENCES

END USER SEARCHING IN THE HEALTH SCIENCES

Edited by
M. SANDRA WOOD, ELLEN BRASSIL HORAK
AND BONNIE SNOW

LONDON AND NEW YORK

First published in 1986 by The Haworth Press, Inc.

This edition first published in 2020
by Routledge
2 Park Square, Milton Park, Abingdon, Oxon OX14 4RN

and by Routledge
52 Vanderbilt Avenue, New York, NY 10017

Routledge is an imprint of the Taylor & Francis Group, an informa business

© 1986 The Haworth Press, Inc.

All rights reserved. No part of this book may be reprinted or reproduced or utilised in any form or by any electronic, mechanical, or other means, now known or hereafter invented, including photocopying and recording, or in any information storage or retrieval system, without permission in writing from the publishers.

Trademark notice: Product or corporate names may be trademarks or registered trademarks, and are used only for identification and explanation without intent to infringe.

British Library Cataloguing in Publication Data
A catalogue record for this book is available from the British Library

ISBN: 978-0-367-34616-4 (Set)
ISBN: 978-0-429-34352-0 (Set) (ebk)
ISBN: 978-0-367-37601-7 (Volume 34) (hbk)
ISBN: 978-0-367-37613-0 (Volume 34) (pbk)
ISBN: 978-0-429-35526-4 (Volume 34) (ebk)

Publisher's Note
The publisher has gone to great lengths to ensure the quality of this reprint but points out that some imperfections in the original copies may be apparent.

Disclaimer
The publisher has made every effort to trace copyright holders and would welcome correspondence from those they have been unable to trace.

End User Searching in the Health Sciences

M. Sandra Wood
Ellen Brassil Horak
Bonnie Snow
Editors

The Haworth Press
New York • London

End User Searching in the Health Sciences is monographic supplement #2 to the journal *Medical Reference Services Quarterly*, Volume 5, 1986. It is not supplied as part of the subscription to the journal, but is available from the publisher at an additional charge.

© 1986 by The Haworth Press, Inc. All rights reserved. No part of this work may be reproduced or utilized in any form or by any means, electronic or mechanical, including photocopying, microfilm and recording, or by any information storage and retrieval system, without permission in writing from the publisher. Printed in the United States of America.

The Haworth Press, Inc., 28 East 22 Street, New York, NY 10010-6194
EUROSPAN/Haworth, 3 Henrietta Street, London WC2E 8LU England

Library of Congress Cataloging-in-Publication Data

End user searching in the health sciences.

    "Monographic supplement to the journal Medical reference services quarterly, volume 5, 1986"—Verso t.p.
    Bibliography: p.
    Includes index.
    1. Information storage and retrieval systems—Medicine. 2. Information storage and retrieval systems—Public health. 3. Medical libraries—Automation. 4. Libraries, Public health—Automation. 5. Library catalogs and readers. 6. Catalogs, On-line. 7. Information retrieval. 8. On-line bibliographic searching. I. Wood, M. Sandra. II. Horak, Ellen Brassil. III. Snow, Bonnie. IV. Medical references services quarterly. Vol. 5. 1986 (Supplement).
Z699.5.M39E53   1986   025'.0661   86-9886

ISBN 0-86656-465-9

CONTENTS

Introduction   ix
    M. Sandra Wood
    Ellen Brassil Horak
    Bonnie Snow

I. THE ENVIRONMENT OF END USER SEARCHING   1

Overview of End User Searching in the Health Sciences:
An Opinion Paper   3
    Winifred Sewell

Online Education for Health Professionals   15
    Ellen Brassil Horak

Determining Content and Structure of Online Educational
Materials   31
    Bonnie Snow

End User Searching: Implications for Library Planning   53
    W. Ellen McDonell

End User Search Systems: An Overview   65
    James Shedlock

Issues in Mounting a Local MEDLINE Database   85
    Frieda O. Weise
    Gary A. Freiburger

Personal Information Management: An Overview   95
        Nancy G. Bruce
        Anna Thérèse McGowan

II. END USER SEARCHING PROGRAMS   111

Training the End User: The Stanford University Medical
    Center Experience   113
        Gloria A. Linder
        Richard A. Lenon
        Valerie Su
        Joseph G. Wible
        Peter Stangl

Teaching End User Searching in a Health Sciences Center   127
        Alice C. Wygant

U-Search: A Program to Teach End User Searching
    at an Academic Health Sciences Library   137
        Vicki L. Glasgow
        Gertrude Foreman

Implementing End User Systems at the Massachusetts
    General Hospital Health Sciences Libraries   149
        Rhonda A. Rios Kravitz
        Ellen R. Westling

The BRS/AFTER DARK Search Service in a Health Sciences
    Library   163
        Marjorie Simon

III. THE END USER'S VIEWPOINT   179

Search Strategy Outline: An Approach to Assist the
    Occasional End Searcher   181
        George Nowacek
        Robert H. Hodge

Physician Searching: A Rural Hospital Experience   189
Frederick J. Myers

Confessions of an End User   197
David N. Neubauer

End User Searching in the Small Hospital Setting   205
Corrine R. McNabb

IV. BIBLIOGRAPHY AND GLOSSARY

End User Searching: A Selected Annotated Bibliography   213
M. Sandra Wood

Glossary   275
Compiled by Bonnie Snow

Index   283

Introduction

Over a decade has passed since online searching was introduced to library public services. Currently, developments such as electronic publishing, local area networks, full-text online, and the new information technologies have far-reaching implications for online searching and assure its continued evolution. Few aspects of the online industry have sparked as much controversy and have engaged as varied a cross-section of spokespersons as the trend toward end user searching. In the past, professionals such as lawyers have been trained to search online databases; however, the market now includes an inordinate number of products aimed at health sciences personnel. In fact, database producers and vendors have developed sophisticated programs aimed directly at the end user; librarians are being asked by users to recommend search services and to provide courses on how to use these systems.

This current marketing trend will have an extensive impact on the future role of librarians and on information management education. Involvement with remote, computerized information resources is no longer the province of trained search intermediaries only. User-friendly or menu-driven software interfaces, as well as information management education activities, have extended admission into the world of online that was once almost exclusively the domain of librarians. End user searching has also enabled clinical departments, research labs, offices, and virtually any setting having access to a simple data terminal to join libraries as nodes in an electronic information network.

Health professionals have been enticed into searching online databases partly because of market factors, such as the appeal of microcomputers and vigorous promotion of user-friendly software. Much of the popular literature describes end user searching as a market trend and as the latest fancy of computer enthusiasts. Nevertheless, this supplement attests to the fact that it is easier to herald any trend than it is to guide its implementation. The following papers cover the larger context of end user searching, such as personal information management and online education, that far exceeds the sometimes oversimplified perspective offered by the computer industry.

Many published accounts of end user experiences and training efforts in health sciences libraries have heretofore been scattered and diffuse. Instead, this monographic supplement consolidates the viewpoints of both information specialists and end users, and documents programs already in existence. Many facets of end user searching and its effect on the roles of both information specialists and health professionals are explored. While the focus is on health sciences libraries, educational and information management principles discussed within the papers are applicable to all types of libraries.

This supplement also reflects the commitment of many libraries to ensure effective online searching by their users. As user advocates, libraries are relaying the concerns of information consumers to the commercial sector. In addition, libraries are helping users compare available products by hosting seminars or providing consultant services. As a result, librarians have become more conversant with related disciplines, such as education, business, and computer science.

Librarians who teach end users must themselves develop more diversified skills than those warranted by a custodial approach to reference service. The end user searching debate is in some ways merely a variation on early opposition to bibliographic instruction. Even before online searching, many librarians and users charged that bibliographic instruction was tantamount to librarians pushing their responsibilities onto users instead of perfecting their own craft. This work takes off at a point well beyond the controversy over whose role is appropriate to what function, however. Instead, the reader will encounter many positive approaches that are based on the assumption that end user searching is here to stay. The authors share a number of ideas that will be useful simultaneously to users and librarians.

M. Sandra Wood
Ellen Brassil Horak
Bonnie Snow

EDITORS' NOTE

Terminology is always a problem in any new field or subject area. The concept of users performing their own searches has been referred to in a variety of ways, including "end user searching," "nonmediated searching," and "patron searching." Of the terms in use, "end user" seemed the most descriptive and was therefore selected as the preferred term by the editors. The most difficult decision, however, involved the spelling of "end user." Three versions are found in the literature: "end user," "end-user," and "end-user." "Enduser" was not considered since it is not truly a word. Grammatically, "end user" is the noun, while "end-user" is the adjective. For simplicity, "end user," as two words, unhyphenated, whether in the noun or adjective form, was selected in an attempt to standardize the format.

I. THE ENVIRONMENT OF END USER SEARCHING

Many converging environmental forces have influenced the trend toward end user searching. These include: technological developments of "user-friendly" systems and front ends; increased sales of microcomputers and modems; and aggressive marketing by database vendors directly to the end user. The papers in this section explore these and other environmental factors. Sewell views end user searching as part of the health information transfer process, and traces these needs full circle from the creator of knowledge to the end user. Horak explores online searching as a content area and an educational activity in the health professional curriculum. Snow presents a detailed look at how to determine the content and structure of online educational materials—how and what to teach the end user. McDonell considers the role of fundamental library assets in planning for a future of extensive end user searching. An overview of the user-friendly online search systems currently available is provided by Shedlock. Weise and Freeburger discuss factors to consider when deciding whether to mount a subset of the MEDLINE file on a local computer. One of the final uses for information which is accessed online by end users is to download the data into a personal information file; Bruce and McGowan overview the area of personal information management.

Overview of End User Searching in the Health Sciences: An Opinion Paper

Winifred Sewell

ABSTRACT. End user online searching is a part of the health professional's information transfer process. That searching is affected by each participant in the process—creator of knowledge, primary publisher, secondary publisher, vendor, librarian, and end user. Critical needs for optimizing such searching are categorized under: awareness, accessibility, and assistance. Satisfying all of those needs will facilitate the incorporation of online searching into end users' problem solving.

The term "end user" has appeared frequently since the advent of online searching. It refers to that scientist or practitioner who consolidates into his own thinking some or all of the information that has been transmitted to him through an information transfer chain. Sometimes he serves a dual function by writing a paper about findings, thus becoming the creator of information, which starts a new trip through the information transfer path.

THE INFORMATION TRANSFER PATH

The information transfer process traditionally proceeds in turn through the information's creator, primary publisher, secondary publisher, librarian, and user—or end user. Recently, there has been an addition. Between the secondary publisher and the librarian, the vendor of online bibliographic databases has been inserted.

This work has been partially supported by NIH Grant LM 03758 from the National Library of Medicine.

Winifred Sewell is an adjunct lecturer at the University of Maryland College of Library and Information Services and a consultant. She has formerly held positions with the University of Maryland School of Pharmacy, the National Library of Medicine, Squibb Institute for Medical Research, and Wellcome Research Laboratories. She holds a B.A. from Washington State University, a B.S. (M.S. equivalent) in Library Science from Columbia University, and an honorary doctorate from the Philadelphia College of Pharmacy and Science.

Originally there was no formal information transfer process, because end users performed all the functions. At first they communicated directly with one another either face to face or through letters. Separate steps in the information transfer continuum were needed to improve access to information when an increasing number of scientists made direct communication difficult. From the time of Oldenburg,[1] when letters among scientists were distributed in the first periodical, researchers and practitioners have edited and refereed their journals and are primarily responsible for their content. Like primary periodicals, secondary publications were started by the creators and users of knowledge to make it easy to find information that had appeared in journal articles. The first librarians in health sciences libraries were also physicians. Libraries were started because of the need to collect in one place the large number of primary and secondary publications that health scientists had created.

As the number of health scientists has increased and publications have grown exponentially, professionals in the fields of primary and secondary publication and librarianship have emerged to perform many of the functions in the information transfer chain formerly carried out by physicians and other health professionals. Each of the new professionals has, in turn, made refinements to improve the performance of his or her part of the information transfer process. For example, the secondary publisher has added classification schemes and tree structures to bring hierarchically-related information together. Librarians have added not only classification schemes but, more recently, integrated systems that ease access to bibliographic records and publications containing wanted information.

While the information transfer chain is logically a continuum from the creator of knowledge through the various intermediaries to the end user, in fact the various participants often deal directly with one another. Librarians work with all of the other participants in the process. As the new role of librarians as outlined in the Matheson report[2] develops, their involvement is likely to become even greater.

ONLINE INFORMATION TRANSFER

Other direct communication across the information transfer continuum includes transmission of scientific data between scientists through online conferences and bulletin boards sometimes bypassing journal publication. The concern of this *Medical Reference Services Quarterly Supplement* is that the vendor is beginning to market online services directly to the end user, omitting the mediation of the library. That is what is meant by end user online searching: searching by end users themselves in an online database, with library assistance optional and frequently skipped.

Omitting the library is of concern because online searching was a refinement developed primarily by librarians from their need to do searches for their clientele more quickly and satisfactorily than could be done manually. The first online searching in a medical library was initiated by Irwin Pizer and others at the State University of New York (SUNY) using the National Library of Medicine's MEDLARS (Medical Literature Analysis and Retrieval System) database.[3] Soon afterwards, AIM/TWX, the predecessor of MEDLINE, was begun by the National Library of Medicine with the same database.[4]

As these systems evolved, specialized groups, or vendors, took over their management and became new participants in the information transfer chain. The vendor's function was thus created out of the needs of librarians to serve end users rather than being initiated directly by end users themselves. For example, the early SUNY operation was the predecessor of BRS (Bibliographic Retrieval Service).[5]

Online searching has had an influence on, and been influenced by, virtually every participant in the information transfer chain. The author of this paper has supported information transfer for end users over more than forty years, as a librarian in the pharmaceutical industry, as a participant in the creation of MEDLARS, and as a resource person in an academic health sciences center. To understand academic scientists' needs, she instituted a study in the fall of 1974. She observed pathologists and pharmacists as they searched National Library of Medicine online databases by themselves at the University of Maryland in Baltimore. Transaction logs, questionnaires, interviews, and a *Micromanual** to aid end user searching have all been used to analyze end user attitudes and behavior.[6-9] Throughout the remainder of this paper, this work will be referred to as the Maryland study.

From the background of her previous experience and the

---

*The *Micromanual* can be obtained from Drug Intelligence Publications, 4720 Montgomery Lane—Suite 807, Bethesda, MD 20814. Single copies, prepaid, are $6.50; five or more, prepaid, are $5.50 per copy. If billed, the price is $8.00 per copy.

Maryland work, the author will discuss the needs of medical end users which she believes will be critical in determining future trends in their online searching. These needs fall broadly into three categories: awareness of possibilities, accessibility of services, and assistance. Since all participants in the information transfer cycle play a part in creating the needs and in satisfying them, their roles will be described in turn, with special emphasis on the librarian.

CREATORS OF INFORMATION

Today scientists and practitioners are using computers in every phase of their work from data collection and statistical analysis to reporting their findings with a word processor. These activities create the proper climate for online searching by the end user. It is made convenient by access to microcomputers purchased for other purposes.

One observation of the Maryland study was that online searches were sometimes performed during research discussions, so that use of information coalesced during online searching into creation of knowledge. There has always been a critical need for end users to incorporate recorded knowledge into their thinking as they create new ideas. As such incorporation becomes more feasible, end user online searching will be an important part of problem solving by health professionals.

PRIMARY PUBLISHERS

The computer revolution has had a profound effect on all publication, and primary publications are no exception. Journal and book publishers are providing full-text information directly to online vendors, without benefit of the manipulation of the secondary abstracting and indexing services. Concurrently, references to the same text are indexed and abstracted by the secondary services for their bibliographic databases. But finding a reference to a paper through such secondary publications is only the first step in reaching the knowledge in the original. End users want to read the article itself as soon as its existence is discovered.

Full-text searching as it is available in online services today is more difficult for both the librarian and the end user than simple bibliographic searching. There is a critical need to combine the ease of traditional searching for references with immediate and direct access to the full text of those references. Ideally, end users would find a citation on a topic of interest through a simple MEDLINE-like search. If the title looked interesting, they would then ask for and see the full article online as easily as they now display abstracts.

SECONDARY PUBLISHERS OF ABSTRACTING AND INDEXING PUBLICATIONS

Publication of virtually all abstracting and indexing services has been computerized for many years. Such mechanization has made it possible to create multiple outputs from the single input of a piece of bibliographic information. Making their databases available through an online vendor was simply an additional revenue producing innovation of secondary publishers. Though marketing of online databases may decrease the sale of their printed counterparts,[10] the incorporation of secondary service products into vendor databanks is at the heart of the online industry.

In health sciences abstracting and indexing services, there are special practices that add to the power of the systems, but are difficult for end users to comprehend and remember. In MEDLINE, these are subheadings and explosions. Explosions increase recall by collecting hierarchically subsidiary terms when a single term is exploded. Subheadings improve precision by subdividing the topic of a term into just one aspect of it. In EMBASE, EMTAGS and EMCLAS numbers perform some of the same functions. In all systems, if one knows these practices well, one also knows when to revert to natural language to locate topics too obscure or recent to have found their way into a controlled vocabulary such as MEDLINE's *MeSH (Medical Subject Headings)*, or EMBASE's *MALIMET.*

Librarians have contributed substantially to the power of secondary services, either directly, as in MEDLARS, or indirectly through users groups or individual suggestions. Meanwhile, the health scientists, whose antecedents created the secondary services, are barely aware of the services' names, let alone the retrieval power added by the refinements just discussed. Though secondary publishers have always promoted their products to end users as well as to librarians, there has been an implicit assumption that the librarian or other intermediary would do the online searching. Little has been done to make the changes accessible to other than a sophisticated professional searcher.

The Maryland study confirmed health professionals' difficulty with MEDLINE subheadings and explosions. Failure to explode when it was possible accounted for 91 of 174 problems in a follow-up study, but usually caused searchers to miss less than a third of what they would have liked to retrieve. Problems with subheadings represented only 13 percent of the failures observed, but when they occurred, searchers missed 85 to 100 percent of what they wanted.

There is a critical need for secondary services to make the power of their systems more easily accessible in end user searching. In the case of MEDLINE, for instance, the end user would be helped if the system automatically defaulted to explosions for all terms that had additional terms listed under them in the tree structures. There would be a number of problems to be solved to make such defaults work smoothly. Until the system they are using contains such defaults, however, end users will miss some references they want, no matter how well they are trained or how much a vendor's "user-friendly" interface tries to guide them.

VENDORS

Vendors are a new phenomenon which have appeared in the online age. They are the organizations which have built up large computer databanks of bibliographic and other databases for access at a terminal or personal computer through communications networks.

Once they had saturated the market of libraries and other intermediaries who provide services to end users, vendors naturally turned to end users themselves as potential consumers who would expand their sales. In addition to their traditional systems, major vendors have created simpler systems for end users.[11-13] In this discussion, vendors also include those marketing directly to physicians,[14-15] producers of software that makes it easy for an inexperienced user to search one of the available online systems,[16-21] and such variants as a separate computer (Easynet)[22] that is a "one-stop shopping" means of access to any major databank. Most of these "user-friendly" systems are based on the premise that end users want few options and need menus to aid them in performing their searches. But vendors have concentrated on the parts of the systems that are easiest for end users to learn: the techniques of the search.

Errors with techniques occurred without correction in fewer than 15 percent of the sessions in the Maryland study. Problems with explosions, subheadings, and natural language were far more frequent. In fact, the Maryland end users soon learned to tailor their print commands to include the abstract, or list just title and source. For them the limited options of the newer user-friendly systems would be inhibiting.

Subheading and explosion capabilities are available in all of the user friendly systems that have mounted MEDLINE, but it is difficult for an inexperienced user to find or use them. Such vendor products as miniMEDLINE[23] and PaperChase,[24-27] which cover only MEDLINE, have made these special features easier to use than have the systems sold by major vendors. There are critical needs for vendors to assist secondary publishers in making the special features of their systems easily accessible to end users, to make full text more readily displayable as already discussed, and to improve the flexibility of their systems.

LIBRARIES AND LIBRARIANS

Health sciences librarians have been involved in online searching by end users since the beginning of such searching. The end user was in the minds of the creators of AIM/TWX, the predecessor of MEDLINE,[28] as well as of those librarians who developed the even earlier SUNY[29-30]—the original system, not the SUNY backup to MEDLINE which became familiar in the later 1970s.

There were early experiments by librarians to test the success of end user searching. In this country, Lancaster experimented with health professional searching of MEDLINE[31] and EARS (Epilepsy Abstracts Retrieval System).[32] A little later, Olson had sixteen end users run their own MEDLINE searches in the library of Washington University (St. Louis) to see how they interacted with the system while online.[33] Perhaps the most extensive early experiment was carried out in Great Britain.[34-36] Special programs were written for end users as part of the overall MEDUSA project, which studied use of MEDLINE by intermediaries and end users in various settings throughout the United Kingdom. The end user portion of the project was eventually dropped because of the expense and time required.[37] In 1974, the Maryland study introduced National Library of Medicine databases to pathologists and pharmacists in their work places, and these groups have continued to search ever since. More recently, library staffs have designed systems to make MEDLINE user-friendly.[38-40]

Health sciences librarians can continue to assist the end user with online searching in three ways. First, the Maryland study suggests that librarians will retain their searching function. End user searchers who also had library searches done were usually ready to acknowledge those from the library as better and more exhaustive. The librarian should prepare for the most difficult searches as end users learn to perform the simple ones.

Second, the librarian will instruct the end user. The Maryland study indicated that it is unwise to attempt to teach end users a great deal of detail at any one time. Long training sessions may bolster the physicians' image of librarians. Short sessions or one-on-one training as needed, however, are more helpful and better remembered. As other papers in this supplement suggest, there are many ways to teach which can and should be shaped to individual situations. The critical needs are for librarians to mold their training methods to their particular end users and to be readily available and well prepared to answer questions by end users on search strategy, hardware, and software.

Third, the librarian can help in developing systems expressly for end users. One example is miniMEDLINE. As libraries obtain subsets of MEDLINE for local use, the critical need is for them to make modifications that will help end users with subheadings, explosions, and other key features. In addition, librarians should suggest such modifications to secondary services and vendors.

END USERS

End users have been discussed as creators of information and in their relationships with other participants in their information transfer process. Now the basic principles of how they search online will be summarized. End users may fall into three broad groups: those for whom bibliographic searching is a part of their primary job, such as drug information specialists; "hobbyists" who enjoy the "game" of making the computer serve them in a variety of ways; and the run-of-the-mill scientists or practitioners who have a need for bibliographic information and will search for themselves to find it if that method is easy and convenient.

Most of the Maryland study searchers belong to the last group, representing all academic levels, in proportions corresponding fairly closely to those of the total group of searchers and nonsearchers. One frequent searcher at Maryland wrote that she chose to be a scientist rather than a computer specialist because she found biological sciences more interesting, and that her contact with the computer was "best kept to a minimum." In short, the average end user is interested in the results of the search rather than the search process—that is, in the end, not the means.

Nearly half of the pathologists and pharmacists who had a need for information from MEDLINE or other NLM databases actually searched for themselves in the Maryland study. Though specific figures have not been found, this appears to be a higher proportion than in other studies, except possibly those of miniMEDLINE[41] and PaperChase.[42] The only criterion that separates searchers from nonsearchers in the Maryland study is a perceived need by online searchers to get answers quickly. The Maryland study group showed little concern with cost. Though searching by themselves was free, one of the major reasons for preferring library searches was that they were "cheaper" even though there was a charge. A major component of costs in the minds of end users appears to be that of their own time.

A critical need is for end user searching to reach all to whom it could be useful, so that those who are still "afraid" of the computer or unaware of its advantages will use online searching as an option whenever it is their best alternative for problem solving.

The Maryland study confirms that convenience is the primary reason for deciding to search for onself. Besides being the first choice as a reason for nonmediated searching on a questionnaire, convenience was demonstrated to be a motivator in practice. The average number of searches performed by the 100 active searchers was 900 to 1000 a year, but the numbers fluctuated substantially as the terminals became more or less easy to use or were moved to more or less convenient areas.

There is thus a critical need to assure that end user searching is convenient. This will most likely mean making it available in the health professionals' work area, with librarians readily accessible when assistance is desired.

CONCLUSIONS

If end users in general are to search for themselves whenever such searching is their best option for problem solving, the critical needs discussed throughout this article must be met. They are consolidated and restated as follows:

1. *Awareness*. All health professionals who could use online services, whether they are now computer literate or not, should be made aware of the potential of such searching for their problem solving. They should be able to evaluate various systems for their use and to avoid those which do not make the full power of a database readily available. At least, they should know what they are missing if they choose an overly simplistic system. The librarian should be an impartial adviser in these evaluations.
2. *Accessibility*. Online retrieval services should be conveniently accessible to end users in their work places so that health professionals can incorporate recorded knowledge into their thinking as they create new ideas. Secondary services and vendors should modify their systems so that end users can take advantage of their special features. Librarians should also consider such modifications if they make subsets of MEDLINE available locally. Vendors should provide immediate and direct access to the full text of a paper once a reference to it has been found. Other display capabilities should be more flexible than they are at present.
3. *Assistance*. The librarian should be readily available when and where help is needed with end user searching, and should be thoroughly acquainted with hardware and software as well as all health sciences databases. Training for end users should be carefully adapted to their individual needs.

If everyone involved in the information transfer process helps to fulfill their online searching needs, end users can become more productive health scientists than they have ever been.

REFERENCES

1. Kronick, David A., assisted by Winters, Wendell D. *The Literature of the Life Sciences. Reading, Writing, Research*. Philadelphia, PA: ISI Press, 1985, pp. 22, 24.
2. Matheson, Nina W., and Cooper, John A. D. "Academic Information in the Aca-

demic Health Sciences Center. Roles for the Library in Information Management." *Journal of Medical Education* 57 (October 1982, Part 2): i-iv, 1-93.

3. Pizer, Irwin H. "Looking Backward, 1984-1959: Twenty-five Years of Library Automation—A Personal View." *Bulletin of the Medical Library Association* 72 (October 1984):335- 48.

4. Katter, Robert V., and McCarn, Davis B. "AIM-TWX: An Experimental On-line Bibliographic Retrieval System." In: Walker, D. E., ed. *Interactive Bibliographic Search: The User/Computer Interface.* Montvale, NJ: AFIPS Press, 1971, pp. 121- 41.

5. Pizer, *loc. cit.*

6. Sewell, Winifred, and Teitelbaum, Sandra. "Preliminary Observations of Nonmediated Search Behavior of Pathologists and Pharmacists." *Proceedings of the 45th ASIS Annual Meeting* 19(1982):276-8.

7. Teitelbaum, Sandra, and Sewell, Winifred. "Survey of Attitudes of Pathologists and Pharmacists Toward Nonmediated Online Searching." *Proceedings of the 45th ASIS Annual Meeting* 19(1982):298-300.

8. Sewell, Winifred, and Bevan, Alice. "Nonmediated Use of MEDLINE and TOXLINE by Pathologists and Pharmacists." *Bulletin of the Medical Library Association* 64(October 1976):382-91.

9. Sewell, Winifred, and Teitelbaum, Sandra. "Observation of End User Online Searching Behavior Over Eleven Years." *Journal of The American Society for Information Science* 36(1986). Accepted for publication.

10. Hitchingham, Eileen; Titus, Elizabeth; and Pettengill, Richard. "A Survey of Database Use at the Reference Desk." *Online* 9(March 1984):44-50.

11. Tenopir, Carol. "Dialog's Knowledge Index and BRS/After Dark: Database Searching on Personal Computers." *Library Journal* 108(March 1, 1983):471- 4.

12. Clancy, Stephen. "BRS/Saunders Colleague: An Information Service for Medical Professionals." *Database* 8(June 1985):108-21.

13. Baker, Carole A. "Colleague: A Comprehensive Online Medical Library for the End User." *Medical Reference Services Quarterly* 3(Winter 1984):13-26.

14. Nathanson, Michael. "Physicians Tap into AMA/NET." *Modern Healthcare* 12(November 1982):86, 88.

15. "Minet Transmits Disease Alerts." *Online Review* 8(August 1984):291.

16. Levy, Louise R. "Gateway Software: Is It for You?" *Online* 8(November 1984):67-79.

17. Kesselman, Martin. "Front-end/Gateway Software: Availability and Usefulness." *SR Library Software Review* 4(March/April 1985):67-70.

18. Tenopir, Carol. "Online Information in the Health Sciences." *Library Journal* 108(October 15, 1983):1932-3.

19. Tenopir, Carol. "Database Access Software." *Library Journal* 109(October 1, 1984):1828-9.

20. Tenopir, Carol. " 'Other' Bibliographic Systems." *Library Journal* 109(November 1, 1984):2008-9.

21. Tenopir, Carol. "Systems for End Users: Are There End Users for the Systems?" *Library Journal* 110(June 15, 1985):40-1.

22. O'Leary, Mick. "EasyNet: Doing it All for the End-User." *Online* 9(July 1985):106-13.

23. Broering, Naomi C. "The miniMEDLINE SYSTEM: A Library-Based End-User Search System." *Bulletin of the Medical Library Association* 73(April 1985):138- 45.

24. Bleich, Howard L.; Jackson, Jerome D.; and Rosenberg, Harold A. "PaperChase: A Program to Search the Medical Literature." *MD Computing* 2(March/April 1985):54-9.

25. Horowitz, Gary L.; Jackson, Jerome D.; and Bleich, Howard L. "PaperChase. Self-Service Bibliographic Retrieval." *JAMA* 250(November 11, 1983):2494-9.

26. Horowitz, G. L.; Jackson, J. D.; and Bleich, H. L. "PaperChase: Computerized Bibliographic Retrieval to Answer Clinical Questions." *Methods of Information in Medicine* 22(October 1983):183-8.

27. Horowitz, Gary L., and Bleich, Howard L. "PaperChase: A Computer Program to Search the Medical Literature." *New England Journal of Medicine* 305(October 15, 1981): 924-30.

28. Katter, *loc. cit.*

29. Pizer, *loc. cit.*

30. Egeland, Janet. "User-Interaction in the State University of New York (SUNY) Biomedical Communication Network." In: Walker, D. E., ed. *Interactive Bibliographic Search: The User/Computer Interface.* Montvale, NJ: AFIPS Press, 1971, pp. 105-20.

31. Lancaster, F. Wilfrid. "Evaluation of On-line Searching in MEDLARS (AIM-TWX) by Biomedical Practitioners." Occasional papers no. 101. Urbana, IL: University of Illinois Graduate School of Library Science, February 1972.

32. Lancaster, F. W.; Rapport, Richard L.; and Penry, J. Kiffin. "Evaluating the Effectiveness of an On-line, Natural Language Retrieval System." *Information Storage and Retrieval* 8(1972):223-45.

33. Olson, Paul E. "Mechanization of Library Procedures in the Medium-sized Medical Library: XV. A Study of the Interaction of Nonlibrarian Searchers with the MEDLINE Retrieval System." *Bulletin of the Medical Library Association* 63(January 1975):35-41.

34. Barber, A. Stephanie; Barraclough, Elizabeth D.; and Gray, W. Alexander. "On-line Information Retrieval as a Scientists [!] Tool." *Information Storage and Retrieval* 9(August 1973):429-40.

35. Barber, A. S., and Emmerson, J. S. "Development of Medlars Services in Newcastle upon Tyne." In: Jeffreys, A., ed. *The Art of the Librarian.* Newcastle upon Tyne: Oriel Press, 1973, pp. 94-114.

36. Barber, A. Stephanie; Barraclough, Elizabeth D.; and Gray, W. A. "Closing the Gap Between the Medical Researcher and the Literature." *British Medical Journal* 1(February 5, 1972):368-70.

37. Harley, A. J. "The UK MEDLARS Service: A Personal View of its First Decade." *Aslib Proceedings* 29(September 1977):320-25.

38. Broering, *loc. cit.*

39. Doszkocs, Tamas E.; Rapp, Barbara A.; and Schoolman, Harold M. "Automated Information Retrieval in Science and Technology." *Science* 208(April 4, 1980):25-30.

40. Doszkocs, Tamas E., and Rapp, Barbara A. "Searching MEDLINE in English: A Prototype User Interface with Natural Language Query, Ranked Output, and Relevance Feedback." *Proceedings of the American Society for Information Science* 16(1979):131-9.

41. Broering, *loc. cit.*

42. Horowitz and Bleich, *loc. cit.*

Online Education for Health Professionals

Ellen Brassil Horak

ABSTRACT. Online searching has become both a content area and an educational activity in the health professional curriculum. In their new role of online educators, librarians should emphasize the principles and concepts of online searching along with its mechanical aspects. As a means of augmenting the knowledge gained during formal schooling, online searching renews learning and lessens user reliance on memorization. Health sciences librarians conducting online training for users have become key participants in their institution's educational program. Subsequently, they should adopt formal educational procedures and ensure that planning is consistent with the aims of their institution.

Memory . . . is primarily a collection of inference rules describing mechanisms that can be used to reconstruct facts . . . knowledge of mechanisms is therefore central both to learning new things and to solving problems.—J.H. Larkin

INTRODUCTION

Converging trends in the information industry and the health sciences curriculum are forging a new alliance between librarians and educators. The exponential growth of medical knowledge, widespread formalization of library user education programs for

---

Ellen Brassil Horak is Director, Health Sciences Library, The Mount Sinai Hospital, Hartford, Connecticut. She was previously Head, Information Management Education Services at the Health Sciences Library, the University of North Carolina, Chapel Hill. Ms. Horak received an M.S.L.S. from Simmons College, Boston, Massachusetts and edits the User Education Column for *MRSQ*.

I wish to acknowledge Mr. Samuel Hitt, Director, Health Sciences Library, the University of North Carolina, Chapel Hill, as an early proponent of the library's educational role and the importance of effective information management by users. I am also grateful to Jack for his encouragement.

health professionals, the application of information technology to medical education, and other factors are fostering a climate charged with cooperation—an atmosphere where everyone is becoming better acquainted with one another's trade. It has become commonplace to find librarians appointed to the curriculum committees of medical schools and clinicians participating in online user group sessions or consulting *MeSH* volumes. Both librarians and health scientists are promoting database searching as a means of keeping pace with the steady growth of biomedical knowledge. Within the present milieu of professional retooling and interaction between information providers and health professionals, the Matheson report advocates diversifying information specialists' functions to create a "boundary spanning" of teaching and information management skills.[1] The report also urges medical educators, health sciences professionals, and librarians to join forces in support of formal training in information management.[2]

This paper examines end user searching within the overall context of formal health professional education. End user searching is presented as a method of clinical problem solving and as a means of independent learning for both students and professionals in the health sciences. The association between end user searching and education in the health professions is evidenced by the integration of online training into a variety of medical education programs. Whether or not an end user searching program enjoys curriculum support, sponsoring libraries are emerging as significant teaching arms within their institutions. It is hoped that the following treatment of end user searching as an educational issue will challenge popular emphasis on the role of the microcomputer. How many librarians can recall users expressing interest in doing their own online searching but dismissing the need for any training because they already use one of the information utilities such as CompuServe, or they know all about their microcomputer's operating system *and* how to program. It is possible that librarians who feature online demonstrations in conjunction with computer fairs perpetuate the myth of an exclusive association between end user searching and microcomputers. Although the mechanical aspects of online searching are important, and without denying that searching with a microcomputer offers new and unique capabilities, the implications of end user searching as an educational pursuit are stressed here. Many of the following ideas that cite examples from medical education are applicable to all education in the health fields and in any health care environment.

Even though information management concepts predate mainframes and microcomputers, the dazzle and visibility of computer technology has captured the attention of both information scientists and health professionals. Unfortunately, inclusion of courses on traditional information management topics is not a contingency for launching an online training program. Any library's user education roster that excludes coverage of research strategy formulation, or that omits discussion of the printed indexes and abstracts that correspond to online databases, equips its user population with a limited command of available information. Instead, libraries should emphasize that online searching is only one method of information retrieval or one phase of the process of information management. User education programs that are limited to online searching per se, ignoring subject matter that is independent of online searching, such as principles of file management or sources of health statistics, deny users a balanced appreciation for traditional information formats. Similarly, an online instruction program ought to include preliminary sessions that cover topics in manual searching. Such classes could be optional and designed to accelerate learning for less sophisticated users.

Some of the information world's own enthusiasm can mislead users to equate online searching with microcomputer searching, and confuse information literacy with computer literacy. One cannot help but consider the disproportionate share of the online industry's end user product line that is targeted at health professionals. The health professional, on the other hand, is inundated with promotional material that does little to suggest the intellectual aspects of online searching. Health sciences librarians must intervene to help users appreciate the dimensions of online searching other than equipment that the commercial sector sometimes ignores. The computer vendors are not solely responsible for user misconceptions, however. Owing to the visible costs of equipment, users themselves might assign greater importance to the mechanics of software installation, communication protocols, and terminal settings, rather than the conceptual aspects of information management.

Nevertheless, user fascination with new technology has helped librarians gain access to the classroom, after years of undaunted effort infiltrating curriculum groups, saturating the agendas of library committees, and negotiating with department chairpersons. Since end user searching often implies "on site" searching in the office, clinic, or any one of a number of places away from the library, users can anticipate preparing for the absence of trained intermediaries that are available on demand.

Some librarians might object to the concept of end user searching because of a possible decline in the quality of searches done by their libraries' users. To others, end user searching threatens the professional stature of the search intermediary. Nielsen bemoans widespread belief that the intermediary role is the "core task" of librarianship, and that it was the arrival of online searching in the early 1970s that finally elevated the profession to its rightful place.[3] User dependency on the librarian's expertise might have seemed assured by the search intermediary role. Rather, one might consider that the search intermediary's role is expanding into that of educator and consultant instead of being rendered obsolete. Professionalism should not be equated with exclusive mastery over online searching and its machinery. Librarians can take pride in de-mystifying the new technology and ensuring that health professionals are informed connoisseurs and skilled users of online products.

Advocates of the librarian's new educational role can count among their allies persons far afield from librarianship. Many leaders in health professional education have acknowledged the importance of information management education and have echoed the major recommendations of the Matheson report. In 1983, a group of health professionals and other faculty convened for the Macy Conference on Basic Science Education. The conference set out to rethink the preclinical component of medical education by integrating the viewpoints of three fields: the biomedical sciences, information science, and cognitive science.[4] Pointing to medical education's current emphasis on the acquisition of vast quantities of information, the Conference concluded that:

> Computer science, cognitive science and information science are emerging as fields basic to medicine. The information technology produced by these fields will play an ever-increasing role in medical practice and biomedical research. Yet, these fields have not yet penetrated the curricula of most medical schools, despite their adaptation by other segments of the educational system, and by society at large.[4]

Considering the rate at which information is being generated, medical educators have concluded that the factual knowledge mastered by a graduating medical student soon becomes obsolete or incorrect.[5] The problem has moved many medical educators to question their traditional emphasis on memorization, and instead employ information technology as a resource for augmenting existing knowledge.[6]

ONLINE TRAINING AS A CURRICULUM COMPONENT

As with other subjects in a health sciences curriculum, online searching is either integrated into a larger course of study or is taught as a freestanding class or series of classes. As online training accompanies other subjects in a school or department's curriculum, librarians are teaming up with instructional designers and other experts. Accordingly, information specialists are key participants in medical curriculum planning and are becoming more familiar with formal educational theory and teaching skills. However, end user training by no means implies a greater teaching commitment than do traditional user education programs. In some respects, end user instruction merely amplifies basic principles of information management that have application to both manual and online information access.[7] Expertise in online searching is distinct from computer literacy and shares with manual searching such concepts as controlled subject access and search strategy formulation.

As a curriculum component that is featured within a roster of courses, instruction in end user searching must adhere to the school or institution's overall educational philosophy. Also, an end user searching program that is based within a curriculum must incorporate formal educational considerations such as course evaluation. No matter what teaching methods are used, planning for online training includes formulating a program goal and objectives. The course framework of goal, objectives, and content should progress in descending order from general to specific. For example, the goal of a course might be to help users decide whether or not to do their own searching. Enabling objectives could include the following: that users be able to discuss the economic components of online searching, to describe the elements of database construction and to compare online information retrieval with manual searching. Course content could include discussion of equipment and training costs and vendor charges, defining basic terminology, and comparison of MEDLINE with *Index Medicus*. Each course offering, based on a precise set of goals and objectives, should be commensurate with the precepts of the library's instructional program as a whole.

Another two-tiered, essential phase of an end user training program is instructional evaluation, which applies to the program, and learner evaluation, which measures user competency. Whether at the "class roots" level, or characteristic of an entire school, justification for a curriculum follows from prior identification of a problem or an educational assumption.[8] For example, a program in end user searching might cite as its underlying rationale the problem of information growth in the health sciences.

During users' orientation to online searching, instructors should inject a note of skepticism and point out an interesting paradox of information retrieval in general: more information without useful learning creates a greater burden of selection. The potential overload of information created by online searching is acknowledged by programs in clinical epidemiology, which warn that additional quantities of information will only compound the problem of sifting out relevant material.[9] As a result, practitioners should be schooled to make critical, evaluative decisions by appropriate and maximal use of both printed and online information sources.

Although online searching can be regarded as a subject, the term "end user searching" resists simple definition and is too multifaceted to serve as a workshop title. Like information management itself, end user searching implies a wide range of topics and lends itself to modular instruction. Unless publicity and course description specify content, such as "microsearching," "searching MEDLINE on the NLM system," or "interfacing search results with a personal information file," user expectations and content won't necessarily converge. Libraries might take into account the diverse topics, competencies, subject interests, and experiences that a training program in end user searching can address before designing the online training curriculum.

The instructional context of information technology is only one factor related to educators' interest in end user searching. Widespread curriculum review by health schools has also stimulated appreciation of online searching as an academic skill applicable to both clinical and research proficiencies. The integration of information management into a revised curriculum reflects substantial change in educational philosophies, especially when change has come from within.

It might be useful to first review some background issues in medical education before considering the place of end user searching in formal training for health professionals. Many curriculum concerns during the 1970s related to federal government policies and were of a quantitative nature: minority student admission quotas, fiscal incentives for expanding training programs in certain primary care specialties, distribution of graduate specialties, and improving physician-patient ratios through Area Health Education Centers, to name a few. Flexner's revolutionary report, *Medical Education in the United States*, proposed that medical education be consonant with the scientific method and be subject to federal government regulations.[10] Since that time, accrediting bodies, review boards, licensing organizations and other groups apart from the schools' own administrative offices have also influenced and controlled curricular issues. More recent curricular review has been to a greater extent self-imposed and experimental.[11]

In terms of a health curriculum, educators have distinguished between the broad cognitive categories of preclinical and clinical studies. Training in the basic sciences, clinical care, or social aspects of health and illness all address competency areas deemed essential to the practice of good medicine. Wilson and Smythe have identified four distinct components of medical education relevant to both basic science and clinical training: (1) strategies for transmitting cognitive knowledge, (2) practice skills, (3) definition and transference of attitudes and values, and (4) methods for achieving life-long learning.[12] The first and fourth points make a strong case for including an online searching component in a health sciences curriculum. The significance of online searching as a new learning skill to help keep pace with an ever-growing knowledge base was articulated by Barondess in his assessment of curricular needs for the physician in the future:

> Another need will relate to information management. The future physician will have to cope with a continuing increase not only in the volume of information, but also in its complexity. Computer techniques, including centralized storage capabilities for purposes of literature review and for consultative help with specific clinical problems, will undoubtably require some degree of acquaintance with technology.[13]

Online searching offers health professionals a means of achieving self-directed, independent learning. Furthermore, online training in the health sciences curriculum promotes skills that are useful for adapting to changing medical practices. Clinicians can use online searching for applications other than literature review. The immediacy of online searching can expedite clinical decision making and even assist with diagnosis by combining keywords that express symptoms.

ONLINE SEARCHING AS BOTH A SUBJECT AND A SKILL

Prospective end user searchers should nonetheless consider that effective use of online systems requires familiarity with manual information systems and knowledge of how information is structured and organized. Even use of a library's online catalog is helped by prior understanding of the bibliographic record. Users already familiar with an online catalog will likely have greater confidence when beginning to search than would users with no exposure to interactive systems. In addition, online instruction should reinforce concepts already used successfully to acclimate users to an online catalog. It is essential, therefore, that librarians emphasize the conceptual aspects of online searching that pertain to other methods of information retrieval and that will remain intact even as technology evolves.

By stressing online searching's underlying principles, librarians help users appreciate the similar capabilities that are offered by most systems across most databases. Typical cross-system, cross-database functions include expressing search concepts that are selected from a controlled vocabulary or coding scheme, combining concepts by using Boolean operators, limiting retrieval to certain parameters, and printing according to desired format. If users are aware of the larger framework of product-transparent concepts, they should be better able to grasp the specifics of either user-friendly prompts or full system commands. As information counselors, librarians have a responsibility to help users appraise online products critically. If vendors' promotional literature and marketing tactics lead users to perceive online searching as fairly automatic and always friendly, it is understandable that users might reduce the process of online searching to its procedural mechanics. User misconceptions can be compounded by ignorance of system capabilities, which leads to dysfunctional searching.

User underestimation of online searching is understandable, however. Health professionals encounter computer technology in many forms that suggest ease of use and automatic capabilities. Physicians employ computers in their practice management for diagnostic testing or for physiologic monitoring, using programs such as MYCIN or INTERNIST.[14] Hospital data processing and laboratory testing are other common examples of how computers have penetrated the health sciences environment.

Long before the advent of laser-activated optical disc technology, health science educators have promoted computer-aided instruction (CAI) for self-paced learning, or have used computer technology to design clinical simulations. Educators recognize how CAI increases the learner's attention and active participation, and individualizes user needs through branching program construction. CAI also requires the learner to start the tutorial, and lets the student control the pacing of new information. Health professionals have seen the potential for computer-aided instruction as a teaching technique ever since the Lister Hill National Center for Biomedical Communications launched its experimental biomedical computer-assisted instruction network in 1972. As a medium with which many health professionals are already familiar, CAI can supplement the classroom portion of a library's online training program. A single CAI program can furnish simulation exercises, help identify problem areas, and provide practice drills. Many health sciences librarians consider MEDLEARN, the National Library of Medicine's CAI introduction to MEDLINE searching, to be an effective instructional method in their own introduction to online searching.

The relationship between CAI and end user searching goes beyond their similarities of terminals, user interaction, and transport of knowledge. Faculty resistance to featuring online instruction in a curriculum is reminiscent of early opposition to CAI. The CAI adversaries largely protested against the time-consuming aspect of authoring CAI programs, and questioned available curriculum time for its implementation.[15] Even the earliest strides in bibliographic instruction in the health sciences during the 1930s and 1940s suffered for lack of curriculum support and the need to compete with required courses for students' limited free time.[16,17]

Regardless of what instructional method is used, planning for an end user training program should be concerned with achieving subject relevance. A case problem can illustrate the practical application of several information sources to a health care issue and, at the same time, portray online searching as just one solution among a gamut of strategies from which to choose. A clinical problem can contain multiple concepts, each geared to a unique phase of the information management process. One phase might be systematic problem analysis, followed by identification of what types of information are needed for clinical decision making. It is just as important that students recognize when an online search would be an inappropriate solution to a problem. A case problem can mimic a realistic scenario which might typify an instance where online searching is not a suitable approach. Instructors would then stress the association between type of information needed and its likely format or method of access. For example, the need for therapeutic equivalents or mortality rates would suggest handbooks or other sources of primary data that would obviate an online search. A case problem can also furnish relief from an overly didactic presentation.

There are ways other than use of a case problem that can help to enhance the relevance of online instruction. Teaching materials should be adapted to the lay person's command of information science, be relatively free of jargon, and feature examples drawn from user subject interests. Just as traditional user education would refrain from casual reference to a monograph precis, online trainers should monitor their use of search jargon. As self-explanatory as "thesaurus" might sound, users might need definitions for this and other examples of online terminology.[18] Materials should not presuppose a level of knowledge on par with the search intermediary, but include ample definitions and references to basic terminology.

Also in the interest of clarity, instruction should establish a hierarchy of concepts, carefully synthesizing subordinate points and relating them to major ideas. Instructors should review content from preceding modules and refer back to material presented earlier in any given session. For example, coverage of the print command might refer to retrieving data elements that are useful for evaluating records. Users would then be reminded how evaluation of search retrieval affects document procurement decisions.

The concept of controlled subject access warrants special attention and thorough explanation. Confusion is likely to stem from ambiguities such as the difference between major and minor descriptors in *Medical Subject Headings—Annotated Alphabetic List* and the designation of major emphasis for controlled vocabulary terms. Users' first encounters with controlled vocabularies often foster a new appreciation for the skill involved in online searching.[19] If the health professional's initial experience with MeSH headings is so sobering that he or she decides to leave searching to the intermediaries, that same user will probably come better prepared for future search interviews. Discussion of principles such as controlled subject access should be included in training follow-up, whether through user group meetings or individual consultation.

Online trainers should be attuned to user frustration not unlike that experienced during their own indoctrination period, and consider their role in influencing user perceptions of online searching. In his work on information technology in health professional education, Deland stresses the importance of user attitudes for any computer application to win acceptance.[20] Perceptions of ease of use will vary considerably according to the user's degree of familiarity with computers. Even definitions of computer literacy often rank levels of sophistication according to an understanding of concepts such as computer hardware versus software, microcomputer versus terminal, and explanations of machine architecture, multiprocessing, and the structuring of databases.[21]

Although incoming students in higher education will increasingly demonstrate facility with computers and their educational applications, a great deal of learner trepidation can persist. During the transition to clinical training, students might be well versed in the use of computers for "drill and practice" but deficient in their understanding of telecommunications and interaction with computers to obtain information.[22] Information systems and advanced diagnostic aids might represent sophisticated applications whose fundamentals have not been taught previously. If any of the information technologies, including online searching, are ever to become as familiar to students as the stethoscope, they must first be integrated into the entire educational process.[23]

CONTINUING EDUCATION THROUGH ONLINE SEARCHING: PROBLEM-BASED LEARNING

As one means of ensuring the health professional's ongoing education, online searching helps faculty continue the knowledge gained during their student years. Compared to their earlier methods of learning, however, online searching can coincide with actual need. Faculty development should be a major effort of any curriculum-based end user searching program. At the very least, librarians should educate faculty about basic information management concepts and applications before asking them to sponsor an online training module. The success of most instruction can be influenced by the modeling behavior of faculty, showing students how to ask questions and how to obtain new information.[24] Library educators should encourage faculty to apply all information management skills visibly and require it of their students. Faculty can tailor course examinations to give credit for problem-solving abilities and critical use of information resources.

A faculty development program in online searching will also strengthen faculty's pedagogical role and advance their skills beyond those of incoming students. Consequently, students will perceive faculty information management skills as desirable scholarly behavior that is to be emulated. Faculty can participate in a curriculum-based program on many levels. Initial faculty instruction will stimulate the integration of information management concepts into a variety of learning activities staged throughout an entire course of study. Those faculty whose own courses include information management requirements should be targeted for online training. Faculty involvement in the library's online program can provide positive reinforcement away from the terminal. In addition, health sciences faculty can to some extent serve as surrogate library faculty and monitor students' online skills on site or away from the information specialist.

Clinical training in all of the health fields consists of clerkships, or apprenticeships, where learning is achieved by observation and repetition of other faculty practices. Clinical problem solving differs from either rote memorization or learning by repetition, however. Through clinical problem solving, specific rules can be generalized to similar situations, instead of expecting the learner to uncover the process by which a solution is reached. Problem-based learning asserts that the student can draw upon learned knowledge when he or she confronts another problem where the information is relevant.[25] Like problem-based learning, whereby strategies can be generalized to specific topics, online searching is a method or inquiry and contrasts with conventional learning methods that are based on memorization.

Richard B. Friedman cited information science as a means of stimulating problem solving in pre-clinical education:

> The successful application of computers and the information sciences requires training in the ability to analyse one's own reasoning process and then to break this reasoning into a series of logical, machine-oriented steps; it requires the expertise needed to take a specific case and develop a generalized set of

rules: neither skill is taught in medical school. . . . The student must then progress to the application of therapeutic principles in the care of specifically assigned patients. Other elements include biostatistics, epidemiology, and use of the library and computer.[26]

Similarly, in the process of teaching online searching to health professionals, instruction should aim toward an economy of detail and not allow larger concepts to be subsumed by considerations that will vary considerably according to the search topic. Initial practice should focus on only those rules that are relevant to the problem or online principle. For example, a practicum on searching by authors' names should not involve using codes or cascaded search terms as well. According to the principle of minimalist training, the learner will achieve more if given less to learn in each increment.[27] Librarians should consider that a few bold strokes of information might be better retained than endless minutia.

Problem-based learning in a health curriculum encourages students to work with issues related to a patient or clinical situation, and to apply broad principles through small group interaction. Similarly, online searching can be viewed as an application-oriented learning methodology that is consistent with curriculum efforts to decrease the volume of lectures and required memorization.

Students and faculty can be introduced simultaneously to file management concepts and online searching as co-adjuncts to memory. Instructors should emphasize that information files and online searching are ultimately interdependent entities. If a reprint file, for example, compares to memory, online searching assures updating and new knowledge. Since online searching can directly interface with a professional information file, involve similar retrieval techniques, and occur in the individual's work environment, libraries should consider offering joint coverage of online searching and file management content. Many arguments for integrating file management and online training into undergraduate health sciences education redouble when applied to continuing education. Since a professional information file organizes existing knowledge, then online searching, like continuing education, keeps knowledge fresh. In a similar vein, Jeghers distinguishes between undergraduate medical knowledge learned by precept versus the professional's technique of self education that expands and individualizes the student's knowledge base.[28]

Apart from a graduate medical curriculum, inservice activities in hospitals are a standard continuing education forum for many health professionals. Inservice training typically includes equipment operation and updates in medical technology for nurses and many allied health personnel.[29] Inservice sessions often employ other hospital units to develop training modules from their own areas of expertise. Many inservice programs extend training through a series of related classes, which enables the hospital librarian to introduce end user searching after adequate preliminary coverage. The convenience of having quick and easy access to clinical information right at the patient-care setting appeals to many hospital staff who already use microcomputers for office management tasks. Online searching by hospital clinicians can be an efficient means of clinical problem-solving and continuing education.

Manning distinguishes between formal continuing medical education and practice-linked continuing education. The former is readily dispensed, counted, and recorded, whereas practice-linked continuing education requires greater personal initiative for identifying knowledge gaps that often relate to clinical problems.[30] Online searching was widely viewed as an essential source of new clinical knowledge by respondents in Singer's survey of health practitioners' attitudes towards computers in medicine.[31]

The Accreditation Council for Continuing Medical Education presently awards to physicians continuing medical education credit for completing National Library of Medicine sponsored MEDLINE training.[32] Online trainers should consult with their institution's office of continuing education and inquire about continuing education eligibility. Notice of continuing education credit available can be useful for workshop promotion.

Health professionals and information specialists together are looking to their libraries to influence and lead their institution's adjustment to change brought about by new information technology. The concept of a teaching library does impose new requirements for librarians, especially in their new role as educators and consultants. In the process of refining existing skills and contemplating the future, it is important to value the knowledge and information gained over and above the method used. Instead of preoccupation with machines and technical considerations, online education for health professionals concerns itself with the significance of what has been retrieved, and the computer-based enhancement of teaching and learning.

REFERENCES

1. Matheson, N.W., and Cooper, J.A.D. *Academic Information in the Academic Health Sciences Center: Roles for the Library in Information Management.* Washington, D.C.: Association of American Medical Colleges, 1982, p. 76.
2. Ibid., p. 44.
3. Nielsen, B. "Teacher or Intermediary: Alternative Professional Models in the Information Age." *College & Research Libraries* 43(May 1982):186.
4. Friedman, C.P., and Purcell, E.F. eds. *The New Biology and Medical Education: Merging the Biological, Information, and Cognitive Sciences.* New York: Josiah Macy, Jr. Foundation, 1983, p. 74.
5. Du Val, M.K. "The Library as an Educational Instrument, the Problem." *Journal of Medical Education* 42 (August 1967, Part 2):4.
6. Anderson, J., and Graham, A. "A Problem in Medical Education: Is There an Information Overload?" *Medical Education* 14 (1980): 4-7.
7. Brassil, E.C. "Information Management Education: Policies and Procedures for a Reference Department Manual." *MRSQ* 2 (Winter 1983): 59.
8. Stritter, F.T., and Jessee, W.F. "Setting Goals and Objectives." In: Cooper, J.A.D. ed. *Teaching Quality Assurance and Cost Containment in Health Care: A Faculty Guide.* San Francisco: Jossey-Bass, 1982, p.2.
9. Fletcher, R.H., and Fletcher, S.W. "Clinical Epidemiology: A New Discipline for an Old Art." *Annals of Internal Medicine* 99 (September 1983): 401-3.
10. Jonas, S. *Medical Mystery: The Training of Doctors in the United States.* New York: W.W. Norton & Company, 1978, pp. 199-222.
11. Rosinski, E.F. "Curricular Trends: Critical Review and Analysis." In: McGuire, C.H., ed., *Handbook of Health Professions Education.* San Francisco: Jossey-Bass, 1983, pp. 162-94.
12. Wilson, M.P., and Smythe C. "Medicine." In: McGuire, C.H. ed. *Handbook of Health Professions Education.* San Francisco: Jossey-Bass, 1983, pp. 24-5.
13. Barondess, J.A. "The Future Physician: Realistic Expectations and Curricular Needs." *Journal of Medical Education* 56 (May 1981): 381-9.
14. Hammond, K.R. "Teaching the New Biology: Potential Contributions from Research in Cognition." In: Friedman, C.P. and Purcell, E.F., eds. *The New Biology and Medical Education: Merging the Biological, Information, and Cognitive Sciencies.* New York: Josiah Macy, Jr. Foundation, 1983, p. 58.
15. Rubin, M. et al. "Experimental CAI Network Evaluation." In: Deland, E.C. *Information Technology in Health Sciences Education.* New York: Plenum, 1978, p. 582.
16. Cunningham, E.R. "Instruction Given to Medical Students Regarding Use of the Medical Library." *Journal of the Association of American Medical Colleges* 12 (1937): 376-85.
17. Postell, W.D. "The Formal Training of Medical Students in the Use of the Library." *Journal of the Association of American Medical Colleges* 15 (July 1940): 241- 4.
18. Snow, B. "Why Use a Database Thesaurus?" *Online* 9 (November 1985):92-6.
19. Worthington, W.C. "The Biomedical Information Crisis: A User's Viewpoint." *Perspectives in Biology and Medicine* 27 (Winter 1984): 252.
20. Deland, E.C., ed. *Information Technology in Health Sciences Education.* New York: Plenum, 1978, p. 2.
21. Norman, D.A. "Worsening the Knowledge Gap: The Mystique of Computation Builds Unnecessary Barriers." In: Pagels, H., ed. "Computer Culture: the Scientific, Intellectual and Social Impact of the Computer." *Annals of the New York Academy of Sciences* 426 (1984):222.
22. Ball, M.J., and Shannon, R.H. "Vertical and Horizontal Curricula: How Can they Work Together in the Integration of Computer Science and the Classic Medical Sciences." *Medical Informatics* 9 (1984): 283.

23. Rabkin, M.S. "As Familiar as the Stethoscope." In: Friedman, C.P. and Purcell, E.F., eds. *The New Biology and Medical Education: Merging the Biological, Information, and Cognitive Sciences.* New York: Josiah Macy, Jr. Foundation, 1982, p. 170.

24. Duban, S. et al. "Teaching Clinical Skills to Pre-clinical Medical Students: Integration with Basic Science Learning." *Medical Education* 16 (1982): 186.

25. Barrows, H.S., and Tamblyn, R.M. *An Approach to Medical Education.* New York: Springer, 1980, p. 13.

26. Friedman, R.B. "The 'Art' of Medicine." In: Friedman, C.P. and Purcell, E.F., eds. *The New Biology in Medical Education: Merging the Biological, Information, and Cognitive Sciences.* New York: Josiah Macy, Jr. Foundation, 1983, p. 148.

27. Carroll, J.M. "Minimalist Training." *Datamation* (November 1, 1984): 130.

28. Jeghers, H. "Medical Care, Education, and Research." *New England Journal of Medicine* 271 (December 17, 1964): 1297.

29. Munk, R.J., and Lovett, M. *Hospitalwide Education and Training*, Chicago: Hospitalwide Research and Educational Trust, 1977, p. 2.

30. Manning, P.R. "Continuing Education: the Next Step." *JAMA* 249 (February 25, 1983):1042-5.

31. Singer, J. et al. "Physicians' Attitudes Towards Application of Computer Data Base Systems." *JAMA* 249 (March 25, 1983): 1610-4.

32. Accreditation Council for Continuing Medical Education. *Essentials and Guidelines for Accreditation of Sponsorship of Continuing Medical Education.* Lake Bluff, Illinois, ACCME, 1982, p. 2.

Determining Content and Structure of Online Educational Materials

Bonnie Snow

ABSTRACT. Designing online training for medical end users requires careful planning. Assessing goals and determining desired outcomes in clearly stated performance objectives is a preliminary step. A structured examination of the cognitive processes involved in learning computer searching can lead to more effective design of training programs. Introductory online instruction must deal with at least four areas: (1) capabilities of major retrieval systems, (2) topic analysis and strategy formulation, (3) software system protocols, and (4) database-specific idiosyncrasies. A checklist approach is suggested for determining content in each area. After requisite decisions have been made about what components to include, the task of developing instructional aids remains. Several problems can be anticipated; a detailed discussion of desirable attributes for training materials is included. References to some of the published literature about end user characteristics and documentation design will, hopefully, provide useful background reading for new online educators.

INTRODUCTION

As more and more online searchers assume the role of online educators, the volume of publications devoted to "end user" searching increases. Much of this literature reports data gathered *after* educational programs have been initiated. Relatively little has appeared which focuses on preparation for end user education. What factors need to be considered *before* instituting a training program? How can intermediaries prepare themselves to become online educators? What problems need to be anticipated?

Recognizing that these questions are important, in May 1985 the

---

Bonnie Snow is Biomedical Information Specialist and Staff Regional Representative for DIALOG Information Services, Inc., 2100 Arch Street, Philadelphia, PA 19103. She worked in DIALOG's Washington DC office from June 1980 to December 1985. Ms. Snow received her M.S. from Drexel University. She is the author of the *DIALOG Seminar for Medical Professionals* and *Database Search Aids: Health Sciences*.

31

Medical Library Association (MLA) sponsored the presentation of a course on "Designing Online Education for Medical End Users" at its annual meeting in New York.* An outline of topics covered in this workshop provides an overview of some items which need consideration in planning an educational program (see Figure 1). Several articles in this volume discuss in detail how specific institutions have addressed one or more of these design issues. This article will concentrate on that portion of the MLA course devoted to *determining content* of instructional materials.

GOALS

Due to the interest generated by reports in medical journals of successful experiences in using online information systems, many health science practitioners have already asked medical librarians for instruction in searching. The information professional's immediate response is usually to concentrate on conveying facts about the search process, often without prior consideration of long-range goals and future outcome. Thus, MLA workshop attendees were asked to list their goals in designing a training program. What emerged was a list of competency-based or "performance" objectives. Figure 2 summarizes the results of this survey/discussion. Not every educational program will attempt to achieve all of these competencies. Nonetheless, determining desired outcome is a necessary preliminary step to determining content. The mere act of enumerating skills assists the intermediary besieged by requests for instruction in shifting from the stop-gap approach of the reactor to that of the proactive planner.

Yet deciding what health professionals need to know in order to search effectively for themselves can be more difficult than a plainly stated competency such as "ability to perform simple searches" implies. Analysis of search topics requested by the extant library user group will help define the information needs of prospective end user trainees. But what is often missing from data collected regarding search requests is *purpose*. The selection of techniques to be

---

*Sponsored as part of the "New Perspectives" series of the MLA Continuing Education Program, CE856 was developed jointly and team-taught by Joseph Wible (Lane Medical Library, Stanford University) and Bonnie Snow (DIALOG Information Services, Inc.). Ellen Brassil Horak (then affiliated with the University of North Carolina at Chapel Hill) also helped in preliminary planning for the workshop.

FIGURE 1. DESIGNING ONLINE EDUCATION FOR MEDICAL END USERS
(MLA Course Outline)

I. The Context for Online Searching by Health Science Professionals
   A. Users
      1. Identification of target user group(s)
      2. End-user characteristics
   B. Anticipated Problems: Pros & Cons of End User Searching
II. Review of Currently Available End User Software Interfaces
   A. Terminology
   B. Characteristics and Comparisons
III. Designing a Training Program
   A. Goals
   B. Administrative Aspects
      1. Participants - enrollment policy
      2. Scheduling
      3. Promotion
      4. Equipment
      5. Costs
      6. Instructional formats
      7. Instructors - staffing
   C. Determining Content: Intellectual versus Mechanical Aspects
      1. Commonly asked questions about microcomputer access
      2. What needs to be included about the "generic" process of searching?
      3. System protocols: vendor-specific techniques, problems
      4. Database specifics
   D. Desirable Attributes of End User Training Materials

covered in instruction will be influenced by the purpose behind information gathering. And that purpose may, in fact, be different when the health professional is able to perform his or her own searches, than it is for requests heretofore only answerable via an intermediary. For example, many topics requested currently are likely to serve immediate needs, such as information for basic research work or information gathered in support of patient care.

FIGURE 2. DESIGNING A TRAINING PROGRAM: PERFORMANCE OBJECTIVES OR STUDENT COMPETENCIES

A. Basic Knowledge of What's Available
   1. Differences between hardcopy and online access
   2. Distinctions among vendors and producers or suppliers
   3. Types of databases - bibliographic, nonbibliographic, fulltext
   4. Database structure - access points
   5. How to evaluate vendors, software systems
   6. Understanding "lag time"
   7. Understanding of costs involved in online searching
   8. Vocabulary - definitions of standard jargon

B. Ability to Perform Simple Searches
   1. Topic Analysis, concept identification
   2. Logical connectors
   3. Database selection - what factors to compare
   4. Telecommunications - how to connect, disconnect
   5. Interactive techniques - evaluating results and using data obtained to improve output
   6. How to proceed from one database to another
   7. Cost-effective techniques

C. Understanding of Indexing Principles
   1. Controlled vocabulary versus natural language searching
   2. User aids needed and how to use effectively

D. Search Follow-Up - Locating Source Documents

E. Integration of Online into Overall Information-Seeking Behavior

---

Yet the end user may anticipate expanded use of online service when he or she has direct access. This may include: (1) broader surveys of the literature for general review purposes—characterized by Neubauer[1] as "online explorations," (2) regular access for current awareness, (3) more searching performed in support of writing for publication or spoken presentations, (4) generating bibliographies to locate the names of individuals as resource persons with the general intent of widening professional contacts in the "invisible college," and (5) quick research on non-medical topics, such as business investment queries.

Timing is crucial when attempting to survey potential trainees regarding their anticipated information needs and purposes in seeking instruction on nonmediated use of online systems. The health professional needs to know some general facts about what is available online and some of the practical applications for output before identifying projected uses. Information obtained from individuals who have been given a general orientation to online searching is usually more substantive and specific than that collected from a relatively uninformed user group. Thus, accomplishment of one of the objectives listed in Figure 2—conveying a "basic knowledge of what's available"—may be necessary before further objectives can be addressed. It will be noted that several training programs described in this volume tacitly acknowledge this need by offering a general orientation or "consciousness-raising" session as a separate course.

In such programs, enrollment in the second segment covering actual online search mechanics seems to be accepted as adequate "needs assessment" on the part of the trainee, whose mere perseverance implies that his or her needs and purposes will be met by additional instruction. Further exploration of trainee motivation prior to plunging into more advanced techniques is lacking in many programs. Even an informal survey of projected applications, using a multiple choice questionnaire, administered after orientation is completed, could serve two purposes: (1) assist educators in selecting which system features to emphasize, and (2) indirectly define training goals to prospective participants. Confronted with the variety of possible uses and applications, the medical end user is encouraged to form realistic expectations and focus on specific, attainable goals when attending training.

FIRST STEPS

Then, of course, it is the responsibility of the educator to "deliver the goods." Introductory online instruction must deal with at least four areas:

1. Capabilities of Major Retrieval Systems;
2. Topic Analysis and Strategy Formulation;
3. Software System Protocols;
4. Database-Specific Idiosyncrasies.

Recognition that there are several steps involved in learning the search process is necessary in designing effective training. Huq[2] describes the process as beginning with the "confidence phase": familiarity with basic capabilities, terminology, and format of online information must be achieved before an individual can progress to the "insight phase," when potential applications are perceived realistically and concepts of topic analysis can be introduced.

Some orientation programs address both of these objectives in one session. For training in system mechanics to succeed, it must build upon these essential first steps. Immediate introduction to command protocols via hands-on experience in even the simplest of "user-friendly" systems may lead to woefully inadequate search techniques and lack of integration of online retrieval into overall information-seeking behavior on a long-term basis.

TOPIC ANALYSIS AND STRATEGY FORMULATION

Behind every successful search experience lies careful presearch formulation. Yet it is sometimes difficult for an intermediary searcher, to whom the process has become almost intuitive, to determine how best to convey to novices the basics involved in topic analysis and strategy formulation. Dolan and Kremin[3] have, in fact, speculated that this part of searching involves innate aptitude. In surveying results of research on online searching skills, Fenichel[4] has pointed out that findings seem to indicate search strategy is difficult for experienced as well as inexperienced users.

Despite these somewhat humbling reflections found in the literature of professional librarianship, instruction in the basic "rules of thumb" for search strategy formulation is included in most training programs. The method favored seems to be sample question analysis by the experienced searcher/instructor. Such a practicum approach can be effective, provided that (1) examples are perceived as relevant to the trainee's anticipated needs, (2) care is taken to enumerate underlying principles along the way, and (3) the process is illustrated as consisting of logical component parts which may be replicated, rather than as intuitive insight. A practicum teaching technique requires extrapolation by trainees: parallels with their own questions must be easily deducible, and a wide variety of information problems must be illustrated. Yet a rapid succession of sample solutions to ad hoc queries can undermine the effectiveness of this approach. In a critique of database documentation, Smith[5] warns that "providing consistency among examples is extremely important. . . . The experts suggest developing a sample . . . situation and planning ahead so that all examples are interrelated." In medicine, a case study method is familiar to trainees and thus recommends itself as an "instructional approach . . . relevant to user needs, thereby assuring [and maintaining] a reasonable level of motivation"[6] in this preliminary phase of introductory online education.

MLA course attendees mentioned some of the following as "search strategy fundamentals" to be conveyed:

> Identifying individual concepts to be searched—
> > Establishing priorities among concepts.
> > > What words must a record contain to be relevant?
> > > Which concepts might be considered as secondary?
> > Rules-of-thumb:
> > > Searching low-occurrence terms first.
> > > Eliminating redundancy.
> > > Avoiding abstract concepts not easily or consistently expressed in words (e.g., "direction," relative quantities).
> Developing lists of alternate search terms or synonyms for each concept.
> Truncation—understanding word roots, possible ambiguity.
> Choice of logical connectors—when to use Boolean logic versus proximity operators.

SOFTWARE SYSTEM PROTOCOLS

The choice of software system (i.e., vendor or databank) to be taught is yet another problem facing the online educator. In fact, preparation for the initial orientation session mentioned above may include material which is helpful to the instructor as well as potential trainees, who ask: *What factors need to be evaluated when selecting a software system* to learn? The medical searcher in the United States has a fairly extensive menu of mainframe systems to compare: National Library of Medicine (NLM) MEDLARS, DIALOG, BRS, KNOWLEDGE INDEX, BRS/Saunders Colleague, BRS/AFTER

DARK, MEDIS, and AMA MINET (to name a few). Linder[7] and Myers[8] mention some criteria in vendor selection, augmented below.

>   Databases available—
>   exclusive offerings in medicine
>   access provided to potentially relevant nonmedical sources.
>   Cost—
>   start-up fees?
>   monthly minimum or annual fees?
>   telecommunication charges?
>   availability of reduced rates for classroom instruction?
>   Hours of availability.
>   Local access on networks.
>   Other special features—
>   stop word list
>   logical operators available: word proximity?
>   left-hand truncation
>   online sorting
>   output options
>   online thesauri
>   cross-file indexes and other database selection aids
>   automatic sdi's
>   electronic mail
>   document ordering and delivery
>   quality and extent of user aids
>   customer assistance
>   Timeliness—
>   database updating
>   online response time
>   Degree of "user-friendliness"

The last of these factors has received an increasing amount of attention in the past few years. Menu-driven systems are often more attractive to both novice users and educators. However, some of the initial enthusiasm for such user-friendly features has waned upon closer examination. Rudin[9] laments: "The major drawbacks . . . are directly related to the promoted benefits. For example, one may find menus helpful, yet time-consuming and costly online. Once the user becomes fairly proficient in using the system the deluge of choices becomes frustratingly tedious." Williams[10] points out that "user-friendly front ends remove from the user the interactive aspect of the search service and the facility for iteratively developing and improving search strategies." She warns that "lower level operations are removed, and online system user contact is decreased."

Viewing the issue from a different perspective, Kirby and Miller[11] conclude that the nature of the search topic is probably the most important determinant of search success on a user-friendly system: "It is relatively easy for an untrained user to search a topic which is wholly expressed by a single descriptor term or by a unique phrase consistently used in titles and abstracts." They found that more difficult MEDLINE searches required more sophistication than a menu-driven system usually demands or encourages, and expressed their concern about end users who "may believe that with their simple search, they have done all that it is possible to do: 'That's all there was in the computer!'" Inattention to individual database refinements weakens the appeal of user-friendly interfaces. When these doubts are added to the attractive incentives for instructional use provided by major online vendors, many medical librarians find that familiarity with the full system capabilities of NLM, DIALOG, or BRS does *not* breed contempt when choosing which system to teach.

After selecting a vendor, still another problem remains: what commands and features need to be taught? It is helpful for experienced searchers to make a list of all commands and software features they commonly use. This list should then be considered in light of the purposes for searching expressed by potential trainees. What is the minimum which must be covered to achieve these purposes? Information professionals use more special features than an end user may need to learn. It is important to remember that "although a command-by-command approach and detailed analysis of software and indexing refinements holds some fascination for individuals whose livelihood may depend on mastering this new skill, it will not serve as well the medical practitioner for whom online is not a vocation, but rather an avocation."[12] Software will be regarded as a means to an end, rather than as an end in itself.

Thus the wise educator will select only those commands which are clearly essential for success, and avoid unnecessary "frills." When developing search examples to introduce individual commands, those features which seem to require elaborately contrived case studies to show their utility are usually those which are not needed by novice searchers. Figure 3 lists some vendor system capabilities to consider when deciding what to teach.

If classroom instruction has been chosen as the mode of delivery, time constraints will dictate a concise search vocabulary. In designing instructional material, many modes of delivery are possible. MLA course participants were encouraged to consider their list of commands and features in light of what might be taught via handouts or other self-instructional aids, versus what really required oral discussion and the immediate reinforcement of hands-on experience with expert help available.

DATABASE-SPECIFIC IDIOSYNCRASIES

Knowledge of indexing policies is generally considered essential to effective use of online databases. In this respect the problems facing online educators in medicine are somewhat unique. Medical databases tend to be less than user-friendly, in that major files differ dramatically from one another in special indexing features and consequent search techniques. There is also an ethical problem confronting the health science educator. End user searchers in medicine often begin as avocational "dabblers," but may progress to relying on their results in patient care and research. In other words, what begins as avocational interest may merge with vocational applications, in the sense that important decisions, which may either affect the quality of someone's life or investment of research time and dollars, may be based on the outcome of medical end user searches.

Most MLA workshop participants agreed that teaching MEDLINE without reference to the *MeSH* thesaurus[13] and the *Tree Structures*[14] would amount to "information malpractice." Sewell and Teitelbaum's[15] frequently cited retrospective study of nonmediated MEDLINE searching by pathologists and pharmacists reinforces this belief. In a database with less than fifty percent abstracted records, there can be major differences between free-text or natural language retrieval and that produced by searches which take into account the controlled vocabulary, with its inverted phrases, and the classification scheme, which is searchable but not displayable. The penalty of missed opportunities in health care is obvious. As Kirby and Miller[16] have pointed out, the problem is not only "unanswered questions," but also "unquestioned answers."

Still another obstacle faces the educator. Because the trainer's

FIGURE 3. VENDOR SYSTEM FEATURES: A CHECKLIST OF COMMON SEARCH VOCABULARY

1. Entering a database/file
2. Searching command or response to user entry cue
3. Logical operators or connectors
   a. Boolean
   b. proximity, degrees of proximity
   c. order of processing
   d. phrase searching without connectors
4. Word variants
   a. open-ended truncation
   b. controlled-length truncation
   c. embedded variable character
5. Index browsing command (e.g., EXPAND, NEIGHBOR, ROOT)
6. Stop words
7. Punctuation - rules for searching
8. Output commands
   a. format options
   b. offline printing
   c. sorting or rearranging output
9. Saving search strategies
   a. temporary
   b. permanent or long-term
   c. SDI's
   d. execution
   e. releasing, erasing
10. Subject-oriented field or paragraph qualification
    a. defaults
    b. title word searching
    c. abstracts
    d. descriptors or indexer-added keywords
11. Other qualifiers
    a. language
    b. dates - publication and/or accession, ranging
    c. document type (e.g., letter, review)
    d. journal name
    e. author
    f. author address
    g. number searching
12. Inventory and/or editing (e.g., DISPLAY SETS, ERASEBACK, etc.)
13. Typographical error correction
14. Exiting a database/file
15. Cross-file indexes
16. Online ordering of source documents
17. Disconnecting from system

role is often that of mentor or model, medical librarians must be acutely aware of their own search behavior. Wanger, McDonald, and Berger[17] found that many MEDLINE searchers do not take advantage of the interactive capabilities of online systems. Accustomed to careful presearch formulation using *MeSH*, MEDLINE searchers are inclined to employ a "fast batch"[18] searching style. While this has not been shown to yield worse results than a more iterative approach, it does presuppose effective use of the thesaurus, and may serve less well health science end users involved in research which requires creative augmentation of *MeSH* terminology, or which may necessitate use of databases other than MEDLINE. Poor free-text searching skills have been observed as a characteristic trait among habitual MEDLINE searchers.[17] Thus although great emphasis has been placed on teaching *MeSH* in medical end user training programs, it may be advisable to include search problems which also cultivate use of natural language.

Several useful publications exist which introduce *MeSH* but, being designed for professional searchers, may contain more detail than is really needed by end users. Again, a "list" approach is useful in making decisions about what to teach and what not to teach. MLA course participants worked with a checklist of MEDLINE-specific indexing features and discussed what was essential to know for effective use of the database. A sample of elements which might be included on such a checklist is illustrated in Figure 4.

TRAINING MATERIALS: DESIRABLE ATTRIBUTES

After requisite decisions have been made about what components to include in each of the three areas discussed above, the task of developing instructional materials remains. Rarely can training publications intended for librarians be adopted "carte blanche" for use in end user instruction. Differences in vocabulary, educational background, and philosophy or motivation in searching between intermediaries and medical practitioners dictate that many database-supplier-sponsored pedagogical publications need considerable adaptation for end user education. Problems to anticipate in such adaptation have been discussed elsewhere,[12] but it may be useful to review desirable attributes in instructional materials designed for end users. Figure 5 summarizes the results of forty-two MLA course participants' collective consideration of the topic.

FIGURE 4. MEDLINE FEATURES - WHAT TO TEACH, WHAT NOT TO TEACH?

1. Subject scope - comparisons and contrasts to other online resources
2. Document coverage, including
   a. number of journals
   b. monographs
   c. journal priorities - indexing depth and lag time
3. Abstracting policies
   a. percent of abstracted records
   b. dates of availability
   c. length limitations
   d. how to retrieve abstracted records only
4. MeSH
   a. major versus minor headings
   b. dates of availability, history notes
   c. backwards cross-referencing (X, XU, XR)
   d. data forms (DF:)
   e. nonMeSH entries in MeSH
   f. SPEC; SPEC QUALIF
   g. IM or NIM
5. TREES classification scheme
   a. explosion
   b. preexplosions
   c. multiple tree numbers for some concepts
   d. possible ambiguity
   e. sequence (not a decimal scheme)
   f. use of asterisk in hardcopy
6. Subheadings
   a. references in MeSH annotations
   b. allowable dates
   c. allowable categories
   d. internal hierarchy
   e. common combinations
   f. free-floating
   g. main heading versus subheading, when both are available
7. Permuted MeSH
8. Check tags
9. Document types in titles (rubrics)
10. Author indexing policies
11. Named person as subject
12. Contract/grant number indexing
13. Country of publication
14. Author address
15. Journal names, codes, ISSN
16. Language
17. Publication date
18. Other dates: entry month/update, accession
19. Subfiles or special lists
20. Registry numbers, Enzyme Commission numbers

43

FIGURE 5.   END USER TRAINING MATERIALS: DESIRABLE ATTRIBUTES

1. Avoid online in isolation.

    Proceed from known to unknown.
    Relate online search process with past experience in hardcopy sources.
    Draw parallels from printed counterparts.

2. Problem orientation versus product orientation.

    The unit record and its searchable fields should *not* dictate the sequence of materials.
    'How to' aaproach, versus 'What is.
    Relevance. Use examples directly pertinent to specific user group's research needs.

3. Language clarity.

    Avoid unnecessary jargon.
    Be consistent in use of specialized terminology and define it in context, through examples.

4. Freedom from choice.

    If there are multiple ways of searching the same thing, choose *one* and stick to it.

5. Flexibility.

    Arrange material in brief modules or units which stand by themselves and can be consulted separately as questions arise.

6. Accessibility.

    Section titles indicative of content *and* application.
    Extensive annotation for examples.
    Detailed subject keyword indexing.
    Multimedia approach, if possible: CAI, printed manuals for self-tuition, customized quick-reference guides, classroom instruction, etc.

Several authors have mentioned these and other factors to consider. Budavari[19] found that life scientists were sometimes less familiar with printed (hardcopy) research tools than instructors had anticipated; drawing parallels from printed counterparts, as suggested in Figure 5, would obviously be less useful to such trainees. Shelton and Scharf [20] cite "lack of formal bibliographic training" as a characteristic common among end users interviewed.

Materials which present information in the traditional field-by-field "unit-record" format are frequently criticized. Warning that "real users want to perform a specific task," Smith[5] counsels manual writers "not to tell 'what is' but rather 'how to.'" Linder [21] also mentions creating customized examples for each audience; end user task orientation must be met with sample problems directly pertinent to trainee information needs. Ifshin and Hull[6] include relevance in their "five planning criteria."

Language clarity is an attribute frequently lacking in user manuals. Findings from one end user survey indicate that: "The wording and language of database documentation are thought to be in need of closer editorial scrutiny. The choice of language often requires existing familiarity with retrieval systems; words or terms used to convey information and instructions are neither standardized nor consistently applied."[20] A librarian-turned-educator needs to scrutinize all materials carefully. Use of jargon is a habit so ingrained in most professional searchers that detecting it is one of the greatest challenges in designing handouts and other teaching tools. Trying to avoid "buzz words" completely is probably neither practical or desirable; introducing basic terminology and defining it is a necessary part of online training. End users will, after all, need to communicate with experienced searchers and will, inevitably, encounter certain terminology in search manuals consulted long after the training program is completed. Writing a glossary of specialized terminology used in training material is, in itself, a useful "consciousness-raising" exercise for the would-be online educator. Providing definitions which do not use terms that, in turn, also need further definition will be an act of contrition for many specialists.

Consistency is desirable not only for use of terminology to describe search procedures, but also in the language used to conduct searches. Command languages developed by major vendors are like the "last will and testament" written for a youthful testator: an attempt is made to provide for every eventuality. Despite this contingency planning, changes in the user community and the availability of hitherto unanticipated resources and technology lead to the introduction of new features each year. Layer-upon-layer the command language grows, incorporating ever-increasing refinements—just as codicil after codicil is added to a will in response to life "passage" events and acquisition of new property. The result is encyclopedic database documentation and a bewildering array of alternate ways to perform a search.

Choosing one way and adhering to it consistently throughout all examples is a method recommended by experienced educators. Pritcher[22] advises, "focus on content, minimize commands," and Smith[5] adds that "it is not necessary to provide information on how to perform every conceivable task." A practical example will illustrate the careful planning needed for consistent results. On DIALOG, one may range publication years by using prefixes and a colon (*SELECT PY = 1983:1985*) or by applying the four-digit codes as suffixes, ranging with a colon or a hyphen (*SELECT ONLINE/ 1983:1985* or *SELECT ONLINE/1983-1985*). One may also range line numbers from an "expand" display (similar to "neighbor" output on NLM or "root" on BRS) or consecutive "set numbers" using either a colon or a hyphen (*SELECT E3-E6* or *SELECT R1:R10* or *SELECT S2-S5*). But one may range prefix fields other than publication year (such as "concept codes" on BIOSIS PREVIEWS or "annual sales" in financial directories) *only* by employing a colon, not a hyphen. Thus the best choice to teach ranging to end users in DIALOG introductory training would probably be the colon, and reference to the isolated exception of publication years being applicable as suffixes as well as prefixes should probably be omitted. In other words, prospective instructors should emphasize the "generic" methodologies in command languages and avoid introducing too many variants.

This recommendation for "freedom from choice" in end user training may seem to contradict the next requirement in Figure 5: flexibility. However, striving for simplicity in command language is part of a general effort toward increasing accessibility. Reporting their experiences in CAS ONLINE training for end users, Ostrum and Yoder[23] comment: "the message was becoming increasingly clear to us—various end-user audiences will desire different levels of discussion on various system features and capabilities depending on their needs and background. This is hardly a new—or, with 20/20 hindsight, unexpected—guideline." It would seem that even among a very specialized user group such as chemists, workshop materials and presenters must be easily adaptable. Wygant[24] cites "flexibility" as a desirable trait for online instructors, who must be prepared to deal with sometimes disastrous equipment problems and a variety of student skill levels and capabilities. Although hardware can, indeed, be intractable, training material need not be.

A modular approach, already encouraged by the task-orientation typical of end users, lends itself to many different presentation situations and learning styles. Constructing "how to" units which can stand by themselves and be consulted separately as questions arise incorporates flexibility into printed user aids. To be successful, "material relating to individual areas should assume minimum prior knowledge or exposure" and be "self-contained . . . accessible according to one's own schedule and priorities."[6] Elaborately "hierarchical" manuals, intricately interweaving cross references and predicating completion of one section upon consultation of another, will be less effective and, incidentally, much more costly to revise. Anything published about online searching is doomed to rapid obsolescence. Provision for frequent amendments is thus part of designing "flexible" educational material.

Hand in hand with a modular approach comes the need for several access methods. A detailed table of contents is helpful, but only if section titles are indicative of both content *and* application. For example, "reprint address," "source," "document type," or "check tags" simply won't help the end user find what he or she needs. Similarly, a detailed subject index is desirable in user manuals, but selecting appropriate terminology is a challenge. A good indexer will attempt to anticipate every conceivable situation when the index will be consulted. Entries will need to include not only the formal labels for system commands and each "field" or "paragraph" or "record element" used by database suppliers, but also synonyms for each label and "functional" or task-oriented terminology, such as "start," "stop," "end," "sign-off," "English," "names," etc.

Providing a means for end users to locate the appropriate section of a manual via a table of contents or subject index is only the first step in fulfilling the accessibility requirement. A second, equally essential step is providing a "real life" example of exact entry format, fully but succinctly annotated, and preferably in a context which does not require consultation of previous examples. As Smith points out, "Nowhere in most search manuals will you find a section titled, 'How to find articles by a particular author.' What you will find is a section about how author names are indexed and possibly a list of exceptions to general rules."[5] Fortunately, unlike reference manuals, online pedagogical tools frequently feature extracts from sample printouts. But often little attempt is made to highlight commands in order to distinguish them from output, or to annotate them with brief explanations. The assumption is that the trainee will fill in any notes required as the instructor covers the material. The problem is that what seems straightforward and easy to the student during class may later need more extensive annotation than was included at the time.

Another aspect of accessibility is format. Ideally, a multimedia approach, as suggested in Figure 5, will accommodate different learning styles and situations. Chapman's[25] findings provide food for thought in deciding modes of delivery for end user training. He compared search performance following completion of a computer-assisted-instruction program versus in-person instruction. Both groups studied used commands stressed by trainers, but the latter showed more varied and individualized searching "styles" than did the machine-trained group.

Much more literature is published about developing printed material than about other formats, probably because typewriters, paper, and copying machines have long been standard equipment available to most educators. That which can be produced with these humble tools remains the cheapest to produce, the easiest to revise quickly, the most "portable" for both instructors and learners, and therefore, not surprisingly, the most flexible and accessible. However, there is still room for improvement in the products of these time-honored tools. Simple embellishments, such as use of different typefaces (provided this use is consistent), shading, symbols (arrows, boxes, etc.), page tabs, colored paper for section divisions, and looseleaf format for easy updating can all enhance the utility of printed materials intended for classroom and self-instruction and ready-reference applications.

FOLLOW-UP

Bellardo,[18] in summarizing "What do we really know about online searchers?", states that "the type, amount, and quality of training seem to have a considerable effect on beginning searchers but there is evidence that differences are not retained over time." Perhaps even more surprising, research has yet to show that experience plays a major role in improving search results. In study after study, type of training and subsequent search experience have proved to be poor predictors of long-term search performance in intermediaries. However, evidence has yet to surface that there will, in fact, be a "long-term" for end user searchers. Preliminary reports directly from pioneers such as Myers[8] and Nowacek[26] indicate that one of the chief problems is maintenance of skills.

Training program design should take this into account. Several author/instructors in this volume mention that follow-up sessions have been requested by trainees. Plans range from weekly "search clinics," to ad hoc trouble-shooting sessions, to abbreviated adaptations of user aids. Janke[27] discerns "a clear shift away from traditional *online searching* to the new phenomenon of *online reference*," and predicts that "presearch counseling" will be "considered an essential component in any client search service." Providing for ongoing consultation and instruction by intermediaries can be assisted by circumstances such as location of public-access terminals, as is shown in the Stanford program.[21] Sewell and Teitelbaum[15] have also conjectured on the effect of "socialization" in acquiring and maintaining skills, observing that searches on a terminal located in an area where peer review (by end users, not intermediaries) was readily available were different from those performed in a more isolated location. Fifty-seven percent of trained end user searchers surveyed in another informal study reported that they had taught colleagues to search.[28]

Sixty-five percent of the same sample no longer request online searches from library and other sources. Many of these respondents may not have used intermediary search services in the first place, but such data reinforce the need to recognize that avocational searching may become vocational, and that in preparing to assume the role of online educators in medicine, librarians assume a weighty responsibility. Although the training methodology chosen may not, indeed, be crucial, it is reasonable to suppose that follow-up may be an important factor in maintaining adequate search skills. Wanger hypothesized that "after a certain period of time, perhaps within six months or a year, the effects of experience may also be 'washed out' because the length of time searching no longer contributes to advancement in search skills."[17]

Quantity may not, in effect, be as crucial as quality in follow-up. Attributes mentioned as desirable in training materials could equally well be applied as planning criteria in designing ready-reference aids. Arranging for staff availability to provide in-person consultation, preferably encouraging use of any self-tuition aids developed, is part of the training design process. An added advantage of in-person follow-up is feedback to the trainer as well as the trainee. Recurrent problems in certain areas of searching point to weaknesses in training. Evaluations obtained immediately following a classroom session are but poor indicators of the success of the effort. Search consultation services can provide ongoing feedback regarding the efficacy of a training program. Mechanisms for pooling results of such interviews will increase their utility in larger organizations.

CONCLUSION

This discussion of factors to be considered in designing online training for medical end users emphasizes careful planning, including a structured examination of the cognitive processes involved in learning computer searching, as well as suggestions for content and format of instructional materials. References to some of the published literature about end user characteristics and documentation design will, hopefully, provide useful background reading beyond the necessarily subjective viewpoint of one online educator.

REFERENCES

1. Neubauer, D.N. "Confessions of an End User." In: *End User Searching in the Health Sciences*, edited by M.S. Wood; E. Brassil Horak; and B. Snow. New York: The Haworth Press, 1986, pp. 197-203.
2. Huq, A.M.A. "The Challenges, Rewards and Pitfalls in Teaching Online Searching." Paper presented at the Mid-Year Meeting of the American Society for Information Science, Lexington, KY, May 22, 1983.
3. Dolan, D.R., and Kremin, M.C. "The Quality Control of Search Analysts." *Online* 3 (April 1979): 8-16.
4. Fenichel, C.H. "Online Searching: Measures that Discriminate among Users with Different Types of Experience." Ph.D. dissertation, Drexel University, 1979.
5. Smith, P.K. "Database Support Documentation—Good and Not So Good." In: *Proceedings of the Sixth National Online Meeting, New York, April 30-May 2, 1985*. Medford, NJ: Learned Information, 1985, pp. 421-5.
6. Ifshin, S.L., and Hull, D.M. "CAI Plus: A Strategy for Colleague Training." In: *Proceedings of the Sixth National Online Meeting, New York, April 30-May 2, 1985*. Medford, NJ: Learned Information, 1985, pp. 233-40.
7. Linder, G. "Choosing a Vendor for Medical Databases." (Course handout, Stanford University.)
8. Myers, F. "Physician Searching: A Rural Hospital Experience." In: *End User Searching in the Health Sciences*, pp. 189-96.
9. Rudin, J. et al. "Comparison of In-Search, SciMate and an Intelligent Terminal Emulator in Biomedical Literature Searching." In: *Proceedings of the Sixth National Online Meeting, New York, April 30-May 2, 1985*. Medford, NJ: Learned Information, 1985, pp. 403-8.
10. Williams, M.E. "Highlights of the Online Database Field—Gateways, Front Ends and Intermediary Systems." In: *Proceedings of the Sixth National Online Meeting, New York, April 30-May 2, 1985*. Medford, NJ: Learned Information, 1985, pp. 1-4.
11. Kirby, M., and Miller, N. "MEDLINE Searching in BRS Colleague: Search Success of Untrained End Users in a Medical School and Hospital." In: *Proceedings of the Sixth National Online Meeting, New York, April 30-May 2, 1985*. Medford, NJ: Learned Information, 1985, pp. 255-3.
12. Snow, B. "Making the Rough Places Plain: Designing MEDLINE End User Training." *Medical Reference Services Quarterly* 3 (Winter 1984): 1-11.
13. *Medical Subject Headings—Annotated Alphabetic List*. Bethesda, MD: National Library of Medicine, 1985.

14. *Medical Subject Headings—Tree Structures*. Bethesda, MD: National Library of Medicine, 1985.

15. Sewell, W., and Teitelbaum, S. "Pathologists and Pharmacists as Nonmediated Online Searchers." Paper presented at the 25th meeting of the National Federation of Abstracting and Information Services, Arlington, VA, February 27, 1983.

16. Kirby, M., and Miller, N. "Medline Searching on BRS Colleague: Search Success of Untrained End Users in a Medical School and Hospital." Paper presented at the Sixth National Online Meeting, New York, NY, May 1, 1985.

17. Wanger, J.; McDonald, D.; and Berger, M.C. *Evaluation of the Online Search Process*. Santa Monica, CA: Cuadra Associates, 1980.

18. Bellardo, T. "What Do We Really Know About Online Searchers?" *Online Review* 9 (3, 1985): 223-39.

19. Budavari, S. "End User Searching in the Sciences." Paper presented at the 76th annual conference of the Special Libraries Association, Winnepeg, Canada, June 11, 1985.

20. Shelton, A.L., and Scharf, D. "Online Database Documentation for End User Training." In: *Proceedings of the Sixth National Online Meeting, New York, April 30-May 2, 1985*. Medford, NJ: Learned Information, 1985, pp. 415-9.

21. Linder, G.A. et al. "Training the End User: The Stanford University Medical Center Experience." In: *End User Searching in the Health Sciences*, pp. 113-26.

22. Pritcher, P.N. "Strategies for Training the Information End User: Training the Manager How to Use Information." In: *Proceedings of the Sixth National Online Meeting, New York, April 30-May 2, 1985*. Medford, NJ: Learned Information, 1985, pp. 365-76.

23. Ostrum, G.K., and Yoder, D.K. "Training in CAS ONLINE for End Users." In: *Proceedings of the Sixth National Online Meeting, New York, April 30-May 2, 1985*. Medford, NJ: Learned Information, 1985, pp. 343-9.

24. Wygant, A. "Teaching End User Searching in a Health Sciences Center." In: *End User Searching in the Health Sciences*, pp. 127-35.

25. Chapman, J.L. "A State Transition Analysis of Online Information-Seeking Behavior." *Journal of the American Society for Information Science* 32 (1981): 325-33.

26. Nowacek, G., and Hodge, R.H. "Search Strategy Outline: An Approach to Assist the Occasional End Searcher." In: *End User Searching in the Health Sciences*, pp. 181-7.

27. Janke, R.V. "Presearch Counseling for Client Searchers (End-Users)." *Online* 9 (September 1985): 13-26.

28. Snow, B. "End User Searching in the Sciences." Paper presented at the 7th annual conference of the Special Libraries Association, Winnepeg, Canada, June 11, 1985.

End User Searching: Implications for Library Planning

W. Ellen McDonell

ABSTRACT. Increased interest in end user searching has been stimulated by widespread computer literacy, system enhancements, and direct marketing by database vendors. Such factors as the reality of full-text databases and inflexible library policies also encourage health sciences library users to bypass the search intermediary. This article considers the role of fundamental library assets in planning for a future of extensive end user searching.

End user searching of bibliographic databases began nearly twenty years ago with the SUNY project in late 1968. The system was too difficult and the time spent waiting for equipment too long for the concept to take hold with most SUNY users.[1] Instead, librarians accepted the role of search intermediary and no longer encouraged library users to perform their own searches.[2] In the years since, end user searching has been kept alive in the medical community by scattered projects,[3,4] and has been fueled by system enhancements, widespread computer literacy, and recent direct marketing by database vendors. Interest continues to grow at a steady rate. Although the medical reference and online searching literature abounds with articles on end user searching,[5] few libraries have taken positive steps to plan for their role in this new aspect of information transfer.[6] This article proposes a framework around which libraries can plan organizational change in preparation for extensive end user searching programs.

Naisbitt, in the much quoted *Megatrends*, predicts a furthering of

---

W. Ellen McDonell is currently Manager, Technical Information Center, Buckman Laboratories, 1256 N. McLean, Memphis, TN 38108 and a Doctoral student in Information Sciences at Nova University. Previously she was Reference Librarian, University of Tennessee Center for the Health Sciences Library in Memphis.

the move from institutional help to self help.[7] He applauds the return to independence and reliance on our personal abilities. His prediction is particularly applicable to the concept of end user searching. In years past, scholars searched the maze of printed knowledge for clues to their needs. They took notes and memorized, as they might have difficulty returning to the exact passage at a later date. The *Index Catalog of the Surgeon General* and *Index Medicus* filled an important gulf in the access to medical information.[8] As bibliographic databases became accessible through search intermediaries, many scholars and practitioners passed on this part of their information-gathering activity to search intermediaries. It is reasonable and exciting to anticipate that the new electronic age of scholars will again search the maze of stored knowledge, often unaided, and obtain answers to their information needs more quickly than ever. Direct electronic access will allow them to pursue diverse, even eccentric, needs "outside the conforming structures of institutions."[7] As librarians, we should also applaud this return to self-reliance. By embracing end user searching now, librarians will be able to plan proactively for their future role in the transfer of information.

EXTERNAL ENVIRONMENT

If one accepts that end user searching is not a transient fad, but a true change in the information-seeking behavior of individuals, then a close look at the needs and environment fostering this change is in order. There are five major environmental factors which have encouraged end user searching: (1) widespread computer literacy, (2) direct marketing by database vendors, (3) full-text databases, (4) varying quality control in intermediary searching, and (5) obstacles with which users are faced during each intermediary search encounter. Each of these factors continues to play an important role in the development of the trend toward end user searching.

Computer Literacy

The proliferation of microcomputers in the last few years has been astounding. Surprenant recently reported a Louis Harris survey which found that 45 percent of the general public stated that they knew how to use a computer. The percentage rose greatly for higher income (over $35,000) individuals and professionals.[9] Most offices and many homes are now supplied with computer power. Fortunately, modem connections were standardized as early as 1969 with the Electronics Industry Association's adoption of the RS-232 for serial communications. Telecommunications systems are now widely available. The time is right for individuals to use their microcomputers to the greatest advantage, especially if that use is tax deductible. Many health science practitioners and researchers have become comfortable with the microcomputer and the concept of databases; both are necessary in an environment which fosters end user searching.

Direct Marketing

In the same vein, the marketing of databases to end users has increased the awareness of the direct access possibility. BRS, AMA/NET, DIALOG, PaperChase, The Source, CompuServe, Mead Data Central, and others, recognizing the opportunity to serve end users' needs, have utilized direct marketing with good results. Home and office markets represent totally new buyers for these vendors.[10] Many studies of underutilized library services have determined that one of the primary reasons for lack of library use is ignorance of the service. Friedman, in his recent article, "Future of Medical Information and Medical Libraries," admonishes librarians for not always sharing their knowledge and expertise in the area of online databases, automated catalogs, and inventory systems.

> Many health care practitioners are only now becoming aware of the existence of online databases through advertisements and presentations by commercial concerns. They are not aware of their own library's experience and existing capabilities in this area.[11]

A good example of this is the recent comment aimed at end users of bibliographic and full-text databases in *Creative Computing*: "Telecommunications can replace the limitations of the local library with the virtually boundless resources of huge databases."[12] Marketing plays an important role in the use of services. Direct vendor marketing to the end user will enlighten many individuals to the availability of these services and create a level of interest not seen previously.

Full-Text Databases

Full-text databases of books, journals, and consensus reports, although currently limited in coverage and scope, will be an important force in the future expansion of end user searching. The primary literature will become available in electronic formats to a greater extent each year.[13,14] When an end user locates references on a bibliographic database, he must still limit himself to his private journal collection or come (or send) to the library for the complete article. With full-text databases, even this final step becomes unnecessary. The end user simply scans the full text for the needed information or displays it on his personal printer. The time saved to the client is economically valuable, so that despite the fee charged by the vendor, it is cost-effective.

Cost savings might be more important to practitioners than to researchers and also may be a factor encouraging direct access to full-text databases. Practitioners' needs are often for immediate access to just one or two good articles rather than an extensive literature review which might take days or weeks to have the original articles in hand. Clinicians who have previously used intermediary searchers will often be spared delays and the frustration caused by those dreaded words, "It's gone to the bindery." Full-text databases will be a significant resource to libraries and end users. It is a weighty component of the new information technology which libraries must recognize and integrate into a strategic plan for change.[15]

Quality Control

Another factor in the move toward end user searching is the quality of searches. Many topics could easily be searched by users on BRS/Saunders Colleague, BRS/AFTER DARK, DIALOG's KNOWLEDGE INDEX, or PaperChase with minimal instruction. Other requests could, no doubt, use the added help of a search analyst. The distinction here goes beyond that of exhaustive versus brief search. An exhaustive search on acupuncture could easily be done by the novice searcher, while the nutritional aspects of a disorder would be the type of search for which an experienced trained searcher could be valuable. Even on PaperChase this search would be difficult. An algorithm has yet to be suggested to differentiate a difficult search from an easy one. If the user wants only a couple of articles, an inexperienced searcher could meet the need. But if more is required, an experienced search analyst may be necessary. Unfortunately, the quality of searching in libraries has not kept up with the proliferation of libraries offering search services. This is evidenced at the National Library of Medicine Online Updates by the types of questions posed by librarians who are considered to be experienced MEDLINE searchers. It also becomes evident to anyone who consistently reruns searches previously conducted at other libraries. There are many end users now doing their own searching who were not satisfied with the searching performance of intermediaries.

Library-Placed Obstacles

There was a time when medical libraries produced manual bibliographies as a regular activity. Back then, the requester expected some delay but was also aware of the time necessary to do the same search himself. As a result, the number of health science librarians, especially reference librarians, grew. Later, as searches could be requested through a regional center, the client knew that a good deal of time would pass before the results would be delivered. Because requests often went through several people, the results were not always what was expected. When online searching as we know it today became available, the delays were reduced, but still existent. Some institutions still have restrictive policies concerning the number of citations which may be printed online or the online printing of abstracts. Even for those libraries which are able to conduct the search immediately and print output as the client's wishes, the requester still has many obstacles. Free time is necessary to visit the library during its scheduled reference hours. As a result, the user might wait hours or days after the question was posed in his mind.[16] A friend and biomedical researcher once commented, "When a question presents itself I need the information immediately. Any delay is a waste and an obstacle to my work."

Electronic access to information holds the promise and expectation of increased productivity. The energy a practitioner or scholar must expend to obtain information reduces his productivity. Productivity is defined as the measure of the relationship between outcome and the resources or energy consumed to produce that outcome.[17] When library policies and procedures demand increased energy expenditure by the client, then productivity of the individual is diminished. Veaner enumerates some of these expenditures, such as traveling to the library, fetching materials, and negotiating for materials not on the shelf.[18] The costs of reading, digesting, and sorting out unneeded material just add to the price tag. The costs associated with online searches are just as real and sometimes paid with the same frustrations.

Institutional constraints have played a large role in the interest in end user searching today. Mick found that the perceived information environment had an impact on the way people went about seeking information; if information resources were not managed so as to be responsive to the needs of users, use of those resources was lower.[19] Mooers' Law should not be overlooked: "An information retrieval system will tend not to be used whenever it is more painful and troublesome for a customer to have information than for him not to have it."[20] Friedman addresses this obstacle in the process of information transfer as he implores librarians to "become more responsive to user needs."[11] This is not to say that libraries should offer twenty-four hour search service and do whatever else is necessary to remove all delays from the searching process. These may be management impossibilities. End user searching, however, should inspire librarians to re-evaluate the usefulness or necessity of their policies. Flexibility and accessibility are important in all services, but libraries often do not address these needs until pressured by competition.

INTERNAL ENVIRONMENT

If end user searching is just the beginning of a total change in the information-seeking behavior of library users, it becomes obvious that libraries must plan for this change. Are libraries in jeopardy of losing their role in the information retrieval arena? Will even their archival role be minimized with the move toward full-text databases? Libraries have inherent in their structure at least three elements, which, if retained, will ensure their vitality and importance for many decades to come.

First and most importantly, libraries are basically neutral administratively and philosophically.[21] This premise affects the collection of material, its storage, and dissemination. Much has been written over the concerns for the legal and ethical aspects of online full-text,[22] including its relationship to online editing, author corrections, and ownership of the information by private sources.[23] Electronic materials, especially the older or little used information, may no longer be available in our civilization's stock of recorded knowledge.[24] The total loss of low-demand, non-scholarly, or noncurrent information is possible.[25,26] This will come to the forefront as electronic publishing and records management mature. The non-political nature of the library will become important during this period. Broadman[27] reminds us that "Libraries are the insurance policy against trouble."

The library has knowledgeable information professionals as their most important resources. If encouraged by management to keep pace with users' information needs, librarians will continue to rise in professional stature.[28] As the information society grows, those who can effectively manage information—organize, process, select, and disseminate—in a timely manner will come center stage in the organization.

One of the main roles of any library is to provide access to information and materials at a fraction of the cost that would be necessary for the individual to acquire or access the materials himself.[29] Many online search services are currently organized to recoup all direct online costs. This situation lies at the heart of the fear of end user searching. If end users can supply their own bibliographies and perhaps full text at a fraction of the costs (money plus energy expenditure) that it would take if they used an intermediary (the library), the future of the librarian does looks dim.[30]

THE IMPLICATIONS

What can libraries do in the changing environment of end user searching and the shift to direct access between the end user and the information producer? First, policies and regulations for current intermediary search services should be reviewed. Few libraries have yet seen a decrease in online searches performed due to end user searching. In fact, many libraries are looking to end user searching for help in managing the number of requests for online services. As end user searching becomes more prevalent, however, demand for intermediary searches should either decrease, or, at the very least, cease growing at the current rate. At the point that full-text databases become widely available, the number of intermediary searches will be greatly reduced. Searches which are performed for users must meet their needs with utmost precision. Institutionally-placed obstacles should be reduced whenever possible. Needs assessment and policy review are crucial to any strategic management approach, including the management of online services.

Secondly, the quality of present search services should be evaluated. It is important that when an intermediary search is requested, the resultant product should be superior to the user's best effort. To accomplish this, searchers must be trained professionals. The library must support the continuing education of these individuals and emphasize the need to keep up-to-date with database changes. A system of peer review of search strategies might be feasible in a larger institution or among consortium members. A formal feedback mechanism could be developed for the searches performed—difficult in some ways, but important in the ultimate process of providing quality services. Little has been done to develop controls in this area.

Librarians who are in the position to be asked about online databases should be able to answer the questions quickly and intelligently. This will take some work on their part, and a great deal of commitment on the part of the library.[31] Librarians need the opportunity to work with the systems which are being marketed to their clients. They are then in a position to become local resource persons on the strengths and weaknesses of the different systems. They should be aware of hardware and software options for their users. Libraries could provide access to database and system manuals and basic texts.[32] Access to vendor and database newsletters would also be a welcome addition to some end users.[33] Training for end users is an important new task for libraries. It is now common for health sciences libraries to offer formal and informal classes on the use of indexes and abstracts in print form. Training for electronic access is only an extension of this role.[34] A few health sciences libraries are beginning end user training, but most attempts to date have been transitory and not part of the regular services. It is not the place of the computer center to teach online searching of bibliographic or full-text databases. These people can be excellent resources for librarians who train end users to organize their reprints or notes with database management systems. Librarians are aware of this[35] and should be knowledgeable about electronic options. Training for end users in this area is a necessary and logical expansion for the librarian. With these expanded consulting and training roles, the online search intermediary's salary and stature in society can be predicted to rise, not decline, as a result of the proliferation of end user searching.[13]

Other options that librarians have for retaining a primary role in the transfer of information are to provide database access and production. Some libraries are already providing access to library equipment for end users.[36] For those users who do not have their own equipment or password, this service would be readily welcomed. Some systems allow for the library to issue passwords and thereby benefit from volume discounts. This could become an important institutional service. Other libraries have agreed upon a set rate for the in-house user of databases and charge back accordingly.

As they begin to collect electronic formats, libraries will need to provide access to those formats for remote and in-house users.[21] Access to information concerning what is held in the library's own collection on a dial-up basis is fundamental. Priority should be placed on this activity in medium to larger academic libraries. The future prospects of computer-aided access to optical discs is an excellent example of optimal electronic collection and access. Equipment and training for librarians will be a necessity. The library may want to make MEDLINE or its subsets available for user access. Additionally, production of specialty databases unique to the institution's needs may be a real necessity. The library's impartiality, accessibility, and expertise in the organization and dissemination of information will render it a good choice for developer and manager of the institution's information system.

The change which may be the most difficult for library management to accept is subsidizing the electronic format. It is apparent that libraries now subsidize access to print and audiovisual material. As the shift to electronics becomes more evident, libraries must shift their subsidies from paper to electronic formats.[29] Only a few libraries have acknowledged this need and have supported it financially.[37] The investment exceeds training searchers or supplying terminals with paper—although those costs can be substantial. Librarians teach that both the print and electronic format of *Index Medicus* have their place,[38] but they often only truly subsidize the print format. Philosophically, librarians must realize the necessity to discount or offer free access to electronic publications for their primary clientele. In the face of economic austerity, it will be difficult to divert funds to support electronic formats. It is important, nonetheless, to do so for the sake of long term viability. Friedman states:

> If librarians and libraries choose to ignore these changes and continue to adhere to the belief that books and journals are the only reasonable form in which to store medical knowledge,

then the medical library is destined to diminish in importance and be eclipsed by a national network of commercially maintained databases, microcomputers, and videodiscs.[11]

If libraries recognize the need to subsidize the electronic format of material just as they would the access to printed or audiovisual forms, then they have taken a major step toward ensuring their place in the information transfer process.

CONCLUSION

Health sciences libraries have been at the forefront of many ideas that have changed the information transfer process. Any change is difficult, especially when it results in changed roles and responsibilities. Libraries must remember that, although the move to end user searching was ignited by many agents, it continues because of actual need. Through the years libraries have developed many strengths upon which their services are grounded and through which libraries have prospered. It is imperative that libraries build on existing strengths and develop new expertise in adjusting to the changing needs of users. The opportunities are boundless; the challenge is surmountable; the rewards are well worth the effort.

REFERENCES

1. Egeland, Janet. "User-Interaction in the State University of New York (SUNY) Biomedical Communication Network." In: Walker, Donald E., ed. *Interactive Bibliographic Search: The User/Computer Interface.* Montvale, NJ: AFIPS Press, 1971, pp.105-20.

2. Egeland, Janet. "The SUNY Biomedical Communication Network: Six Years of Progress in On-Line Bibliographic Retrieval." *Bulletin of the Medical Library Association* 63(April 1975):189-94.

3. Sewell, Winifred, and Bevan, Alice. "Nonmediated Use of MEDLINE and TOXLINE by Pathologists and Pharmacists." *Bulletin of the Medical Library Association* 64(October 1976):382-91.

4. Olson, Paul E. "Mechanization of Library Procedures in the Medium-Sized Medical Library: XV. A Study of the Interaction of Nonlibrarian Searchers with the MEDLINE Retrieval System." *Bulletin of the Medical Library Association* 63 (January 1975):35-41.

5. Lyon, Sally. "End-User Searching of Online Databases: A Selective Bibliography." *Library Hi Tech* 2(1984):47-50.

6. McDonell, W. Ellen, and Givens, Mary King. "State of the Art in End User Searching." Paper presented at the Annual Meeting of the Medical Library Association, New York, May 26, 1985.

7. Naisbitt, John. *Megatrends: Ten New Directions Transforming Our Lives.* New York: Warner Books, 1984.

8. Kirkpatrick, Brett A. "History of the Development of Medical Information." *Bulletin of the New York Academy of Medicine* 61(April 1985):230-7.

9. Surprenant, Tom. "Future Libraries." *Wilson Library Bulletin* 59(March 1985):475-6.

10. Gaffner, Haines B. "Personal Computers: Key to Mass Market Online Database Usage." In: Williams, Martha E., and Hogan, Thomas H. comps. *National Online Meeting 1983: Proceedings of the Fourth National Online Meeting New York, April 12-14, 1983.* Medford, N.J.: Learned Information, 1983, pp.147-58.

11. Friedman, Richard B. "The Future of Medical Information and Medical Libraries." *Bulletin of the New York Academy of Medicine* 61(April 1985):290-7.

12. "Modem Magic." *Creative Computing* 11(May 1985):14-30.

13. Summit, Roger K., and Meadow, Charles T. "Emerging Trends in the Online Industry." *Special Libraries* 76(Spring 1985):88-92.

14. Goodrum, Charles, and Dalrymple, Helen. "The Electronic Book of the Very Near Future." *Wilson Library Bulletin* 59(May 1985):587-90.

15. Dougherty, Richard M., and Lougee, Wendy P. "As Electronic Publishing Evolves and Libraries Adapt to It . . . What Will Survive?" *Library Journal* 110(February 1, 1985):41-4.

16. Ojala, Marydee. "End User Searching and its Implications for Librarians." *Special Libraries* 76(Spring 1985):93-9.

17. Taylor, Robert S. "Information and Productivity: Definitions and Relationships." In: Benenfeld, Alan R., and Kazlauskas, Edward J., eds. *Communicating Information: Proceedings of the 43rd ASIS Annual Meeting* v.17, 1980. White Plains, N.Y.: Knowledge Industry, 1980, pp. 236-8.

18. Veaner, Allen B. "1985 to 1995: The Next Decade in Academic Librarianship, Part I." *College and Research Libraries* 46(May 1985):209-29.

19. Mick, Colin K. et al. *Towards Useable User Studies: Assessing the Information Behavior of Scientists and Engineers. Final Report.* Palo Alto, CA: Applied Communication Research, December, 1979.

20. Mooers, C.N. "Mooers' Law on Why Some Retrieval Systems Are Used and Others Are Not." *American Documentation* 11(1960):204.

21. *Guidelines for Academic Health Sciences Libraries.* AAHSLD/MLA Joint Task Force. Revised Draft, April, 1985. Erika Love, Chairman.

22. Butler, Meredith. "Electronic Publishing and Its Impact on Libraries: A Literature Review." *Library Resources and Technical Services* 28(January-March 1984):41-58.

23. Drew, Sally. "Online Databases: Some Questions of Ownership." *Wilson Library Bulletin* 59(June 1985):661-3.

24. Betts, Mitch. "Federal Historians Alarmed at Loss of Computerized Data." *Computerworld* 19(September 23, 1985):34.

25. Neavill, Gordon B. "Electronic Publishing, Libraries, and the Survival of Information." *Library Resources and Technical Services* 28(January-March 1984):76-89.

26. Neustadt, Richard M. *The Birth of Electronic Publishing: Legal and Economic Issues in Telephone, Cable and Over-the-air Teletext and Videotext.* White Plains, NY: Knowledge Industry, 1982.

27. Brodman, Estelle. "The Physician as Consumer of Medical Literature." *Bulletin of the New York Academy of Medicine* 61(April 1985):266-74.

28. Givens, Mary King, and McDonell, W. Ellen. "End User Instructions for Searching MEDLARS." *Medical Reference Services Quarterly* 4(Summer 1985):63-7.

29. Lancaster, F. W. *Libraries and Librarians in an Age of Electronics.* Arlington, VA: Information Resources Press, 1982, pp. 152-3.

30. Thompson, James. *The End of Libraries.* London: Bingley, 1982.

31. Hewison, Nancy S. "Making the Time for 'Futures' Work in Reference Services." *Medical Reference Services Quarterly* 4(Spring 1985):85-9.

32. Fenichel, Carol Hansen. "Online Communications Publications for End-Users." *Online* 9(May 1985):129-32.

33. Friend, Linda. "Independence at the Terminal: Training Student End Users to Do Online Literature Searching." *Journal of Academic Librarianship* 11(1985):136-41.

34. Brassil, Ellen C. "Information Management Education: Integrating the Old With the New." *Medical Reference Services Quarterly* 4(Spring 1985):91-5.

35. Matheson, Nina, and Lindberg, Donald A.B. "Subgroup Report on Medical Information Science Skills." *Journal of Medical Education* 59(November part 2, 1984):155-9.

36. Slingluff, Deborah; Lev, Yvonne; and Eisan, Andrew. "An End User Search Service in an Academic Health Sciences Library." *Medical Reference Services Quarterly* 4 (Spring 1985):11-21.

37. Halperin, Michael. "Free "Do-It-Yourself" Online Searching . . . What to Expect." *Online* 9(March 1985):82-4.

38. Egeland, Janet, and Foreman, Gertrude. "Reference Services: Searching and Search Techniques." In: Darling, Louise, ed. *Handbook of Medical Library Practice* vol.1 4th ed. Chicago: Medical Library Association, 1982,pp.183-235.

End User Search Systems: An Overview

James Shedlock

ABSTRACT. Many user-friendly search systems and software packages are now on the market and make it easy for the health care professional to access remote databases without the assistance of a search analyst. This paper describes the major end user search systems and software packages providing an overview of features such as how a product appeals to the user, documentation, costs, and differences between technical systems and the user-friendly versions. A discussion of department management of end user services is provided along with a description of future trends in end user searching.

Along with word processing, computer games, do-it-yourself programming, and information management capabilities, the microcomputer revolution of the 1980s has given us user-friendly online search systems. These new versions of familiar online retrieval systems are designed to appeal directly to the end user, defined for the purposes of this monograph as an individual who personally requests a computer-generated bibliography from a trained searcher and applies the search results to solving a specific health care problem. A computer literate user population is growing and their demands for information, guidance, counsel, and assistance regarding access to these user-friendly systems needs to be met by medical reference librarians and information service managers. Medical reference librarians and managers fulfill a significant professional role by personally disseminating value-added information about end user search systems. This role can be expressed in many ways: as instructors in formal seminars and workshops, as consultants to in-

---

James Shedlock is Head of Public Services, Northwestern University Medical Library, 303 East Chicago Avenue, Chicago, IL 60611. Formerly, he was Coordinator—Online Search Services, Health Sciences Library, University of North Carolina at Chapel Hill. He received an A.M.L.S. from the University of Michigan. Mr. Shedlock is editor of the "Column of Opinion and Exchange" for *Medical Reference Services Quarterly*.

dividuals or departments, and as guides to individuals via the reference interview or other informal contacts.

To assist readers with their role of disseminating information about end user search systems, an overview of existing systems follows. Search features, how a system defines its concept of "user-friendliness," the differences between end user systems and their more technical counterparts, costs, training, and documentation are described. The article concentrates on major products currently on the market and on those that provide access to health care information. Emphasis is also placed on those systems that are directly available to the end user. Finally, front-end and gateway software packages and how they differ in approach from vendor-based systems are presented, as well some comments about the reference department's use of these systems and the future direction of end user searching.

REVIEW OF THE LITERATURE

Generally, the literature on end user search systems can be divided into two categories: the professional literature, written by either the producers of the systems or by reference librarians writing critical reviews and general commentary; or the promotional literature, in the form of announcements, press releases and news items, written by the producers and disseminated in trade publications. There are many articles about training the end user, the impact of such systems on professional roles, as well as vendor newsletter items describing products and features. These articles are not reviewed here.

Much of the professional literature discusses a comparison between three prominent systems: BRS Information Technologies' BRS/AFTER DARK, DIALOG Information Retrieval Corporation's KNOWLEDGE INDEX, and BRS/Saunders Colleague. Tenopir[1] compares KNOWLEDGE INDEX with BRS/AFTER DARK and analyzes the search systems for subject focus, availability and selection of databases, and the mechanics of operating each system. Tenopir evaluates the advantages and disadvantages within each service and concludes with remarks on the future potential of such systems. In another paper, Tenopir[2] writes of user-friendly search systems that appeal to the health professional.

Ojala[3] offers the same kind of comparison between BRS/AFTER DARK and KNOWLEDGE INDEX. She analyzes the differences between end user systems and the comprehensive and technical systems familiar to search analysts, and provides a base for discussing searching mechanics on the user-friendly systems. Janke[4] compares the same two systems for database coverage, ease of use, search commands, hours of access, and costs. His review includes a description of using BRS/AFTER DARK as a reference department search service for faculty and students. A valuable bibliography is also provided[5] and is updated in a recent article.[6] Trzebiatowski[7] describes a similar end user study using BRS/AFTER DARK. Clancy[8] and Kaplan[9] review these major end user services, as does Baker[10] and Slingluff.[11]

Garfield[12] addresses scientists in two articles discussing Sci-Mate. He traces Sci-Mate's historical development and provides insight into the product design, which is intended to facilitate information management and searching. A different perspective comes from Stout and Marcinko who address information specialists in their report of Sci-Mate.[13] Other articles directly from the producers of end user search systems come from Horowitz and Bleich,[14,15] describing the development of PaperChase and subsequent user reaction.

MEDIS, the most recent end user system to be marketed by a major online vendor to health professionals, is described by Collen and Flagle.[16] The National Library of Medicine's user-friendly cancer protocol information system is described by Stonehill,[17] and by Culliton.[18] Haynes et al.[19] provide a useful cost comparison between all the different routes for access to the MEDLINE database. Their study leads to an interesting discussion on the value and price of user-friendly search systems. Lyon[20] provides a useful bibliography on the topic.

Tenopir provides information on software for online searching that includes descriptions of front-end packages for access to one system or many systems.[21] Pisciotta, Evans and Albright[22] discuss SearchHelper, a menu-driven front-end software package for searching Information Access Corporation's databases on the DIALOG computer. Levy[23] and Wible[24] both review gateway systems including Sci-Mate, SearchHelper and In-Search.

Finally, Broering[25,26] discusses the concept of an integrated library system at Georgetown University Medical Library that supports the miniMEDLINE search system. Because miniMEDLINE is a locally available end user search system, it represents the future direction of these search systems for librarians and health professionals.

SEARCH SYSTEM DESCRIPTIONS

BRS/AFTER DARK and BRS/BRKTHRU

BRS Information Technologies announced the availability of its first user-friendly search system, BRS/AFTER DARK, in 1982. The first of many end user searching products, BRS/AFTER DARK was the prototype of the BRS menu-driven systems. Using a menu to assist the search process became the chief characteristic of the BRS line of end user products. Since the arrival of AFTER DARK, BRS has enhanced its search system almost to the point of having very little in the way of differences between the user-friendly mode and the more technical SEARCH System. BRS has also marketed the menu-driven system to professional groups of end users; chief among them is the health professional group for which BRS/Saunders Colleague was developed.

BRS/AFTER DARK. BRS/AFTER DARK is a general, no frills, easy-to-use search system that can appeal to many different types of users. Its unique features include: low cost ($10 to $25 per hour depending on database searched and including telecommunication costs, with a monthly minimum of $12); a limited variety of databases (only twenty-three databases out of more than seventy), but generally something for everyone, taken from the full range of BRS databases. Availability for access runs from 6 PM to midnight Monday through Friday, all day Saturday (6 AM to 4AM), and Sunday from 6 AM to 2PM and from 7 PM to 4 AM. These features make BRS/AFTER DARK especially appealing to the computer hobbyist who wants access to information sources while at home.

BRS/BRKTHRU. BRS/BRKTHRU is a day-time version of BRS/AFTER DARK, with the added advantage of access to all of the BRS databases. BRS/BRKTHRU is likely to appeal to professionals who want access to information while at work. Costs for using BRS/BRKTHRU vary according to the database searched; reduced rates apply after 6 PM. Document charges are also assessed according to database searched, time of day the citations are printed, and format selected.

BRS/Saunders Colleague

BRS Information Technologies joined with the W.B. Saunders Company, a major medical publisher, to produce BRS/Saunders Colleague. This product aims at a highly specialized group of professionals who are eager to tackle the information management problems associated with the health sciences disciplines. Since its beginnings, BRS has always appealed to the medical librarian because of its emphasis on health care information, and it is no surprise to see this product on the market. BRS/Saunders Colleague appeals to the health professional in a number of ways. All of the medically-oriented databases from BRS are separated out and arranged in one special Medical Search Service for users to select their "library" of choice. Included in these libraries are special databases designed for the health professional—namely, the full text of major medical textbooks and journals. Colleague provides access to all of the BRS databases which helps an end user complement his medical search with other, relevant sources of information. Colleague is available during the day (twenty-two hours per day from Monday through Saturday and from 6 AM to 2 PM and 7 PM to 4 AM on Sunday) when the busy health professional most likely wants to track down information.

These BRS products are noteworthy for their approach to the end user. BRS user-friendly services are essentially menu-driven, providing natural, English-language queries and options from which to choose a course of action. The menu acts as the intermediary and covers all the familiar search commands and features of the technical system. Using BRS/Saunders Colleague as an example, the menu provides the following functions:

— Introduces the user to the choice of service (the Master Menu): Medical Search Service (health-related databases) or General Search Service (all other databases);
— Offers a choice of databases to search (databases are grouped by "libraries" in a subject arrangement);
— Describes the libraries and the databases;
— Asks the user if he is inexperienced in searching and requires detailed prompts or is experienced to a degree that only basic cues are needed to proceed through the search.

The queries above greet the user each time he or she logs into the system. Because menu-driven systems can become tedious after a few hours of searching, the "User Experience Menu" is especially significant. By answering "No" to the inexperienced level, the user can save some time in searching and use the available commands along with command stacking to speed through a completed search.

The commands accompany each response in the search and include: Root, Print (in three basic formats of "Short," "Medium" and "Long"), Print Offline, Explode, Display, Change, Return to Master Menu, Return to Database Menu, and Off.

While some basic searching can take place without reading any documentation, the manual that comes with each of the BRS products teaches the user about more sophisticated product features for optimal searching. For example, Boolean and positional operators are all taught through the documentation. Familiar technical concepts like nesting, truncation, back referencing to previous search statements, field qualification, restricting retrieval to year and language, saving, executing, and purging strategies are all explained in the manual.

The documentation for BRS/Saunders Colleague is to be commended for anticipating user's questions. The manual begins with basics like preparing the hardware for communication with BRS, "dialing in and choosing a service," and describing how information is organized. The manual explains all of the different search features and provides database descriptions which include specialized tips for searching. The manual supplies the user with a "quick reference card" and tutorial discs on the basics of searching in general, and specifically, on searching MEDLINE.

What does a product like BRS/Saunders Colleague not do that can only be done in the technical mode? In examining the manual, the item Colleague does not teach the user is the "Limit" command. Other differences with full system access are a matter of degree and emphasis. For example, while the BRS/Saunders Colleague mentions indexing and subject descriptors, it does not stress the use of these terms when searching. Very little is written about planning a search strategy nor about conceptualizing what the search should encompass before going online. Cost-effective techniques are not discussed. This is because Colleague does not try to make over the end user into a search analyst. BRS/Saunders Colleague mirrors the capabilities of the SEARCH System which the manual describes in language written for the layman.

The cost of using Colleague includes a number of components. BRS/Saunders charges a $75 registration fee ($125 for groups); this fee includes account preparation, password and manual. Searching is charged by the connect hour of $32 during prime time (6 AM to 6 PM) and $20 per hour during non-prime time. These rates apply to most of the databases offered in the Medical Search Service; a few databases like PsycINFO and the International Pharmaceutical Abstracts database have a surcharge. Databases from the General Search Service have variable connect hour rates. Charges are also levied for citations and documents printed in the long or full formats. Saving searches and printing and mailing citations in the offline mode are also assessed. BRS/Saunders Colleague accounts have a monthly minimum of $15 ($50 for groups), and volume discounts are available.

DIALOG's KNOWLEDGE INDEX

KNOWLEDGE INDEX has also been available since 1982. It is a scaled down version of the powerful DIALOG search software, offers users a handful of major databases, including all of the MEDLINE file, and presents users with a straightforward approach to searching.

While BRS can be characterized by its menu, KNOWLEDGE INDEX is known as a command-driven search system. Like the technical system, the user must know a command to initiate an action on the part of the computer. DIALOG's sophisticated command language is reduced to the most basic commands in KNOWLEDGE INDEX: Begin, Find, Expand, Display, Recap, Cost, Help, Logoff, Keep, Order and Page. Other technical features, such as Limit, Print, Type, or Prefix and Suffix qualifiers are not utilized.

The training for KNOWLEDGE INDEX is provided in a workbook-manual that teaches the user how to search. The workbook starts by explaining a concept, such as entering a search term, then diagrams how the printout or screen will appear. Each section concludes with a worksheet that suggests a systematic use of commands. The workbook progresses from simple searching, including Boolean operators, to printing and truncation, author and journal name searching, using descriptors, and nesting. The "Help" command provides assistance to users when they go online and forget concepts described in the workbook. Special commands are mapped out for searching with a microcomputer and for displaying more than one citation at a time. KNOWLEDGE INDEX does teach the user how to order documents online if the original material is not available locally. A recent feature added to KNOWLEDGE INDEX is electronic mail. Individuals can communicate with one another or any other user participating in KNOWLEDGE INDEX by sending messages, sharing files, conferencing, reading bulletin boards, and sending and receiving correspondence via U.S. mail.

KNOWLEDGE INDEX offers the user access to only thirty-one databases from the more than 230 databases available on the full service. With these thirty-one databases, KNOWLEDGE INDEX has something for everyone: health, legal, life science, medicine, drug information, some full-text files, business, government-produced, psychology, news and general information. KNOWLEDGE INDEX is also characterized by the fact that it is only available after 6 PM. This time factor may discourage health professionals who want to search during regular business hours. Another special characteristic of KNOWLEDGE INDEX is its price: a flat rate of $24 per hour, which includes telecommunication costs and database royalties for all thirty-one databases. DIALOG has traditionally offered a pricing scheme that charges the user only for the time used on the system; this policy is true for KNOWLEDGE INDEX, and means there is no monthly minimum charge for having a password. Start-up costs for a password, manual and newsletter subscription are held to $35, which also includes two hours of search time. Accounts are generally established with an individual's credit card; however, DIALOG recently changed this policy, and institutions are able to subscribe to KNOWLEDGE INDEX and receive an invoice.

PaperChase

PaperChase has a number of unique characteristics that make it stand out among all the end user search systems. Privately developed at Beth Israel Hospital in Boston with assistance from National Library of Medicine grants, PaperChase grew out of attempts by physicians to design a management system for their department's reprint files. With the success in software design, PaperChase essentially became a user-friendly way of searching citations available in the hospital library's journal collection. Originally a small database, PaperChase was made larger to include the entire MEDLINE database from 1972 forward. In 1984 PaperChase was made available on CompuServe, a publicly available search system offering a wide variety of general information databases.

Besides its user-friendly approach to searching, PaperChase has a number of unique characteristics that make it particularly noteworthy. These include:

—a non-commercial operating philosophy;
—its attempt to solve some of the information management problems in health science disciplines;
—its instructional stance that emphasizes how medical literature is organized so that better search results are achieved; and
—its ability to link a search system with locally available journal literature.

The chief interest in discussing PaperChase is its user-friendly approach to searching MEDLINE. PaperChase is menu-driven, but much different in concept than other such systems. Because PaperChase was initiated to find citations that were available locally, it started as an in-house system that required very little in the way of documentation. There is no introduction to the system, nor is there any brief description of how to start the search process. The first menu asks the user what the computer should "LOOK FOR." The user enters a topic either by single word or phrase, and the computer responds with options of author names, journal names, subject headings, or title words from which to choose. The menu leads the user gradually, but quickly, into building sets of citations that can be matched against each other (implied Boolean AND) or reviewed for relevance.

Another chief characteristic of PaperChase is its instructional capability to lead the user from key title words to relevant terms from *Medical Subject Headings*.[27] After the initial look-up for a given term, PaperChase responds with suggested subject headings that could be explored for a more comprehensive search. This suggestion demonstrates that more citations are in the file that might be relevant to the topic at hand, and teaches the user about the importance and value of controlled vocabulary. More than any other search system available to end users, PaperChase emphasizes the value of indexing to information management in the health sciences.

Documentation for PaperChase is virtually non-existent, and there are no start-up costs to get into the system. Search costs vary depending on whether access is through CompuServe or direct to Boston via one of the telecommunication networks. Access charges are: $13 per connect hour; $6 per hour for telecommunications; $4 per hour royalty; $.10 per citation or abstract displayed or printed; and $.10 for each search statement or list created. Offline printing is available for an additional $6 to cover postage and handling. Volume discounts are also available.

Protocol Data Query (PDQ)

As part of their mission to disseminate information to health practitioners, the National Cancer Institute and the National Library of Medicine cooperated in a joint venture to produce the PDQ database. This single database takes a menu-driven approach to searching and is designed for use by the nation's oncologists, physicians, and other health care workers interested in finding the latest information about cancer treatments. The database provides extensive menus which search four files of information: (1) state-of-the-art cancer information, (2) a physician directory, (3) an organization directory; and, (4) protocols. The database is available only in this user-friendly version.

Searching in PDQ is strictly limited to the menu options made available at each step of the search process. There is no good way to bypass a predefined menu in order to retrieve desired information; i.e., there is no way to enter a search term without a menu prompt from the computer. Because PDQ is a prototype of similar databases still in planning stages, the existing documentation does not instruct the user with all the possibilities for manipulating the menu options. Becoming familiar with PDQ's capabilities requires the time to explore all the options for each of the different subfiles.

Like other NLM databases, PDQ is available for searching around the clock; late evening and weekend hours are not guaranteed and some down time for system maintenance is scheduled each day from 11:00 PM to 11:15 PM. Searching costs can be estimated at $22 per hour for prime time (10 AM to 5 PM) and $15 per hour for non-prime time. The *PDQ User Guide* provides basic information on connecting to PDQ, using the menus and commands, and explaining the different files and how they can be searched.

AMA/NET

In 1982 the American Medical Association joined with the GTE Corporation to form the basis of GTE's Medical Information Network (MINET). The intent of AMA/NET is to provide physicians with easy access to up-to-date information sources. The information found in AMA/NET supports clinical, administrative, and medical practice decision making; electronic mail is also available. The search system is designed to be user-friendly and can be accessed via microcomputers or data terminals.

AMA/NET has six services for subscribers to access: Drug Information, Disease and Diagnostic Information, Patient Management, Educational Services, Business and Professional Services, and General Medical Information and Literature. AMA publications form the base for some of these services. For example, *AMA Drug Evaluations* and *Current Medical Information and Terminology* support the drug information and disease information services.

Access to the literature was limited to citations about the socioeconomic aspects of health care. In 1984, AMA/NET loaded an additional file, EMPIRES, which gave subscribers access to clinical literature. EMPIRES is a subset of EMBASE, the Excerpta Medica database covering all aspects of human medicine. EMPIRES dates to 1982 and represents the literature from approximately 200 major clinical journals. To search the file, a subscriber must use the structured command language available on AMA/NET.

AMA/NET can be used around the clock; prime time is defined as 7 AM to 6 PM and non-prime time is 6 PM to 7 AM. Prices for searching depend on the specific file that is used. Rates vary from $25 to $39 per hour; EMPIRES costs $39 per hour for time searched in this file. Other charges include a registration fee of $100 (waived for AMA members); a user registration fee of $25 for each additional password; $15 for instructional materials and documentation; $15 for profile changes; and $20 monthly minimum.

As AMA/NET exists currently, the system offers little competition to services like BRS/Saunders Colleague. Access to the literature for clinical problems is limited. The full-text information files are online versions of existing print tools, readily available in personal or hospital and academic libraries. The search system requires a user to master a command language that takes time and effort to learn.

MEDIS

MEDIS is the newest of the end user search systems aimed at the health care professional. MEDIS is the product of Mead Data Central of Dayton, Ohio, known primarily for its success in developing and marketing full-text information systems for legal literature and for news services. MEDIS, like BRS/Saunders Colleague, provides access to both the MEDLINE database and the full text of some seventy publications, including journals and books. MEDIS provides MEDLINE access back to 1981 and is accessible by telephone connections through computer terminals linked to modems, or by using dedicated Mead Data Central terminals that are specially programmed to handle searching functions.

Searching takes place through commands, menu options, and specialized function keys if a user has a dedicated terminal. Costs for searching MEDIS are based on connect hour charges plus search session charges. The connect hour rate is $20; session charges range from $6 to $12; adding extra levels during the search process costs $3. There is no extra charge for online printing, but offline printing is charged at $.02 per line; a $15 handling charge is applied for offline prints sent by Mead Data Central.

FRONT-END SYSTEMS

Front-end or gateway software packages are sometimes interchangeable terms that refer to programs that act as an interface between the end user and some online search system or database. Front-end packages generally work with one specific vendor, database or even a group of databases, while gateway software may provide access to multiple vendors.

Sci-Mate

Sci-Mate is probably the most prominent of the current front-end systems on the market, due primarily to its appeal to scientists who manage their own professional literature files. Sci-Mate is a product from the Institute for Scientific Information in Philadelphia, the producers of *Science Citation Index, Social Science Citation Index*, and various other hard-copy indexes and databases. Released in 1983, Sci-Mate now consists of three separate but complementary software packages: the Universal Online Searcher, the Personal Data Manager, and the Sci-Mate Editor.

The Universal Online Searcher allows the end user to search any one of the major online vendors: ISI, DIALOG, BRS, NLM, or SDC/ORBIT. The program acts as an interface between the user and the host vendor. By using menu options, the program will log the user into the system of choice and translate the menu options into the technical command language of the host vendor. A three-step process occurs which is invisible to the user. As the menu prompts the user for the search strategy, the responses are: (1) translated into host computer commands, (2) transmitted to the host computer, and lastly, (3) a response is sent back to the user's terminal. The Universal Online Searcher suggests a solution to the problem of all the technical commands associated with online searching. The potential user should be aware of the fact that translating menu responses and search statements takes time, and the user pays for time when accessing remote search systems. While this package can translate natural English-language queries from the menu into system commands, the user is still responsible for initial communication with each host—namely, to get a password in order to search the vendor's databases. Sci-Mate does not provide the passwords or assist in this first essential step in making the online connection.

Sci-Mate's Personal Data Manager lives up to its name as a program that helps the user create his own database of citations retrieved from searches using the Universal Online Searcher, from searches conducted for the user, and from personal reading, notes, and correspondence. The Personal Data Manager relies on templates to construct a specific file of information. Templates establish record formats which define the fields of data for the database records. Without established formats, the manager cannot retrieve information filed in the database. The templates are essential to the sorting feature available in the program. The Personal Data Manager also uses menu options to lead the user to a desired function, depending on the application that needs to be done during a given session.

The third program of the Sci-Mate Software System is the Sci-Mate Editor. The Editor package allows for the automatic renumbering and reformatting of bibliographic references within a manuscript. The Editor formats according to the specifications required by a journal's editor.

The packages come with detailed manuals which instruct the user in the intricacies of searching, database creation, and editing. Help features are built into the software. The programs can be purchased separately, but work well in conjunction with each other. The prices for the various programs are relatively high: Manager costs $540, Searcher costs $440, and Editor costs $399. Discounts are available when all three programs are purchased together.

Other Front-End Software

Specialized software packages are available to assist users with access to single or multiple search systems. These packages for the most part are user-friendly and rely on menu-driven features to take the user through the search process. For example, a package called

SEARCHWARE is used to access DIALOG and operates at three different levels of search experience. Novice searchers are instructed to plot their search strategy by filling in blanks on the menu screens. SEARCHWARE is unique in its approach to subject searching; the software is sold by subject areas which include appropriate documentation for DIALOG databases that concentrate in the chosen subject. SEARCHWARE is priced at $290 for the first subject module and $100 for each additional module. When purchasing the software a user is also buying a DIALOG password and bypasses any contact with the DIALOG corporation.

Pro-Search is another example of new software on the market that will act as an interface with DIALOG and BRS. Pro-Search is targeted for the intermediary searcher with special features that make searching easier. A package such as this one could be used by searchers unfamiliar with an infrequently used search system. Knowledgeable end users would also be able to take advantage of these same features. The special features include: pre-formulation, single keystroke functions for printing and logon, search interruption to allow changes in uploaded strategy, and detailed accounting for all online searches. Pro-Search can be used to access other systems, like NLM, but these are searched in the native-language mode which does not accommodate the special features mentioned above. Pro-Search is priced at $495.

A number of other programs are available but generally serve as front-ends to specific databases, not all of them oriented toward the health sciences literature. While the packages mentioned here fall into the category of end user "search systems," users should remember that these packages provide access to vendors or databases, but they do not teach the user the intellectual aspects related to online searching. User-friendly search systems open the door to searching, but at the same time can leave the user who is unfamiliar with information management and bibliographic structure only at the threshold of fully utilizing a desired source of information. User-friendly search systems or packages are not necessarily database-friendly.

REFERENCE DEPARTMENT USE OF END USER SEARCH SYSTEMS

While medical reference librarians have concentrated on teaching their users about the new, user-friendly search systems, reference department managers should consider using the same systems or packages as part of an information service. The reference department receives the benefit of a number of advantages when an end user system is managed from the department. Using an end user search system provides an information service to users who lack the essential equipment and investment required for personal searching. Many users are still inquisitive about searching in general and desire to learn more about searching via a real information need. End user searching helps the reference staff teach more users about information management principles, whether the teaching takes place formally in an introductory session or informally at the terminal. An end user system managed by the department demonstrates to users that the library is utilizing the latest technology to update information services and replace the old way of doing things (i.e., manual searching by the user).

There are, however, a number of problems associated with establishing this new service, which mirror the problems managers encountered when intermediary search services were first established. Acquiring terminals, their number, kind (dumb or smart), and location pose a significant funding problem. Telephone connections and costs, as well as telecommunication access, must be considered in this service. Telecommunication quirks like line noise and downtime, while not always significant for experienced searchers, can frustrate novice searchers, especially if terminals must be scheduled among many anxious users.

Education and training, even for user-friendly systems, must be planned, designed, scheduled, and offered with the new search service. A certain amount of handholding is to be expected as part of the search service. This of course affects scheduling and even setting assignments for those reference librarians more skilled at training. These significant educational and personnel issues require policy decisions.

Password security is a new issue tied to end user searching within the reference department. Fortunately, vendors have addressed this problem and most have resolved the issue. However, a manager's options are limited to systems and software that provide multiple password security.

Finally, pricing and billing decisions must be established before the service is initiated. The old questions about how much to charge the user for a service (online) acquired from an outside information source (database producer and vendor) in a new format (i.e., self-service) must be raised again and an acceptable decision reached by department and library management.

Examples of end user systems that can be managed from a reference department include PaperChase and BRS/PROMPT. While PaperChase is directly available to the end user, a manager's program also exists that controls usage within the reference department. Significantly, PaperChase allows managers to register users, specify billing arrangements and indicate expiration dates for passwords. PaperChase also allows the manager to specify local library holdings that are matched against retrieval and are displayed first to assigned passwords. A report feature also exists in PaperChase and includes usage by billing group, comments from users, daily use questionnaire responses, an expiration report for passwords, a listing of temporary passwords, the holdings list, usage and costs by individuals, and ledger sheets.

BRS/PROMPT is a specially designed accounting software package that assists managers in tracking usage of BRS/Saunders Colleague. The software is available for $75, plus a $15 monthly minimum for the Colleague password itself. The software is designed for managers to input policy decisions regarding access via menu prompts. Once data are entered into the software, the parameters are set and need not be changed. Software is required for each terminal that will access the BRS computers since BRS/PROMPT also acts as a communication package.

FUTURE DIRECTIONS: IN-HOUSE SEARCH SYSTEMS

End user search systems, including front-end or gateway software, represent an interim between intermediary search services and future in-house search systems. An in-house system consists of databases stored on the library's own computer and accessed through an easy-to-operate, natural-language retrieval software. An in-house system could be integrated into the other automated systems which the library employs to control its bibliographic records, forming a totally integrated search system. Because the system is locally available and does not require long distance communications with another computer, it would be free to use by anyone walking into the library. By storing databases in-house, the library staff offers its users a favorable alternative to manual searching.

There are three significant problems to be solved before in-house search systems can be implemented: acquiring the hardware, the data, and the software. Hardware problems center on costs; is the library in a position to obtain funding to purchase and then maintain minicomputers, software, and data? Compatibility issues can be resolved once funding is secured and software and data are ready to be purchased. Data for an in-house system are now available from the National Library of Medicine through its subset policy.[28] The new policy is an extension of NLM's distribution of MEDLINE tapes to major commercial vendors. Search software is currently on the market that enables libraries to complete an in-house system. For example, BRS sells the software used for its SEARCH System and is the only commercial vendor to do so.

An example of an in-house search system is miniMEDLINE of the Georgetown University Medical Library. MiniMEDLINE is a user-friendly, menu-driven search system that appears similar to PaperChase. MiniMEDLINE is integrated into Georgetown's Library Information System (LIS) and has been operational since 1982. A number of libraries have already purchased miniMEDLINE for use in their institutions. MiniMEDLINE uses subsets derived from the MEDLINE database and is updated monthly. The subset is based on a selection of basic science, clinical medicine, and nursing journal titles available within the medical library. The aim of the search system is to satisfy the immediate needs of users, and to respond to their educational and clinical questions; intermediary search services are recommended for intensive and scholarly information needs of researchers.

SUMMARY

One of the primary messages medical reference librarians can relate to their users it that "user-friendliness" is a relative term which each health care professional has to accept when reviewing the many systems and software described here. Each end user needs to decide whether a product is acceptable to meet his specific information needs. Another message important both to information professional and end user is the amount of change that many of these systems will undergo in their development. Online access to information will continue to evolve. In-house search systems will soon become the trend rather than the innovation.

REFERENCES

1. Tenopir, Carol. "Dialog's Knowledge Index and Brs/After Dark: Database Searching on Personal Computers." *Library Journal* 108 (March 1, 1983): 471-4.
2. Tenopir, Carol. "Online Information in the Health Sciences." *Library Journal* 109(October 15, 1983): 1932-3.
3. Ojala, Marydee. "Knowledge Index: A Review." *Online* 7 (September 1983): 31-4.
4. Janke, Richard V. "BRS/After Dark: The Birth of Online Self-Service." *Online* 7 (September 1983): 12-25.
5. Janke, Richard V. "Online After Six: End User Searching Comes of Age." *Online* 8 (November 1984): 15-29.
6. Janke, Richard V. "Presearch Counseling for Client Searchers (End Users)." *Online* 9 (September 1985): 13-26.
7. Trzebiatowski, Elaine. "End User Study on BRS/After Dark." *RQ* 23 (Summer 1984): 446-50.
8. Clancy, Stephen. "BRS/Saunders Colleague: An Information Service for Medical Professionals." *Database* 8 (June 1985):108-21.
9. Kaplan, Robin. "Knowledge Index: A Review." *Database* 8 (June 1985): 122-8.
10. Baker, Carole A. "COLLEAGUE: A Comprehensive Online Medical Library for the End User." *Medical Reference Services Quarterly* 3 (Winter 1984):13-26.
11. Slingluff, Deborah; Lev, Yvonne; and Eisan, Andrew. "An End User Search Service in an Academic Health Sciences Library." *Medical Reference Services Quarterly* 4 (Spring 1985):11-21.
12. Garfield, Eugene. "Introducing Sci-Mate—A Menu-Driven Microcomputer Software Package for Online and Offline Information Retrieval. Part I. The Sci-Mate Personal Data Manager; Part II. The Sci-Mate Universal Online Searcher." *Current Contents* 6 (March 21, 1983): 5-12; (April 4, 1983): 5-15.
13. Stout, Catheryne, and Marcinko, Thomas. "SCI-MATE: A Menu-Driven Universal Online Searcher and Personal Data Manager." *Online* 7 (September 1983):112-6.
14. Horowitz, Gary L., and Bleich, Howard L. "PaperChase: A Computer Program to Search the Medical Literature." *New England Journal of Medicine* 305 (October 15, 1981): 924-30.
15. Horowitz, Gary L., Jackson, Jerome D., and Bleich, Howard L. "PaperChase, Self-Service Bibliographic Retrieval." *Journal of the American Medical Association* 250 (November 11, 1983): 2494-9.
16. Collen, Morris F., and Flagle, Charles D. "Full-Text Medical Literature Retrieval by Computer, A Pilot Test." *Journal of the American Medical Association* 254 (November 15, 1985): 2768-74.
17. Stonehill, E. H. "P D Q: A Telephone Accessible Computerized Referral and Protocol Data Query System." *Progress in Clinical and Biological Research* 120 (1983): 163-4.
18. Culliton, Barbara J. "Information as a 'Cure' for Cancer." *Science* 227 (February 15, 1985):732.
19. Haynes, R. Brian et al. "Computer Searching of the Medical Literature, An Evaluation of MEDLINE Search Systems." *Annals of Internal Medicine* 103 (November 1985): 812-6.
20. Lyon, Sally. "End-User Searching of Online Databases: A Selective Annotated Bibliography." *Library Hi-Tech* 2 (1984): 47-50.
21. Tenopir, Carol. "Software for Online Searching." *Library Journal* 110 (October 15, 1985): 52-3.
22. Pisciotta, Henry; Evans, Nancy, and Albright, Marilyn. "Search Helper: Sancho Panza or Mephistopheles?" *Library Hi-Tech* 2 (1984): 25-32.
23. Levy, Louise R. "Gateway Software: Is It for You?" *Online* 8 (November 1984): 67-79.

24. Wible, Joseph G. "Searching Made Easy: Front-End Systems for Medical Databases." *Medical Reference Services Quarterly* 5 (Summer 1986): in press.

25. Broering, Naomi C. "The Georgetown University Library Information System (LIS): A Minicomputer-Based Integrated Library System." *Bulletin of the Medical Library Association* 71 (July 1983): 317-23.

26. Broering, Naomi C. "The miniMEDLINE SYSTEM: A Library-Based End-User Search System." *Bulletin of the Medical Library Association* 73 (April 1985): 138-45.

27. National Library of Medicine. *Medical Subject Headings—Annotated Alphabetic List*, 1985. Bethesda, MD: National Library of Medicine, 1985.

28. "NLM Announces Subsets Program." *NLM Technical Bulletin* No. 185 (September 1984): 5-12.

Issues in Mounting a Local MEDLINE Database

Frieda O. Weise
Gary A. Freiburger

ABSTRACT. Mounting a subset of the MEDLINE file on a local computer is an idea attractive to many health sciences libraries. Recent advances in computer hardware and software along with the National Library of Medicine's issuance of a "Domestic MEDLARS Subset Policy" have also made it feasible. Before a MEDLINE subset is mounted, however, numerous technical, policy and training issues have to be considered. The Health Sciences Library has recently pondered the possibilities of mounting a MEDLINE subset on its own computer. This article is a discussion of both general and specific issues and questions which arose in the library's deliberations. It is offered as a framework for discussion to other libraries who may be involved in a similar venture.

BACKGROUND

Online MEDLINE service has been available nationwide since October 1971, but until recently, only mainframe computers were capable of supporting the system.[1,2] During the past several years, however, developments in computer hardware and software have made it technologically possible to mount large databases locally. As a result of these developments, persons other than search intermediaries, or end users, have been able to access computerized bibliographic databases directly. To meet new user demands for access to its databases, the National Library of Medicine (NLM) announced its "Domestic MEDLARS Subset Policy," which makes it possible for health sciences libraries or other organizations to obtain a subset of the MEDLINE database to mount on a local computer.

Frieda Weise is the Assistant Director for Public Services at the University of Maryland Health Sciences Library, 111 S. Greene Street, Baltimore, MD 21201. She holds an M.L.S. from the University of Michigan. Gary Freiburger is the Head, Information Systems and Technology at the University of Maryland Health Sciences Library. His M.L.S. is from the University of Texas.

Hardware

High capacity mini and microcomputers are now available at a fraction of the cost of mainframe computers. These machines, while not always matching the mainframes in performance, offer computing power sufficient for multiple users to search large databases. Each year, disk drives become smaller as they increase in capacity.

Software

The MEDLARS software was designed to run on large mainframe computers and has not been adapted for mini or microcomputers. Moreover, the complexity of the retrieval system requires a concentrated training effort to take advantage of the system's powerful search capabilities. As a result, most searches on the MEDLARS system are performed by intermediaries for the end user.

In recent years, however, several different approaches have been developed which simplify searching for the end user. Software to achieve this falls into roughly three categories:

1. A user-friendly interface on a central system at the database vendor's site. Examples of this approach are BRS/AFTER DARK, KNOWLEDGE INDEX, and PaperChase.[3]
2. A user-friendly interface which runs on a microcomputer rather than on a central system. Examples of this are Sci-Mate and Pro-Search.
3. A user-friendly system, mounted on a computer at the local library, which contains a subset of a nationally available database, such as miniMEDLINE.[4] Other examples of software available to mount a subset on a local computer are BRS/SEARCH, a mini and microcomputer version of the BRS mainframe software; the D-SIRE module of the Data Research Atlas system based on the SIRE retrieval system; and the SEARCH module of the Washington University BACS system.

Public Expectations

The popular microcomputer literature abounds with articles aimed at demystifying bibliographic searching and encouraging microcomputer users to either subscribe to a user-friendly system or purchase a user-friendly interface to facilitate searching.[5,6] Moreover, library patrons are becoming computer-literate through using online catalogs and through the availability of other end user search systems, and are becoming aware of the possibilities of performing bibliographic searches without a librarian intermediary.

NLM Policy

In July 1984, the National Library of Medicine announced a subset policy and license agreement through which portions of the MEDLARS database were made available to domestic users.[7] Currently, MEDLINE is the only database for which NLM will provide subsets. The software required to store and search subsets is not available from NLM and is the responsibility of the licensee.

FUNDAMENTAL ISSUES

Rationale

Before deciding to mount a subset of the MEDLINE database on a local computer, a health sciences library needs to face numerous technical, policy, and training issues. The questions and issues raised throughout this article comprise a framework for discussion and planning.

The fundamental question libraries must answer is "Why do it?" This is particularly important given the array of databases which are commercially available. Examples include PaperChase, BRS/AFTER DARK, BRS/BRKTHRU, BRS/Saunders Colleague, and KNOWLEDGE INDEX. Both Colleague and PaperChase provide accounting modules for libraries that wish to act as brokers for the systems. Libraries can thus provide access to a large system and control the access to the system, but are spared the work and expense involved in mounting a database themselves.

A major consideration is whether the system will provide enough benefits to the library and its users to justify the costs. The system should offer library patrons benefits in terms of accessibility, ease of use, database content, and low search costs compared with commercially available systems. Additionally, the system should be an integral part of the library's long-range automation plans, as well as those of its parent institution since it will likely have a major impact on the library budget.

End User Perceptions

Libraries that have provided their patrons with access to commercial end user systems such as BRS/AFTER DARK have found that patrons have little understanding of what is in a database, how the information is structured, or how to use the retrieval system efficiently.[8,9] Although user-friendly systems are widely discussed in microcomputer magazines, the information is often sketchy and inaccurate, giving the reader the impression that the system is far more comprehensive and simple than it really is.[10] Furthermore, experience with first time online catalog users suggests that they frequently assume that the catalog contains journal citations as well.[11] The expectation is that the library ought to be able to supply this information, free, through the current system. This situation presents the library with user misconceptions to overcome before it can begin plans for mounting a MEDLINE subset. The library should involve an end user group in the planning process so that the nature of the system is understood and so that user considerations are incorporated.

SPECIFIC ISSUES

Database Content

The library must decide upon the purpose and primary audience of the database before specific decisions about its content are made. A database serving quick information needs of a student will be quite different from a database serving a chemical researcher. Once the purpose has been established, the size and structure of the file can be planned. Although the storage requirements of the MEDLINE subset desired may be influenced by the hardware and software available, the following questions regarding file content should be answered.

1. Who are the primary users of the database?
2. How many journal titles will be included?
3. What type or subject scope of journal titles will be included? What languages?
4. What time span will be covered?
5. What fields will be included in the record?

6. Will abstracts be included?
7. Will all MeSH headings and subheadings be included?
8. Which fields will be searchable?

Software

The choice of software is almost as important as the selection of database content. The two basic questions that must be addressed in selecting retrieval software are: (1) what are the functional requirements, and (2) how are the functions performed?

Functionality can range from a database management system with some searching capability to a system which has multiple searching interfaces, administrative control of passwords, and a sophisticated accounting system. It is important to choose software which will do all that you need, but there is no reason to purchase features which will never be required. How the system performs its functions will affect ease of use. Providing a user-friendly interface for the searching module is a worthy objective, but this may mean different things to different people. A menu-driven system may be appropriate for those who use the system infrequently, but a command-driven system may better serve the needs of those who use the system regularly and become impatient with menu screens. The system should be flexible enough to offer both a menu-driven and a command-driven interface which allows the user to move back and forth between them.

Ease in administering the system is also a major consideration for the library. An accounting module, for example, should be sophisticated enough to handle various billing and password control functions, but not so complicated as to require formal training in accounting.

In the process of determining functionality and ease of use, it is important to talk with those already using the software for similar applications. Any practical information that they can provide will not only supplement the vendor's descriptions and claims, but also will allow the library to better analyze how appropriate the software will be in its particular setting.

Hardware

In many settings, the choice of hardware will be easier than the choice of software. Normally the software will determine the choice of hardware since most commercial software will run only on certain brands of hardware or only under certain operating systems. Although software may run only on one manufacturer's equipment, it will normally run on a range of sizes of that equipment. For example, it may run on the DEC PDP 11 series computers, which are available from the "micro" 11/23 up to the large VAX 780. The software vendor will often be willing and able to offer help with hardware selection decisions. Employing a consultant, though expensive, may prove to be wise when the hardware costs range into the tens or hundreds of thousands of dollars.

Two important factors which will influence hardware selection are: (1) the size of the database, and (2) the number of users expected to be searching the system simultaneously. The disk storage must be able to hold the number of citations in the database; the central processing unit (CPU) must be able to handle the load of processing searches at peak times while keeping response time at an acceptable level.

The number of expected users will also determine whether a data switch will be required to queue dial-in users if all ports are busy. Several ports at different speeds should be available to accommodate modems of various baud rates.

The cost of the computer facility should not be overlooked. A room with special environmental and security safeguards may have to be constructed if none exists in the library.

Staffing

Staff from various library departments might be involved in implementing a local MEDLINE system. Most likely they will be from the systems or automation department and from public services. Staff training needs and staffing levels must be assessed. The library will have to judge whether existing staff will be able to provide the new services in addition to the current services. Some projects or services may have to be terminated if staffing is not sufficient and new positions are not likely.

Costs

Costs associated with mounting a MEDLINE subset include both initial and ongoing expenditures. The funding and budget constraints of each library will of course determine how the project will be financed. Associated costs to be considered include:

Initial costs
1. Computer facility and appropriate environmental controls
2. Computer hardware
3. Retrieval software
4. Terminals for users and staff
5. Software programming (if required)
6. Wiring and phone lines
7. Subset database
8. Staff training

Ongoing Costs
1. Hardware and Software maintenance
2. Database updates
3. Staffing
4. User training

Service

A local MEDLINE system must be convenient for users. Access should be provided through terminals in the library as well as through dial-up ports. The system, moreover, needs to support a reasonable number of simultaneous users to avoid queuing. The assignment of passwords ought to be as straightforward as possible. If there are fees for use, the library should consider whether it will be simpler to bill individuals, departments, or entire schools.

Training Users

Experience that libraries have had in training end users to search has indicated that the conceptual aspects of searching are more problematic than the mechanical.[8] What is included in training to search a local database and how it will be accomplished will, of course, be somewhat dependent upon the retrieval software. Questions to consider when planning the training program include:

1. Should users be required to attend training before a password is issued?
2. Will the training cover conceptual aspects of searching as well as the mechanical aspects?
3. How much background information about databases and their structure should be included?

4. Will training be accomplished through formal or informal means? Or both?
5. Will training be offered on a regularly scheduled basis? On demand? For individuals or groups?
6. Will the system include an online tutorial? Is it feasible to develop a tutorial to run on a microcomputer?
7. What types of printed aids are needed?

Evaluation

The evaluation of the system should be addressed early in the planning stages of the project to ensure that it can be accomplished efficiently and will yield helpful information when it is completed. Some pertinent issues to raise are:

1. What aspects of the system will the evaluation address?
2. What will the data be used for?
3. How formal should the evaluation be?
4. What methods will be used? Can the system handle an online questionnaire? If the system maintains transaction logs will the information in them be useful? Can the system generate reports from the logs?

FUTURE DEVELOPMENTS

When writing about computer technology one can always be assured that something which lies in the future when the article is written will be commonly available by the time the article is published. This article will not be any different. In fact, viable commercial uses for videodisk technology in libraries first appeared between the writing of the outline and the first draft of this article.

At the American Library Association Annual Conference in Chicago in 1985, many vendors were announcing products making use of the CD-ROM or Compact Disk—Read Only Memory technology. IMLAC, a British company, was exhibiting a prototype search system which runs on an IBM PC and uses CD-ROM on which to store the database being searched. IMLAC is working directly with five database producers: Elsevier, the American Psychological Association, and the producers of ERIC, LISA, and PAIS.

NLM has expressed an interest in entering into experimental

agreements with commercial vendors which would allow the firms to work with MEDLINE subsets to develop their own products. The products could run the gamut from twelve inch optical disks through CD-ROM and could include retrieval software.[12] CL Systems, Inc. is testing CL/MEDLINE, a system which stores three backfile years and the current year of MEDLINE on a twelve inch optical disk. Access is provided via a DEC MicroVAX II running BRS/SEARCH software with a user-friendly interface. The system will be available in June of 1986.

So called "super micros" have appeared on the market in the last several years. These machines range from the Alpha Micro, a multi-user microcomputer, to the Digital Equipment Corporation 11/23 and the MicroVAX. Disk storage capabilities vary among this class of machines; the smaller computers are compatible with disk drives holding tens of megabytes of data, while the larger computers can support drives with capacities in the gigabyte range.

As indicated above, new developments are occurring in hardware, software, and in NLM's policies. We are in a period of uncertainty as to which direction or directions will prove to be the most popular or practical. Health sciences libraries should consider all their options carefully before deciding to mount a subset of MEDLINE locally. Not only is the library's commitment in terms of resources extensive, but information technology is advancing rapidly as well.

ADDENDUM

As the final draft of this article was nearing completion, the Health Sciences Library learned that the National Library of Medicine had funded its grant proposal to mount a subset of MEDLINE on a library-based minicomputer and to evaluate the system's performance and use. The issues and questions raised in the foregoing article formed the basis of the library's discussion in determining the feasibility of the project and in writing the grant proposal.

REFERENCES

1. McCarn, Davis B., and Leiter, Joseph. "Online Services in Medicine and Beyond." *Science* 181(July 27, 1973):318-24.

2. Miles, Wyndham D. *A History of the National Library of Medicine: the Nation's Treasury of Medical Knowledge.* Washington, D.C.: U.S. Department of Health and Human

Services, National Institutes of Health, National Library of Medicine, 1982, NIH Publication no. 82-1904, p.387.

3. Horowitz, G.L., and Bleich, H.L. "PaperChase: A Computer Program to Search the Medical Literature." *New England Journal of Medicine* 305(October 15, 1981):924-30.

4. Broering, Naomi C. "The Georgetown University Library Information System (LIS): A Minicomputer-based Integrated Library System." *Bulletin of the Medical Library Association* 71(July 1983):317-23.

5. Friedman, Bernard. "Pharmaceutical Riches Online." *PC Magazine* 4(February 5, 1985):291-5.

6. Elia, Joseph J., Jr. "In-Search." *Popular Computing* 4(November 1984):149-52.

7. "National Library of Medicine Domestic MEDLARS Subset Policy." *National Library of Medicine News* 39(July-August 1984):9-11.

8. Slingluff, Deborah; Lev, Yvonne; and Eisan, Andrew. "An End User Search Service in an Academic Health Sciences Library." *Medical Reference Services Quarterly* 4 (Spring, 1985):11-21.

9. Friend, Linda. "Independence at the Terminal: Training Student End Users to Do Online Literature Searching." *Journal of Academic Librarianship* 11(July 1985):136-41.

10. Tenopir, Carol. "Online Searching in the Popular Literature." *Library Journal* 109(December 1984):2242-3.

11. Simon, Marjorie. "The Online Catalog and Reference Services." *Medical Reference Services Quarterly* 2(Summer, 1983):73.

12. Telephone conversation with Sheldon Kotzin, Chief, Bibliographic Services Division, National Library of Medicine, July 18, 1985.

Personal Information Management: An Overview

Nancy G. Bruce
Anna Thérèse McGowan

ABSTRACT. Personal information management has become easier and more efficient with the widespread availability of microcomputers and filing software. Microcomputers can be used to easily index and manage such diverse information sources as down-loaded database searches, files of correspondence, patient records, or tissue cultures. The software capabilities of three commercially available software packages are compared with the most desirable filing, indexing, and searching needs of a personal file. Basic concepts of indexing and filing theory are reviewed as they apply to microcomputer filing systems.

INTRODUCTION

Personal information management is a process of analyzing information needs, retrieving needed information from appropriate sources, and managing retrieved information for current needs and future reference. The microcomputer has made rapid, thorough indexing and easy retrieval of information possible for today's expanded amount of relevant information sources. Personal files can be constructed to provide convenient access to frequently needed materials and to keep those materials reliably and consistently in order. The purpose of a personal file is to make oneself less dependent on memory to control the information explosion. This paper will discuss the mechanical and intellectual aspects of managing information retrieved from online databases and of integrating it with personal files.

Nancy G. Bruce, M.A., M.S.L.S., and Anna Thérèse McGowan, M.S., M.L.I.S., are members of the department of Information Management Education Services at the Health Sciences Library of the University of North Carolina at Chapel Hill. They wish to acknowledge the technical support of the Health Sciences Library and the illustrations supplied by Ed Tostanoski.

SOME CONSIDERATIONS ABOUT SOFTWARE

Microcomputers in the office setting are capable of serving many diverse information needs. For people who do their own searching of online databases, a nice bonus to a microcomputer filing system is the ability to automatically download information such as bibliographic citations or complete articles into a personal file without typing in each record.

Currently there are many software packages commercially available to build files and manage databases. Specific selection of a program involves "compatibility" with the computer as well as "compatibility" with the various forms in which printouts are needed. The major types of software that may be used include: *file management software* which allow the creation and manipulation of a single database or file; and *database management software* or *relational database systems* which allow the creation and manipulation of multiple files and multiple functions. They provide more control than the more simplistic file management software. Some companies market these various functions of powerful database management systems separately as "utilities" and charge individually for each function of the total package. Cost as well as capability should be kept in mind when examining available software.

Because of the rapid availability of new and more powerful packages on the market, the authors refrain from endorsing any one package, but do suggest that purchasers prepare questions for evaluating and comparing software packages. The Appendix shows a comparative chart which the authors developed for use in a workshop on professional filing systems taught at the Health Sciences Library of the University of North Carolina at Chapel Hill.

A microcomputer file is only as good as the care taken to select software and the care taken to plan the record format. Some programs, such as FYI 3000, can retrieve and produce an index of all significant words in a record. Others can update or change all records containing obsolete subject terms with a "search and replace" feature. Programs such as PFS or Sci-Mate can assign accession numbers automatically, and provide a standard format for all similar points of information among different types of material. Sci-Mate's status report feature is an example of a software program that allows for the creation of retention time reminders.

Regardless of the software selected, the criteria used to evaluate software for ease of filing and retrieval remain the same. Some of the basic questions that must be asked include the following:

1. DATA ENTRY or DOWNLOADING. Is transfer of data among systems simple? Is there a semi-automatic capability to accept transfer from word processing files as well as to accept downloaded online files from telecommunication access?
2. EDITING. Can all records be edited or reformatted *en masse* with a "search and replace" function, or must each record requiring the same change be handled individually?
3. SEARCHING. Can all the significant words in a record be searched? Can all the files in a multi-file database management system be searched with one command?
4. SORTING. Can the records be sorted or rearranged by a common factor? Alphabetically? Numerically? Are all the words within a citation included in sorting or only the first word? Can multiple fields be sorted, *e.g.*, can several titles by the same author be sorted as a subset within the author field? Can records be sorted in descending order 999-1, z-a, as well as in ascending order?
5. OUTPUT. What does the output look like? Bibliographic format or columnar report? Can it be tailored? Can output be viewed on a screen without printing? Can a report style, or printout, be changed easily or is it limited to a prearranged menu?
6. Are ACCESSION NUMBERS automatically added by the software as records are added to the file?
7. Is the system able to handle GRAPHICS, SPREAD SHEETS, STATISTICS, and ORDERING/INVENTORY functions?
8. Is there an AUTOMATIC THESAURUS/INDEXING function that will extract and alphabetize each word in the file? Does this function also include an occurrence number for each word in the alphabetical list?

REASONS FOR BUILDING A FILE

The purpose of a file and the available capacities and convenience of the file's physical storage must be considered at the beginning. The records in a file represent those information resources which must be physically convenient to support future work or research. Resources that comprise a file may be reprints of articles, research notes, patient records, bills, correspondence, tissue culture samples, microscope slides or any other item related to one's research or practice. The file can be a mixed assortment of materials, as idiosyncratic as the individual needs that it serves. The scope and organization of the file should reflect the user's unique approach to retrieving the information. For example, a cardiologist might use the single term "dermatology" to file all material on skin diseases, whereas a dermatologist would use many very specific terms. The index to the personal file may contain a bibliography for reprints which are not physically stored in the office. The bibliography of relevant journal articles in a research field can be interfiled with correspondence from colleagues who are working in that field if storage space is limited.

Preliminary planning should begin with realistic expectations of the capabilities of a personal file. In establishing the criteria for inclusion of materials, the user should confine the file's scope to information which is needed immediately in the office, is unique, or cannot be obtained easily or conveniently elsewhere. An evaluation of the uniqueness, worth, inaccessibility, and frequency of use of each piece of information is essential before it is included in a file. The file will be most successful if its content is quite specific. More skill is required to structure a search in a large database with a broad content scope than is needed to search and retrieve accurately in a very specific database. A personal file is an ideal place to structure a very specific database for a very specific purpose. The more peripheral and supporting materials which are included in building a file, the more skill will be needed to eliminate those materials as irrelevant for a specific information need. If a convenient library has and will always retain particular articles which are not needed on a regular basis, then these items do not need to be physically stored in a personal file.

If the file is to be shared with other staff members or co-workers, a decision must be made about who will file the documents. It must also be determined who will keep the index and update it as new terms are added. At this point, an individual file used by one person may seem simpler than sharing a departmental file. However, just as the tasks seem more rigidly defined in a common file, there are also more people to share the labor of indexing, labelling, filing and weeding.

Considerations about space, equipment, maintenance time and contributions of all those commodities from colleagues should also be included in preliminary planning. The storage of information sources should be simple. File folders, tabs, file cabinets or other items that are easily purchased and easily replaced provide straightforward and consistent storage for reprints and other paper items. One must decide how much physical space to devote to a file. If one file cabinet is all that is available, that may be more than sufficient for a small file of reprints, but it may be limiting for an integrated file of correspondence, reports, and reprints. The physical space allotted to a file will be a determining factor of the size of the file. Size limitations will encourage weeding the materials to only the most useful or necessary sources when it becomes difficult to file even one more reprint.

PLANNING FOR RETRIEVAL

When satisfying an information need, the goal is to retrieve a particular piece of information. The method is the same whether using a file drawer of personal correspondence or an online database search downloaded into a microcomputer to support a personal filing system.

Ideally, a file is constructed to integrate all its contents with an index which leads searchers to information in any format or location. With an index, photographs and articles about photographs may be indexed side-by-side regardless of the actual location of each item as long as that location is clearly noted. Recognizing how one remembers titles, names, subjects, or concepts will help to guide the construction of a file, which then allows for effective retrieval of relevant items. If a file is to be used by a department or a group of colleagues, its structure must be obvious to all users. Accordingly, successful files are indexed and cross-referenced to accommodate multiple users and are independent of any one individual's memory. Along with physical convenience and storage capabilities, a preplanned indexing and filing system are the basic components of a personal information management system.

A one-part system usually made up of a small group of materials is not indexed; it is merely filed in one arbitrary order. The physical arrangement of a one-part file is usually alphabetical by personal name or by subject heading. Simple as this system is, it presents problems for cross references to multiple access points. An access point is any descriptive identifying element about a document, or other source of information, which is likely to be remembered. Examples of access points include author, title, or subject. A one-part system may provide a good experimental file but it is not recommended for a file of over several hundred items. The emphasis of this article is on the capabilities of a two-part system. This is defined as an indexed file which can handle a large number of documents with cross references; it can also be used by several people each of whom remembers a different access point to the same source. A two-part file stores the source items physically and uses an index to locate and retrieve the items as shown in Figure 1.

Before a file is physically stored in file cabinets, or an index is constructed, it is wise to set up a theoretical structure for arranging the materials. This allows experimentation with the way that individuals who anticipate using the file remember information. It is advisable to compile a list of elements needed to remember every type of information integrated into the file. These elements will be placed in individual "fields" in a software program. A field will contain one particular type of information about the document that serves as a point of access, preferably something one can remember. Examples of fields are: author(s), title, journal, date of publication, pagination, registry number, or library location. From this completed list of fields, a standard recording form or unit record for every item in the file can be established. Identifying an item then becomes a simple matter of filling in the blanks. Not every field will be used for every source; for example, a tissue culture will lack a date of publication, and a journal article will lack a refrigerator shelf number.

Establishing a consistent format will provide a memory prompt for each access point which should be recorded for any piece of information in the file. Consistency ensures the future flexibility of the file and is especially critical with computerization since computers are programmed to sort and search by fields. Access points which identify or describe an item are recorded in fields that indicate this document's relationship to the overall scope of the file and delineate each item's reason for inclusion in the file (see Figure 2).

If a personal file is likely to contain records from databases which are constructed using different thesauri (for example, a file on continuing education for oncology nursing might include citations from both ERIC, an educational database, and CANCERLINE), then the record format might include a field to identify the database from which the citation was retrieved. For files containing records from several databases it is useful to choose a software package that can search both the title field and the added subject keyword field in one search, so that subject headings and title words can be combined with a Boolean "OR" to increase retrieval.

FIGURE 1

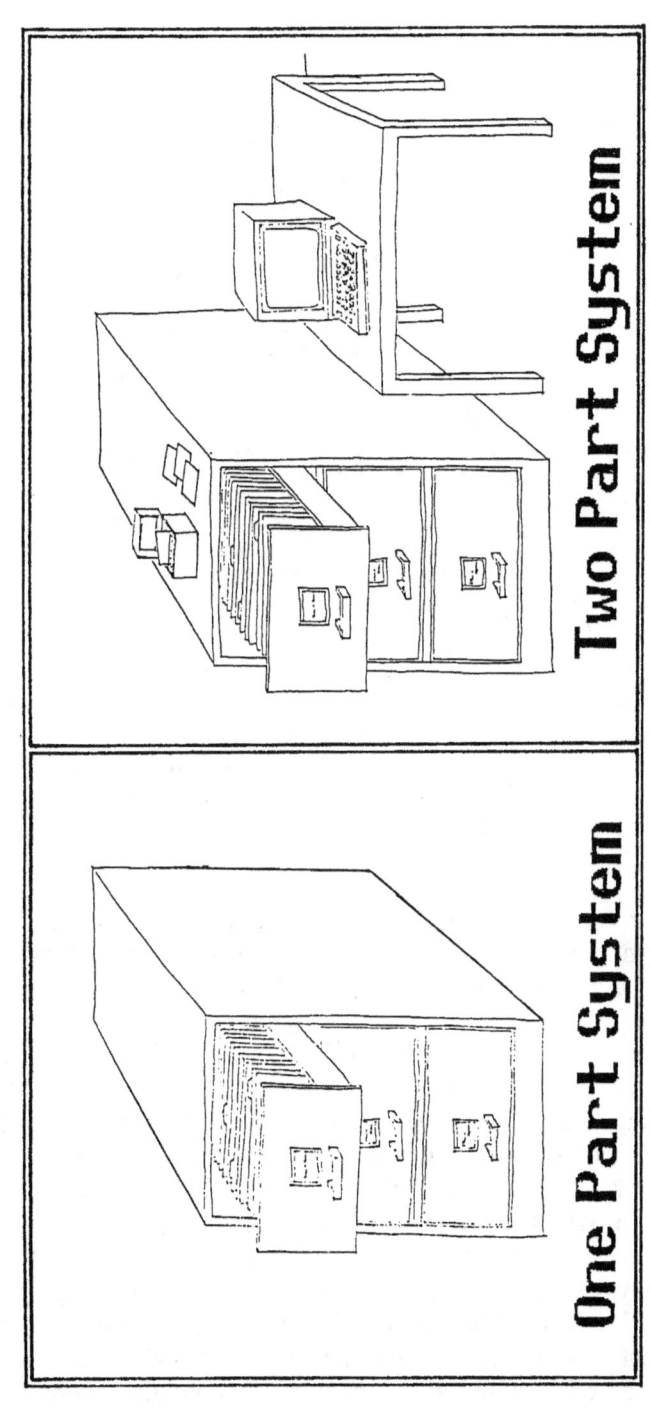

FIGURE 2

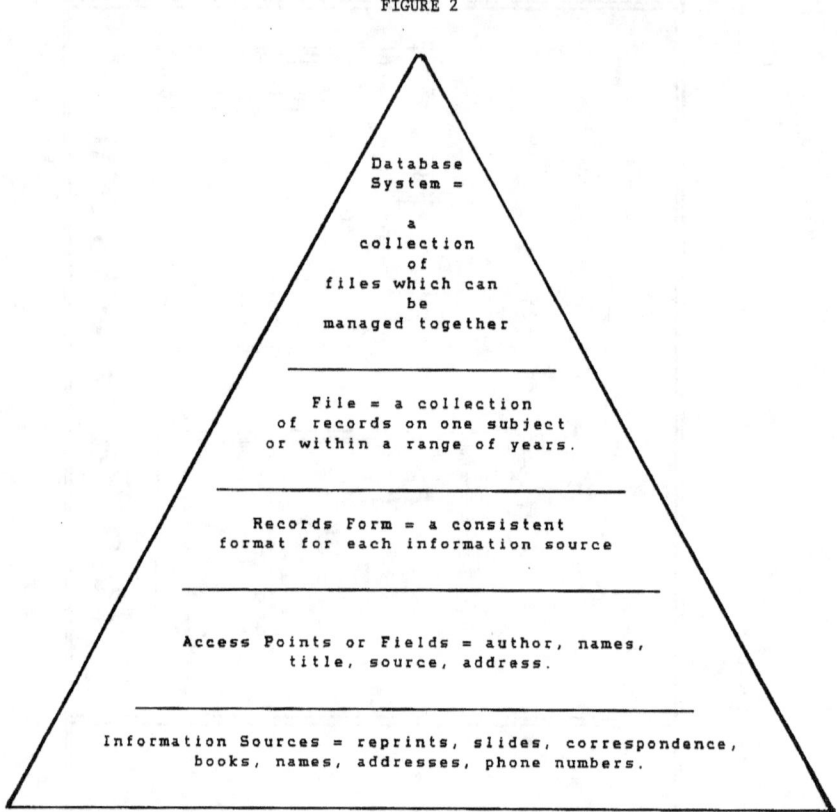

The storage arrangement of documents in the file can also be determined from the list of access points. For example, if documents are to be indexed by author only, they can be filed in drawers by subject. Conversely, if filed by author, they may be indexed by subject. In either of these cases the identification of a source item requires cross references to second authors or synonymous subject headings. Documents which are thoroughly indexed by all authors, all relevant subject terms, and any other useful access points can be filed by an accession number which reflects only the chronological order in which the item was added to the file.

Accession number filing has the attractive aspect of simplifying the physical storage of material. Several people can pull documents from the same accession numbered file and can usually refile them correctly. Accession-numbered files are very useful for those areas of research in which the vocabulary is changing so rapidly that the major subject headings are likely to change and subdivide. A "search and replace" feature on some software packages can change the subject terms used for cross references without disrupting the physical arrangement of the stored documents. Numerically-ordered files are also the easiest to weed, since the lowest numbers represent the oldest information and probably require the closest scrutiny for deselection or weeding.

Just as the format for records of documents must be consistent, the materials in a file must be analyzed and labelled with standard identifying categories of information before they are filed. Document labels should be standardized in content, and may need to include the name of the person who owns a copy of the reprint, the author of the article, a subject heading if filed by subject, or an accession number if the article is filed by number. The identifying label becomes the document's address, indicating its physical location. This location is listed in the index next to each access point. The address allows a document to be retrieved and returned again to the same place. A thorough label for a document is represented in Figure 3. Labelling an item for a file is necessary to ensure that it is not lost from the system once it has been retrieved and removed. Labelling is the physical equivalent of indexing. Figure 4 shows a PFS:File record for the document labelled in Figure 3.

INDEXING

Indexing is the one phase of file construction that is often overlooked by users until the file becomes old, large, invaluable, and costly to reorganize. There are two major stages of indexing. The first stage is identifying the standard bibliographic points descriptive of a document. These identifying points become access points that must be recorded in the fields of a unit record for each document. Access points are taken directly from each document when analyzing it for file inclusion and should at least contain the information on the document's label.

The second stage of indexing, assigning descriptive subject headings, is more challenging. Selection of index terms and other decisions related to filing ultimately relate to retrieval. Hence, efforts to ensure straightforward and simplified indexing and filing procedures should enhance ease of retrieval. Some particularly sophisticated online searchers will soon realize that databases which are

FIGURE 3

```
Your name                           Subject Heading or
R **                                Accession number
Don't Discard  THE LANCET, July 6, 1912.
```

The Croonian Lectures
ON
THE PATHOLOGY OF IMMUNITY,
AS ILLUSTRATED BY THE BEHAVIOUR OF FLUID EXUDATES FROM THE TISSUES AND VARIOUS BODY CAVITIES, IN ACUTE AND CHRONIC BACTERIAL INFECTIONS, MORE ESPECIALLY WITH REGARD TO THE PROBLEM OF AGGRESSINS.
Delivered before the Royal College of Physicians of London
By LEONARD S. DUDGEON, F.R.C.P. LOND.,
BACTERIOLOGIST TO, AND JOINT LECTURER ON PATHOLOGY AT, ST. THOMAS'S HOSPITAL; DIRECTOR OF THE HOSPITAL LABORATORIES.

LECTURE IV.:
Delivered on June 20th.
MR. PRESIDENT AND GENTLEMEN,—In our last lecture I shall endeavour to regard the aggressin problem in its relation to human disease.
ON THE EFFECT OF INJECTING EXUDATES, IMMUNE SERUM, AND NORMAL SERUM INTO ANIMALS SUFFERING FROM BACTERIAL INFECTION.
Large numbers of mice were employed to test the action

Key to Label:

- R = review
- ** = good
- reminder to keep when weeding
- SH = Bacterial Infections, Immunology
       Bacterial Infections, Pathology
- AN = #435

The index will include the following words from the record form in addition to all of the elements of the label:

Croonian Lectures   Dudgeon, L.S.
St. Thomas's Hospital   pathology
immunity   immune
exudates   serum
animals   suffering

---

loaded in no unusual or complicated way tend to be the easiest to search. If an individual always uses the same term to describe a certain subject it will be easy to assign the same subject heading in the files as the one used on the database to find everything collected on that topic. To help increase retrieval one might prepare a thesaurus of synonyms used to index materials. For example, subject headings could be arranged in a list of terms chosen, with cross references added as needed. However, how does one keep track of the synonymous subject headings that are used to cross reference items?

A decision must be made at the beginning, before the file becomes too complicated, between creating an individual thesaurus of subject headings or using an already prepared thesaurus. The user might decide to compile headings by selecting significant words from each document title. This is viable if the authors have chosen descriptive titles. If not, the user might decide that creating headings as they are needed is acceptable. The problem which arises with this method is remembering which term was selected from among the many synonyms. One answer is to compile a list of subject headings into a thesaurus. The software package PFS will compile an index from every word in a record and will list the number of occurrences for each alphabetical listing. This method creates an automatic thesaurus to the index. While such a thesaurus is simple to produce with the right software, it does not produce cross references to favored or preferred conceptual terms, and it does not pull synonyms together when they are separated alphabetically.

These considerations make another choice, that of using an already prepared list, quite attractive. For example, an educator might use terms from the ERIC thesaurus to index a personal file. This has several advantages. First, the person is spared the creative work of compiling synonyms and weighting them to the preferred terms generally used to index the educational literature. Second, when searching ERIC online, the same terms can be used to retrieve articles in the personal file as are used for the online database. This makes the indexing of downloaded citations unnecessary, since the indexing terms can be downloaded with the citations. Third, most published thesauri of large database services are updated on a

FIGURE 4

PFS:FILE

RECORDS FORM

```
DATABASE: old file
AUTHOR: Dudgeon LS

TITLE: The Croonian Lectures on the pathology of immunity: Lecture
       IV; On the effect of injecting exudates, immune serum,
       and normal serum into animals suffering from bacterial
       infection.
SOURCE: Lancet, July 6, 1,912; pp. 1757-1761.
YEAR: 1912
SUBJECTS: bacterial-infections-immunology; bacterial-infections-
          pathology.


LANGUAGE:english
ADDRESS:Director of Hospital Laboratories, St. Thomas's Hospital
PHONE NUMBER:n/a


ABSTRACT (IF ANY) IS ON NEXT PAGE; USE PGDN KEY TO ACCESS:
```

regular basis, and the updates contain a history note on new and old terms. This enables a personal file user to take greatest advantage of a "search and replace" function to change indexing terms.

Like the file that it describes, an index should not be static. As new subject areas or materials are included in the file, and as more terms are needed to describe the file's contents, they can be added easily to an index. The purpose of indexing is to bring together similar items instead of scattering them in separate, unrelated sections. Choosing a prepared thesaurus with major terms to collect synonyms is an invaluable tool for this purpose. By taking advantage of sources that are already tested, one can avoid pitfalls that might not be anticipated until a file becomes very large.

PLANNING FOR FILE MAINTENANCE

The various steps involved in analyzing an item before its entry into the file determine whether or not it is selected for inclusion. Each item must fit the criteria of scope, uniqueness, inaccessibility, and currency which are established by the user. The user may also decide to discard an item after analyzing it, since the analysis may render the content inferior to other items previously evaluated. Planning a time period for retention is as important as planning how and where to file items, since it affects the size and currency of the file. The user may decide that an item is not worth keeping for more than six months and can label the item to ensure removal from the file when it is obsolete. Just as decisions on inclusion, labelling, and indexing are necessary to set up a file, consistent adherence to these decisions is necessary to maintain a file through regular weeding (deselection), indexing of new information, and refiling of retrieved documents.

SUMMARY

In this paper, the focus has been on designing a personal file that will provide for simple and effective storage and retrieval of necessary information with the use of a microcomputer. By using a powerful database management package, the clerical work of filing can seem less overwhelming. The authors describe points to consider when selecting a software package which can simplify construction of an index, provide a number of access points, and help the user maintain a schedule of weeding the material in the file. Since microcomputers are playing such a large role in individual searching of bibliographic databases, it is a logical progression to utilize their capacity for creating a personal database or file of information.

The importance of an initial analysis of information sources selected for storage and an evaluation of the worth of each is stressed. Most of the decision making that is done in adding items to a file can be made at the beginning. These decisions include selection of materials, form of storage, retention time, and indexing and cross-referencing of necessary points of access. How the file's users are likely to remember an item determines how it should be filed and indexed.

Beyond decisions related to individual items in the files, there are decisions that pertain to the file as a whole. These include deciding upon the arrangement of the file, whether or not it will have an index, and whether the index will include original subject headings or an adaptation of available published subject headings. Once preliminary decisions have been made, the construction of the file should be quite straightforward. However, the information should not be subordinate to the system. If so, the system should be revised or modified. Adaptation and flexibility are the characteristics of any vital system; a personal filing system should exhibit them as well.

SELECTED READINGS ON PERSONAL FILE MANAGEMENT

Preliminary reading:

Elkington, J.R. "Where Did I See That Paper?" *Annals of Internal Medicine* 67 (August 1967):459-60.

Subject arrangement of papers:

Singer, Karl. "Where Did I See that Article?" *JAMA* 24 (April 6, 1979):1492-3.
Tyznik, John W. "Taming the Medical Literature 'Monster'." *Postgraduate Medicine* 74 (July 1983):77-80.
Girardet, Roland. "A Surgeon's System for Filing Medical Literature." *Journal of the Kentucky Medical Association* 80 (February 1982):82-4.
Murphy, John E. "Filing Personal Reference Collections." *American Journal of Hospital Pharmacy* 37 (May 1980):618, 621-2.

Accession number arrangement of papers:

Cushing, Ralph. "Improving Personal Filing Systems." *Chemical Engineering* 70 (January 7, 1963):73-88. (Note: This is actually 3 articles back to back.)

Computerized systems:

Bjoraker, David G. "Experience with Microcomputer Management of a Personal Literature Collection." *Journal of Medical Systems* 8 (1984):103-10.

Henderson, A.S., and Craft-Bosley, R. "A Simple System for References and Reprints." *British Medical Journal* 287 (November 12, 1983):1448-9.

McCabe, John B., and McCabe, Bonnie H. "Microcomputer-Based Filing System for Emergency Medicine Literature." *Annals of Emergency Medicine* 10 (February 1981):87-90.

Marks, R.H.L. "A FORTRAN Computer Program for Storage and Retrieval of Personal Journal References." *International Journal of Bio-Medical Computing* 12 (July 1981): 283-90.

Departmental files:

Schutt, David C. "Teaching Reference File for Family Practice Residencies." *Military Medicine* 146 (May 1981):336-8.

Author's records:

Eckert, Allan W. "The Writer's Records." *Writer's Digest* 43 (March 1963):21-4.

APPENDIX

SCI-MATE	PFS: FILE & REPORT	FYI 3000
<u>Sorting</u> —maximum sort of 32,000 records	<u>Sorting</u> —2200 records/disc can be sorted	<u>Sorting</u> —not available without purchasing a separate utility for $125.00
—only first 24 characters of a field can be sorted	—sorts by every word in a selected field	
<u>Editing</u> —very flexible	<u>Editing</u> —insertion always erases existing data	<u>Editing</u> —not available without transferring data to a WP to reformat
<u>Data Entry</u> —easy entry with "templates"	<u>Data Entry</u> —each record must be typed in individually into a work form	<u>Data Entry</u> —must edit for FYI *C—*E on a WP
—can "down load" from Universal Online Searcher packet	—no transfer from WP or remote computer	—indirect downloading through edited DOS file
<u>Searching</u> —sophisticated; only limit—can not refine already retrieved set	<u>Searching</u> —Boolean "and" across fields, not within a field	<u>Searching</u> —backwards Boolean "ands" before "ors"

APPENDIX (continued)

SCI-MATE	PFS: FILE & REPORT	FYI 3000
<u>Searching</u>	<u>Searching</u> —field specific, e.g., same word in two fields = 2 searches	<u>Searching</u>
—whole record searched		
<u>Output</u> —bibliographic through transfer to The Editor utility	<u>Output</u> —FILE: semi-biblio- graphic, must be edited with WP —REPORT: only columnar field report	<u>Output</u> —no way to reformat; what comes out looks like what went in
—text through transfer to text processing software outside of Sci-Mate utilities		
—columnar through the Personal Data Manager utility		

II. END USER SEARCHING PROGRAMS

A prerequisite for end user searching is training and education. The role of training will naturally fall in the domain of the librarian/search analyst, who is considered an expert in database searching. The change in function, however, from searcher to educator and consultant is already underway in many institutions. A training program to search two command-driven systems, NLM MEDLARS and DIALOG, is described by Linder et al.; of special interest is that the NLM training, developed at Stanford University Medical Center, was being taught before NLM's current program for training end users. Wygant describes an end user training program at the University of Texas, Galveston, in which two courses are taught: "Database Searching for the Health Scientist," and NLM's "The Basics of Searching MEDLINE." Glasgow and Foreman describe training for end users at the University of Minnesota Bio-Medical Library on two menu-driven systems, BRS/Saunders Colleague and BRS/AFTER DARK. The processes of planning for implementing and managing end user systems at the Massachusetts General Hospital Health Sciences Libraries is described by Kravitz and Westling; the focus is on PaperChase. Simon discusses the implementation, training, and use of BRS/AFTER DARK at the University of Maryland Health Sciences Library.

Training the End User: The Stanford University Medical Center Experience

Gloria A. Linder
Richard A. Lenon
Valerie Su
Joseph G. Wible
Peter Stangl

ABSTRACT. The Lane Medical Library staff, working with a physician at Stanford University Medical Center, has developed a successful end user MEDLINE training program. Both DIALOG and the National Library of Medicine's (NLM) MEDLARS system are taught. Upon completion of the NLM course, students are eligible to receive academic credit and an NLM password. Several factors are identified as having been crucial to this success: (1) a strong working alliance between library staff and an enthusiastic physician, (2) early and ongoing support from influential leaders in the medical center, (3) minimization of barriers confronting potential end user

---

Gloria A. Linder is currently Head of the Reference Section at Lane Medical Library, Stanford University Medical Center, Stanford, CA 94305. She has an M.S.L.S. from the University of Illinois in Urbana, and an M.S. in Biological Sciences from Stanford University. Dr. Richard A. Lenon is Clinical Assistant Professor of Medicine at Stanford University and is in private practice in Palo Alto specializing in Internal Medicine and Oncology. He has an M.D. from Stanford University. Valerie Su is Deputy Director/Head of Public Services at Lane Medical Library. She has an M.L.S. from Southern Connecticut State College. Joseph G. Wible is a Reference Librarian at Lane Medical Library. He has a Masters of Librarianship from Emory University and a Ph.D. in Biology from the University of Southern California. Peter Stangl, Director of Lane Medical Library, has an M.L.S. from Southern Connecticut State College.

The authors wish to thank Dr. Edward Rubenstein, Associate Dean for Continuing Medical Education, for his help in obtaining the Kaiser Foundation Grant; Dr. Kenneth Melmon, formerly Chairman of the Department of Medicine, Dr. Richard Kempson, Chairman of the Department of Pathology, Dr. Saul Rosenberg, Chairman of the Division of Oncology, and Dr. Edward Shortliffe, Chairman of Medical Information Science, for their early support of the program; and Penny Coppernoll-Blach of DIALOG Information Services for her suggestions following the initial DIALOG seminars. They also wish to thank Elizabeth J. Vadeboncoeur, Michael V. Sullivan and Michael Newman for their critical comments in preparation of the manuscript.

searchers, and (4) strong emphasis on demonstration and hands-on practice. Costs and personnel support to achieve and maintain the program are discussed, and future plans outlined.

INTRODUCTION

The earliest studies to involve end users in searching MEDLINE are succinctly summarized in a 1975 paper,[1] but additional reports exist.[2,3] Although these programs met with limited overall success, intermediary searching dominated the 1970s. Following the advent of personal ownership of microcomputers, Lane Medical Library staff received inquiries from physicians about direct access to MEDLINE; reference librarians referred them to the available vendors. After the successful report of PaperChase,[4] a popular user-friendly system, health professionals began to exert more pressure on librarians to provide information on accessing MEDLINE.[5] This demand, coupled with the Matheson report[6] which outlined new teaching roles for librarians, set the stage for Lane librarians to become actively involved in teaching health professionals to search MEDLINE.

EVOLUTION OF THE PROGRAM

During the Spring of 1982, a physician from the Stanford community made initial efforts directed toward launching a program to teach fellow physicians to search MEDLINE. He had been using MEDLARS since completing the "official" National Library of Medicine (NLM) training course in 1978 and was convinced of its value in clinical work. The convenience and power of MEDLARS, coupled with instant access via a microcomputer in his office, made it practical and worthwhile to search the literature as often as questions arose. Hence the system could be used for everyday clinical problems. At the same time, Lane librarians had discussed the feasibility of offering PaperChase or a similar user-friendly system to the Stanford University Medical Center (SUMC) community. Lack of resources prevented Lane from taking immediate action. In August 1982, the Lane Medical Library staff learned of the physician's efforts and entered into a partnership with him to teach end users online search techniques. At that time, several end user systems, such as BRS/AFTER DARK, BRS/Saunders Colleague, CITE-

HILL, CONIT, KNOWLEDGE INDEX, PaperChase, etc., were under development, but were not yet available on national networks. The National Library of Medicine's course on teaching the end user to search MEDLINE was also not yet available;[7] thus the decision was made to develop and teach courses in the "regular" mainframe system command languages.

By November 1983, a three-hour "MEDLINE on DIALOG" seminar had been developed. DIALOG had approved a demonstration account to conduct these seminars, with follow-up hands-on practice sessions. This short program proved quite popular, resulting in rapid expansion of the local end user community. In addition, a nine-hour NLM course had been introduced and was academically accredited through Stanford's Medical Information Sciences division. Graduates of this course were also eligible to receive NLM passwords. A Kaiser Foundation grant funded the acquisition of five terminals, four of which were strategically placed in the medical center, and one in the library. This made searching by end users a public activity at SUMC.

Figure 1 outlines the chronology of early developments in launching the program. Since 1983, two NLM courses and six DIALOG seminars have been offered each year; a total of 275 people have been trained.

Outlined below are the perceived reasons for the successful program at the Stanford University Medical Center. These observations may be useful to other institutions planning similar programs.

Promotion

Several influential members of the Stanford Medical Center community were helpful in the early development of the program. An Associate Dean worked effectively to help obtain a Kaiser Foundation grant for the public access terminals. Three departmental chairmen committed funds to pay for searches performed by their housestaff and each agreed to house one of the public access terminals obtained with grant funds. Two of these chairmen sponsored Lane's DIALOG seminars for department residents and fellows, which increased the program's visibility.

In turn the initial trainees influenced their peers, and awareness of the program spread quite rapidly. A "ripple effect" was observed by the markedly increased interest in the MEDLINE class (see Figure 2). For example, prior to the initial DIALOG session a flier

Figure 1. Chronology in the Development of Lane Medical Library's Online Training Program

October	1982	DIALOG demonstration account successfully negotiated.
December	1982	First DIALOG seminar.
Winter	1983	Grant proposal for terminals submitted.
		Started negotiations with NLM for recognition as end user training center.
Spring	1983	Departmental sponsorship of Lane's DIALOG classes.
		Grant proposal for terminals approved.
Summer	1983	Formal recognition as NLM end user training center.
		NLM course academically accredited.
September	1983	Terminals installed.
October	1983	Lectures on information retrieval instituted in the general survey "Medical Information Science" course.
November	1983	First NLM class offered.

mailed to each of the 400 medical students elicited no response. Telephone calls to over 100 people attracted only six people to the first class. Yet during the following year, several DIALOG sessions had to be scheduled to meet the growing demand for training. The Oncology Department has a high turnout for MEDLINE classes, no doubt because a very well-respected oncology fellow attended the first session offered and influenced peers who observed him searching.

Publicity in campus newsletters and the local community newspaper generated considerable interest as well. When the terminals appeared in public locations with signs posted on them indicating their purpose and whom to contact for search training, they generated calls too. Signs posted near Lane's copies of *Index Medicus (IM)* encouraged the user to learn to search *IM* by computer, thus eliminating tedious manual searching. These signs described the classes and listed contact names.

Currently, interest in instruction is high, and the classes are

Figure 2

Enrollment in Lane Medical Library's
Online Training Program

DIALOG SEMINAR

Year	Classes	Students
1982	1	6
1983	5	69
1984	6	94
1985 (June)	3	57
	15	226 Total

NLM CLASS

Month/Year	Students
Nov. 1983	10
Apr. 1984	10
Nov. 1984	16
Apr. 1985	13
	49 Total

popular. People regularly come to Lane to add their names to the waiting list for the next class(es). Librarians promote the classes at the reference desk when appropriate. After a class is arranged, it is advertised by announcements in the weekly campus newspaper a week or two before it is scheduled to take place. All people on waiting lists are also notified by telephone and by flier. Promotional fliers are posted at key points throughout the medical center and library. These methods suffice to attract fifteen to twenty students for each class.

Importance of Physician Allies

The early alliance between a physician and the Lane Medical Library staff has been most helpful in developing SUMC's end user program. The physician has contributed professional contacts, considerable enthusiasm, insight into anticipated needs of the target audience, and his time. Lane's staff has contributed expertise, additional contacts, financial support, and considerably more time, both in teaching and in managing the program. The physician functions as a bridge between the library staff and his peers, while the library staff provides resources in the interest of the shared goal.

A few examples illustrate the respective contributions of each in launching SUMC's program. The physician with his many contacts was and is able to promote the program among students and colleagues whom he meets in his day-to-day activities. In addition, his physician status undoubtedly contributed to his influence both with colleagues and with the medical school administration. Lane was influential in contacting key personnel at the Pacific Southwest Regional Medical Library Service (PSRMLS) and NLM when negotiating for recognition as an end user training center. Lane's experienced searching staff played a key role in the negotiation's success.

Barriers

Recruiting potential end users is greatly facilitated if barriers are minimized. Ideally, a training program should be brief, demonstrating the power of MEDLINE, but requiring very little time or financial commitment from participants. Providing access to terminals can be a problem. Initially, the Learning Resource Center (LRC) made two terminals available, while Lane furnished an old terminal for public-access searching. However, all three terminals were slow (300-baud); moreover, a trained searcher and copies of *Medical Subject Headings (MeSH)*[8] were not readily available to users of LRC terminals. Consequently, a grant request was submitted to rectify this situation. It included plans for purchasing five 1200-baud terminals, requisite telephone installation, security "anchor pads," one-year maintenance contracts, and copies of *MeSH* for each location. When funding for the requested items was approved, Lane's staff negotiated terminal locations with each department. In retrospect, placement of one terminal in a frequently inaccessible conference room has been judged to be an error. The best terminal location has proved to be the reference section of Lane, where trainees have ready access to expert searchers. Terminals on the busy medical ward and oncology clinic have also been important in getting searching established as a clinical activity after training is completed by staff.

DIALOG was contacted to provide help with the program because its home office is local and it issues passwords to individuals as well as institutions. After some negotiation, a DIALOG "demonstration" password was obtained to be used in class and for follow-up practice sessions. If the end user participant is still interested in searching after the seminar and hands-on practice sessions, he or she may apply for an individual account, paying full DIALOG rates to search.

In order to provide convenient local training on the less expensive NLM system, negotiations with the National Library of Medicine were initiated to allow Lane to train end users. For busy health care professionals, the necessity to go out of town for three to five days in order to attend "official" NLM training to obtain passwords had always been a strong deterrent. Until this time, NLM did not offer local end user training. Lane successfully negotiated recognition as an end user training center whose graduates qualified for their own passwords.

The first local NLM class was totally subsidized by Lane. For the second class, the students were asked to pay for their online time. This turned out to be excessively tedious to monitor, and only half the cost was recovered. Since then, the "ripple effect" has generated solid interest in the course; a fifty dollar fee, payable at the beginning of the class, has been instituted to recover costs. This fee does not appear to be a barrier to enrollment.

The end user classes are designed to be short and to the point, and are scheduled at times convenient for physicians. The three-hour DIALOG seminar usually meets in the late afternoon to early evening (5 P.M.-8 P.M.). Scheduling of the follow-up practice sessions for hands-on experience is flexible. Students can call any time after the seminar for appointments with a Lane search analyst. The nine-hour NLM class is currently scheduled at noon. This less than ideal time is a barrier; future sessions will be offered at a more suitable time.

As other barriers arise it is important to spot them quickly and to respond. For example, after the terminals were installed on the wards, end users complained that there was never any paper available. Lane responded by reminding the departments that the paper was their responsibility, coordinated the designation of a responsible supply person in each department, and provided the information necessary to order it.

THE TEACHING PROGRAM

The philosophy of Lane's end user program is that full system command languages be taught, rather than the menu-driven or simplified versions of full systems. This offers students maximum access to files and to more powerful searching and printing features. The assumption is that it is worth the effort expended initially to learn the full system. Some current end user training programs share this philosophy,[9-10] while others do not.[11]

Lane has developed two courses: a DIALOG seminar and an NLM course (MIS 208), worth one unit of academic credit. In addition to the online searching courses, lectures on information retrieval presented jointly by a physician and Lane staff are a standard part of a general survey course on "Medical Information Science" (MIS 210).

Course Content

The DIALOG seminar consists of a three-hour didactic presentation during which instructors explain the structure of the MEDLINE database, important system commands, use of *MeSH*, indexing principles, and search strategy preparation. The discussion of *MeSH* emphasizes the importance of its use in searching, including the *MeSH Tree Structures*,[12] and subheadings. Optional hands-on sessions supervised by experienced searchers follow the seminar. Instructors encourage students to list relevant *MeSH* terms and to plan their search strategy before the hands-on session begins. During the session, the instructor reviews the choice of terms, strategy planning, and often gives in-depth instruction on the use of *MeSH*. These initial sessions can only illustrate those system features which are required to search the immediate topic. Thus the end user may not have the opportunity to practice using all system features, such as descriptor code (Tree Numbers) searching, applying subheadings, or limiting retrieval to citations in which descriptors have been designated as "major." Most students do get an opportunity to practice *MeSH* term searching, Boolean logical operators, limiting to English language and human references only, printing results online, and saving a strategy for execution in a backfile.

The NLM course meets for one hour three times a week for three weeks. The initial lecture covers the history of MEDLARS, file structure, Boolean operators, a few basic system commands, and introduces natural language "Text Word" searching. The first assignment following this lecture requires that the student conduct two Text Word searches, thus encouraging immediate hands-on practice. *MeSH* is the subject of the next three class periods. Points covered include why using *MeSH* is important, indexing principles (such as specificity), and an explanation of *Annotated MeSH* and its relationship to the *Tree Structures*. Other points include "pre-explosions," subheadings, and limiting retrieval to the major emphasis of the article. The next lecture covers saving a search and executing it in the backfiles, efficient online search techniques, and search strategy development. The following lecture addresses Text Word searching in more detail, and the "stringsearch" capability. The final two lectures cover TOXLINE, CHEMLINE, and the cancer-related files. The eight required search problem sets are a combination of written and online exercises, designed to reinforce all important points of the lectures and handouts. Students completing this course have practiced all system features. All exercises are annotated and returned to the student.

Lane developed its course prior to the start of NLM's end user training program, and it differs significantly in structure and content from the latter. Required hands-on exercises which are annotated and returned to the students, the coverage of "stringsearch," a final examination, and discussion of databases in addition to MEDLINE are the major distinguishing features of Lane's course when compared with NLM's. NLM's class can be given in a single session, whereas Lane's is presented over a three-week time period.

The content of the handouts for both courses is abbreviated compared to those offered by system vendors for intermediary searcher training. Only essential points are taught. For example, when there is more than one way to perform a particular task, only one is presented. This concept of a "mini-manual" is common.[3,9] The handouts are designed using examples appropriate to physicians. They have been through several revisions in response to initial input from Lane and DIALOG staff and experience, as evidenced by class questions and recurring problems with assignments. A summary page listing useful commands is invaluable when students actually conduct their own searches. The summary page is included in the handout for the DIALOG seminar, but in the NLM course the students prepare their own summary sheets as part of the final examination. This is a particularly valuable learning experience since it forces review of the material and isolation of the most useful points.

Ongoing video monitor demonstrations during class, illustrating important points, are also invaluable in reinforcing handout materials and lecture content. For example, in the NLM course considerable time is spent illustrating with slides as well as with a video monitor the relationship between the *Tree Structures*, "explosions," and results obtained using single terms versus "exploding" a Tree Number. Such demonstrations are part of all lectures in both courses.

Teaching Roles

A physician as one of the instructors no doubt lends credibility to the program. He is perceived as being on "equal footing" with his colleagues and is in a position to emphasize the value of technical proficiency, especially with regard to using *MeSH*, an easily overlooked tool to the uninitiated end user. In class, he draws on his personal experience in searching and his knowledge of clinical medicine to provide examples meaningful to the group. He gears instruction to participants' immediate needs, paces the class appropriately, and helps define what is really important for physicians to learn.

Lane staff's broad searching background has prepared them to serve as resource people in all phases of searching, including use of

MeSH, system software, and search strategy development. Both the physician instructor and librarians are involved in the preparation of handouts and classroom instruction, but Lane's staff handles most hands-on practice sessions following the DIALOG class, tutors students doing NLM exercise sets, and corrects all student exercises and final examinations for the NLM course.

Initially the two types of teachers, physician and librarian, are likely to have differing opinions on material to emphasize in class. However, as a result of joint teaching experience the positions tend to merge—over time the physician shifts position toward including more detail on *MeSH* and search strategy formulation, while the librarian shifts toward including less detail on these points than in the beginning.

Critical Observations

The short, three-hour DIALOG seminar is more popular than the longer, nine-hour NLM course. However, it appears to Lane staff that a larger percentage of participants in the NLM class continue to search after completion of the course. This is undoubtedly due to greater confidence and understanding of online searching gained from successfully completing several required written and hands-on exercise sets over a period of several weeks. The exercises tend to reinforce learning and provide opportunity for a substantial amount of supervised practice.

At first, only a small percentage of the short-course registrants returned for their follow-up sessions with course instructors. More recently the number of students returning for practice sessions has been increasing. Highly motivated students continue to search after the course, and many do quite well. Those DIALOG students who come for practice sessions typically have difficulty breaking down search questions into facets and understanding the use of *MeSH Tree Structures*. Class time allotted for the short course seems insufficient to communicate these concepts. Yet with individualized attention in the practice sessions, students tend to pick up these points quickly.

NLM students, on the other hand, encounter fewer problems in these areas, having three weeks to assimilate the material. A closer rapport between end users and Lane staff is established with students in the NLM class, and as a consequence the students come to rely on Lane staff for future information needs.

Some students learn to use more than one system. Many start with DIALOG because it is a shorter course. Later, those who search regularly take the NLM class to save money. Occasionally students do the reverse to have access to additional databases.

COSTS

Staff Time

Substantial staff time is involved in developing and teaching the end user classes. The actual classroom time is but a small fraction of the time commitment necessary for implementing such a program. Time to prepare and revise documentation is quite substantial. NLM course development and the lecture prepared for the introductory survey course in "Medical Information Science" took well over 300 hours. Repeat presentations require less time, but handout revisions are necessary each time, and depending on their nature, may take hours. Hands-on sessions following the DIALOG seminar also require an average of one hour per person per search.

A major time commitment is obviously involved in teaching the nine-hour NLM class. Grading the required homework sets takes at least twenty minutes per exercise per student, and reviewing the final examinations requires thirty minutes per student. Lecture preparation and review require instructor time prior to each session. Equipment set-up for each class takes thirty minutes or an estimated five hours for the entire nine-hour NLM class. Lane staff spends two to three hours telephoning and mailing notices to students prior to each upcoming class. Time is also required to troubleshoot terminal problems and coordinate maintenance calls.

Staffing adjustments were necessary with the introduction of the program. Initially the program was added to the already heavy workload of existing staff. Temporary part-time reference librarians were hired until new positions in reference could be filled.

Administrative Costs

The cost of maintaining a constant paper supply for the public access terminals is substantial. A thermal printer is used to reduce noise in public areas, but thermal paper is expensive, approximately $3.00 per roll. On a busy day, more than one roll of paper can be consumed. Photocopying costs for handouts are at least $1.00 per handout per person. Database vendor bills are costly if the library is subsidizing, or partially subsidizing, the class. Lane paid an average of $50.00 per student to cover vendor bills for the NLM course, but this fee is now collected from each student at the beginning of the course. Two of the most heavily used terminals require maintenance contracts which the library negotiates and funds.

FUTURE PLANS

A project is underway to develop an evaluation tool which would measure the ability of students to retrieve relevant literature. The methodology involves creating a list of "gold standard" citations for each of several search topics. These topics will be chosen from actual search requests. The search will be done by all members of the committee to create a pool of citations; from this pool, the requester will choose five to ten of the most relevant "gold standard" citations. Course participants running the same searches will be scored according to the proportion of "gold standard" citations they retrieve. This will provide a quantitative measure to determine if one course produces better searchers than another. Preliminary results are not yet available.

Lane's program is dynamic. Plans for additional seminars are in place to be added as time permits. These include offering a seminar comparing available database vendors offering different interactive systems with the same files. Additional interactive systems will be taught as deemed appropriate: under consideration are menu-driven systems designed for individuals who do not search often enough to remember the commands. In addition, Lane has plans to implement a user-friendly interface to a MEDLINE subset on a local computer system in the near future. The need for a permanent teaching facility, wired for ten terminals and individual video monitors, has been addressed in Lane's long-range plan. Arrangements for earning Continuing Education credit for classes would encourage participation and are being made. Plans include working with the curriculum committee on making a search course a requirement for medical students entering clinical training. Budgetary support for a permanent and growing teaching program needs to be negotiated with the medical school administration.

A program of this nature is constantly evolving. It must continue to respond to changes in the needs of health care professionals and to new developments in information science. The long-term goal is to make online literature searching "the standard of practice" in the medical community.

REFERENCES

1. Olson, Paul E. "Mechanization of Library Procedures in the Medium-Sized Medical Library: XV. A Study of the Interaction of Nonlibrarian Searchers with the MEDLINE Retrieval System." *Bulletin of the Medical Library Association* 63 (January 1975): 35-41.
2. Soben, Phyllis, and Tidball, Charles S. "***MEDLEARN***: An Orientation to MEDLINE." *Bulletin of the Medical Library Association* 62 (April 1974): 92-4.
3. Sewell, Winifred, and Bevan, Alice. "Nonmediated Use of MEDLINE and TOXLINE by Pathologists and Pharmacists." *Bulletin of the Medical Library Association* 64 (October 1976): 382-91.
4. Horowitz, Gary L., and Bleich, Howard L. "PaperChase: A Computer Program to Search the Medical Literature." *New England Journal of Medicine* 305 (October 15, 1981): 924-30.
5. "NLM Online Users' Meeting, Medical Library Association Annual Meeting, Anaheim, California—June 14, 1982." *The NLM Technical Bulletin* No. 160 (August 1982): 110-3.
6. Matheson, Nina W. *Academic Information in the Academic Health Sciences Center: Roles for the Library in Information Management.* Washington, D.C.: Association of American Medical Colleges, 1982.
7. National Library of Medicine. *The Basics of Searching MEDLINE: A Guide for the Health Professional.* Bethesda, Maryland: National Library of Medicine, 1984.
8. *Medical Subject Headings—Annotated Alphabetic List.* Bethesda, MD: National Library of Medicine, 1984.
9. Givens, Mary King, and McDonell, W. Ellen. "End User Instructions for Searching MEDLARS." *Medical Reference Services Quarterly* 4 (Summer 1985): 63-7.
10. Snow, Bonnie. "Making the Rough Places Plain: Designing MEDLINE End User Training." *Medical Reference Services Quarterly* 3 (Winter 1984): 1-11.
11. Slingluff, Deborah; Lev, Yvonne; and Eisan, Andrew. "An End User Search Service in an Academic Health Sciences Library." *Medical Reference Services Quarterly* 4 (Spring 1985): 11-21.
12. *Medical Subject Headings—Tree Structures.* Bethesda, MD: National Library of Medicine, 1984.

Teaching End User Searching in a Health Sciences Center

Alice C. Wygant

ABSTRACT. This paper describes the end user training program at the Moody Medical Library, University of Texas Medical Branch, Galveston, Texas. The library staff teaches two classes, "Database Searching for the Health Scientist" and "The Basics of Searching MEDLINE." The first class is a two-hour class designed to acquaint the health scientist with the rudiments of online searching and the various database vendors and producers. The second is a seven-hour class developed by the National Library of Medicine (NLM). It covers searching MEDLINE by author, Text Words, and *Medical Subject Headings* (*MeSH*) and includes two hours of hands-on practice.

The Moody Medical Library (MML) offers two searching classes for end users on a regular basis: "Database Searching for the Health Scientist" and "The Basics of Searching MEDLINE." The first is a two-hour seminar developed by the MML staff, which is designed to acquaint the user with some of the options available for database searching. The second class is an intensive seven-hour course developed by the National Library of Medicine (NLM). The primary purpose of the MEDLINE class is to teach end users how to use authors, Text Words, and *Medical Subject Headings* (*MeSH*) when searching. In both classes discussion of equipment is limited to a simple enumeration of the required basic hardware. The MML has taken the position that it does not advise patrons on equipment purchases nor does it recommend any particular equipment or system.

Alice C. Wygant is currently Reference Librarian/Education Coordinator at the Moody Medical Library, University of Texas Medical Branch, Galveston, TX 77550-2782. She holds an M.S. in Library Science from Louisiana State University, Baton Rouge, Louisiana and an M.S. in Studies of the Future from the University of Houston/Clear Lake, Houston, Texas.

DATABASE SEARCHING FOR THE HEALTH SCIENTIST

In the relatively short time allotted to "Database Searching for the Health Scientist," the instructor makes no attempt to teach the software for any particular system. The emphasis is on theoretical aspects of database searching and a description of the four major vendors of databases: DIALOG, BRS, SDC, and NLM. A comparison is made between the four systems, and their unique features are stressed in order to show that all of the different systems perform approximately the same functions. The system comparison covers start-up costs and the number of databases available on each system, as well as references to files unique to each. It also includes a command comparison between DIALOG, BRS, and MEDLARS. At this point in the class the instructor answers student questions about the different systems.

The system comparison is followed by a brief explanation of Boolean logic. Each operator or connector is discussed individually; the instructor then covers the order of execution (*i.e.*, the order of processing a command statement which contains multiple logical operators), and its impact on formulating search strategies. Search topics are taken from class participants and, using Boolean logic, are written on the blackboard by the instructor, who explains each step as she writes. The segment on Boolean logic leads naturally to a discussion of common pitfalls in online searching.

Areas of concern deal primarily with common searching mistakes as well as misconceptions about searching. Five specific points are mentioned. The first, "You can almost always get something," leads to a description of the enormous size of most files. Novice searchers tend to believe that their retrieval represents the total literature on that particular subject in the database, when it may actually be only a small portion of the total. The injudicious use of the "not" operator is the next topic for discussion. One of the best examples for illustrating this common mistake is the statement "human not animal." Even novice searchers can easily grasp the fact that this way of searching would eliminate many potentially valuable articles that deal with both human *and* animal subjects. A third potential trouble spot involves the use of natural language. Class members are warned of "false drops" or irrelevant retrieval when terms such as "AIDS" or "DRG" are searched. The former is usually intended as an acronym for "acquired immunodeficiency syndrome," but a search on the MEDLINE database using "AIDS" will retrieve citations on hearing "aids" as well as "aids" used as a verb, in addition to the desired citations on acquired immunodeficiency syndrome. "DRG" is an acronym for "diagnosis related group" *and* "dorsal root ganglion." The instructor also points out that in some databases natural language is drawn from a limited field such as the title only; thus, the list of possible words for a given topic must include all the alternatives and synonyms in order to retrieve a majority of the relevant citations.

A fourth pitfall is injudicious use of multiple Boolean operators in one search statement. The order of execution or processing is reiterated, and the following example is explained: INTERFERON I OR INTERFERON II AND VIRUSES. This search statement will retrieve citations about interferon II and viruses or citations about interferon I alone. The searcher probably intended to retrieve citations to articles about either interferon I or interferon II used in conjunction with viruses. To guard against this type of error, the class is advised to use only one type of Boolean operator per search statement.

The final pitfall discussed is the underuse of training, search aids, and controlled vocabulary. In the comparison of database vendors at the beginning of the class, each vendor's searching manuals are mentioned. Their importance to effective searching is stressed again here. The instructor also recommends that the end users seek formal training for the system which they decide to use. The importance of controlled vocabulary and its value as a searching tool is also stressed. An example of a search done using controlled vocabulary versus searching the same topic with natural language is used to illustrate this point.

The last portion of the class is a practicum where the instructor formulates several searches and explains each step in detail. The first search is "canned"; that is, it was designed prior to the class to illustrate a variety of points, such as how to use a thesaurus. Other sample search formulations use topics suggested by class participants. It is advisable for the instructor to have a spare canned search ready in case no requests from the class are forthcoming. As a part of the formulation process, students are advised to think of "Plan B." In other words, the instructor suggests that they have an alternative strategy ready if the first idea does not work online.

All instructional materials for the class were produced at MML using a microcomputer. They are brief handouts that summarize the main points of the lecture and include duplicates of some of the illustrative transparencies used by the instructor. Each class member receives a packet containing the handouts and promotional brochures from different vendors. The packet also contains an evaluation form to be completed at the end of the seminar, and library publicity materials about "The Basics of Searching MEDLINE."

BASICS OF SEARCHING MEDLINE

"The Basics of Searching MEDLINE" is a fairly comprehensive class which covers the rudimentary mechanics of searching the MEDLINE database by author and subject. It is taught using a combination workbook-and-searching manual written by the NLM staff entitled, *The Basics of Searching MEDLINE: A Guide for the Health Professional*.[1] NLM also publishes an expanded edition which gives teaching tips, more extensive explanations, and justifications for some of the material included in the end user manual. On completion of this class the student is eligible to apply to NLM for a password to search the MEDLARS system.

The course begins with a section of introductory material about the MEDLARS system and, specifically, MEDLINE. After this brief introduction the instructor explains the arrangement of the manual and the various program messages that the students will encounter in the class. Those messages covered are the ones most commonly seen by novice searchers such as "NO PSTGS" (no postings) or "USER:" (the searcher's cue to input data). Only those messages absolutely necessary to begin searching are covered at this point.

Searching the system is first presented using the single author approach. Author search problems and solutions are given at the end of this initial section. Numerous problems and answers are included in the manual, usually following the introduction of a new concept. An introduction to Boolean operators, multiple author searching, and simple print commands follow the simple author search.

Subject searching is presented using the *MeSH* thesaurus and then Text Words. A thorough description of *MeSH—Annotated Alphabetic List*,[2] *MeSH—Tree Structures*,[3] and the *Permuted MeSH*[4] begins this section of the course. The "explode" and "pre-explode" features are also discussed at this point and many sample searches done in the INTROMED database are used as examples.

Text Word searching is carefully treated in *The Basics of Searching MEDLINE*. Beginning searchers are given a good idea of when it is most advantageous to use Text Words. They are warned to be careful when truncating words. Good search habits, such as the extensive use of the "neighbor" command, are encouraged.

The instructor then helps each participant to formulate several search strategies before going online for the first time. Usually forty-five minutes to an hour is allotted for online practice using demonstration access codes obtained from NLM. The students need a great deal of help to keep going in the first practice session and the instructor is kept busy answering questions and helping the students refine searches online.

After the first online session and the lunch break, the "neighbor" command is again emphasized and some other useful commands are introduced. This command summary can also serve as a review of the many other searching techniques and principles that have been covered in the previous sections. The "save search" feature is explained in detail and class members are urged to plan a "save search" example for the final practice session.

The rest of the manual is devoted to reference material about NLM, MEDLARS, and the telecommunications systems. The instructor stresses the list of MEDLARS search aids and encourages all class members to complete MEDLEARN, NLM's computer-assisted instruction program for MEDLINE, as a review. Each student also receives an additional hour of free time for practice outside the classroom using one of the demonstration passwords.

After a final question-and-answer period, the class goes online again. Finally, each participant is required to complete two evaluations. The first satisfies the university's continuing education program, while the second is a specially constructed library evaluation form. The library's form asks students to rate each part of the class and provides space for comments. In addition, NLM asks that a form with the participant's name, address, field of study, and other data be completed. This form is returned to NLM by the instructor.

TRAINING MATERIALS

Planning this type of class requires extensive time because the various systems are constantly changing and because there is a scarcity of good teaching materials for end users. Apart from the NLM training manual and the basic search aids such as *MeSH* and the *Online Services Reference Manual*,[5] there is little available for purchase that is suitable for end users. One publication that is highly recommended is the *Micromanual for Casual Users of National Library of Medicine Databases* by Winifred Sewell and Sandra Teitelbaum.[6] Its tables are "cookbook recipes" for various search operations which can also serve as trouble-shooting guides. Its glossary, as explained in the manual's preface, expands the information contained in the tables, provides suggestions for improving the contents of a search, (e.g., by defining MEDLINE subheadings and explaining their use), and can be used to answer specific questions as they arise. For example, the searcher can look up program messages or mnemonics using the glossary while online.

Because end user searching is relatively new, the instructor is forced to develop some original training materials. Even with the availability of resources like the *Micromanual* and the user aids published by NLM, some supplementary material is needed for the class at MML. Much of this consists of one-page handouts, covering such topics as NLM criteria for assigning the "review" check tag or suggested worksheets for formulating practice searches. Other materials originally designed for different purposes have also been used for "The Basics of Searching MEDLINE." MML recently produced a videotape and programmed-instruction workbook, entitled *MeSH . . . A Key to Library Resources*.[7] The workbook can be used separately and is distributed to every end user who takes the class; it provides reinforcement and a review of principles discussed in class.

ADMINISTRATIVE ASPECTS

Advertising for both of MML's end user searching classes has been done through channels such as the campus newspaper, the library's newsletter, and the distribution of flyers describing the classes. Size is limited for both classes, and the response has been impressive.

There are several points to be considered in designing a classroom instruction program. First, scheduling these classes in a busy health sciences center is sometimes a problem. "Database Searching for the Health Scientist" is taught on the third Tuesday of each month in the afternoon from 3:30 pm to 5:30 pm. It was scheduled accordingly to accommodate physicians' clinical responsibilities; this was judged to be the time of day they would most likely be free to attend. If an entire department is interested in taking this class, a special session is held at their convenience.

"The Basics of Searching MEDLINE" is always held on a Saturday. An informal poll showed that prospective attendees would prefer doing the seven hours all at once rather than in several sessions. Saturday was chosen because most of the library's searching equipment is needed for the class, and there is too much searching "traffic" on the equipment during the week to allow for classroom use. Since only four searching stations are available for instructional purposes, enrollment is limited to eight participants. This arrangement assures each class member a total practice time of about two hours, divided into two sessions.

Flexibility is a prerequisite in online instruction. There are so many extra variables to be considered, along with all the hazards normally associated with teaching an art. For example, questions generated during the class, especially during search formulation exercises, sometimes require lengthy explanations. Although questions can be time-consuming and can play havoc with the class schedule, the instructor should allow ample time for them and should be available during breaks and after class. Ideally, class participants should be encouraged to contact the instructor in the weeks immediately following the workshop, if problems arise. End users at the University of Texas Medical Branch have expressed interest in regularly scheduled searching clinics to address problems and questions on the various software systems and databases. The library is currently investigating the possibility of implementing such a program.

Additional ideas have been considered since the MML began its end user instruction program. Some of these ideas grew out of suggestions from the staff at NLM, others were gleaned from the literature, and some resulted from experience after the program began.

One of the most important guidelines is the library's neutral stance concerning vendors and equipment. Most end user searching classes have a limited and relatively short period of time to present many complex ideas that are completely new to participants. Equipment discussions can be lengthy, and equipment needs are impossible to generalize. The instructor could easily end up giving mini-courses to each member of the class on his or her hardware configuration.

An equally important factor for the instructor to stress is the use of vendor documentation and education. It is important to include vendor training schedules in the individual packets and to make available sample copies of vendor documentation in the classroom. For "The Basics of Searching MEDLINE," MML provides each participant with a copy of *MeSH—Annotated Alphabetic List*,[2] *MeSH—Tree Structures*,[3] and the *Permuted MeSH*[4] for use during the class. A demonstration of the relevance of retrieval using both Text Words and MeSH is also useful when stressing the importance of utilizing documentation.

In these and all other demonstration searches it is critical to have run them prior to the class. This is important both from the point of view of eliminating unexpected results as well as to exclude extraneous concepts that can make results difficult to explain. Also, if the instructor is using the MEDLARS database, INTROMED, he or she is likely to get no retrieval on many searches that would be viable in MEDLINE, a much larger database.

Perhaps the most difficult part of teaching end user searching is the logistics of keeping the equipment running properly during demonstrations and practice time, and helping students when they run into difficulties. Instructors must resign themselves to a sometimes frenzied pace and allow for the possibility of equipment or system failure. The MML instructor of "The Basics of Searching MEDLINE" talks frankly to the students before the first practice time about the idiosyncracies of computer equipment and telecommunications systems. This is done on the theory that the sooner they learn about mechanical problems common to all database searching, the better off they will be.

Despite these problems, teaching end user searching is one of the most rewarding of the user education experiences available to librarians. The students are bright, eager to learn, and highly motivated—all characteristics that any teacher would desire. With all of their challenges and time-consuming preparation, the courses still remain a positive experience. The MML staff believes that end user training represents a new and exciting avenue through which librarians can make information more accessible.

REFERENCES

1. National Library of Medicine. *The Basics of Searching MEDLINE: A Guide for the Health Professional*. Springfield, Virginia: National Technical Information Service, 1984.

2. National Library of Medicine. *Medical Subject Headings—Annotated Alphabetic List*. Springfield, Virginia: National Technical Information Service, 1985.

3. National Library of Medicine. *Medical Subject Headings—Tree Structures*. Springfield, Virginia: National Technical Information Service, 1985.

4. National Library of Medicine. *Permuted Medical Subject Headings*. Springfield, Virginia: National Technical Information Service, 1985.

5. National Library of Medicine. *Online Services Reference Manual*. Springfield, Virginia: National Technical Information Service, 1982. *Supplement*, 1984.

6. Sewell, Winifred, and Teitelbaum, Sandra. *Micromanual for Casual Users of National Library of Medicine Databases*. Bethesda, Maryland: Drug Intelligence Publications, 1984.

7. Wygant, Alice C. *MeSH . . . A Key to Library Resources*. Galveston, Texas: Moody Medical Library, 1984. Videotape and workbook.

U-Search:
A Program to Teach End User Searching at an Academic Health Sciences Library

Vicki L. Glasgow
Gertrude Foreman

ABSTRACT. The University of Minnesota Bio-Medical Library has offered classes in end user searching through its U-Search Program since January 1984. A total of more than 150 faculty, staff, and students have been trained to do online database searching on the BRS/Saunders Colleague and BRS/AFTER DARK systems. This paper discusses advantages and disadvantages of teaching end user searching in an academic health sciences library setting and presents the results of a follow-up survey of participants in the U-Search Program.

INTRODUCTION

For several years librarians have demonstrated a growing interest in end user searching. The extent of this interest is well documented by numerous citations in the journal literature, published bibliographies, and presentations at national meetings. End user searching was a topic of discussion at the 1985 Medical Library Association meeting as well.[1]

The literature covers a wide range of topics related to end user searching, and descriptions of the systems designed for end users are readily available. Ojala notes that the database vendors "consider the library market to be saturated and so are turning their attention to the end user" and provides a list of citations to support her view.[2] Typical of the information industry, a computer journal describes database searching for end users as a "key to instant, unlimited information gathering power."[3]

Vicki L. Glasgow, M.S.L.S., M.S., is Coordinator, Bibliographic Search Service and Reference/Bibliographer and Gertrude Foreman, M.A., is Head, Public Services, at the Bio-Medical Library, University of Minnesota, Diehl Hall, Minneapolis, MN 55455.

In her thoughtful article concerning the implications of end user searching, Ojala suggests that one role of the librarian will be that of teacher and trainer.[2] That many librarians agree with this opinion is supported by the increasing number of instructional programs reported in professional journals. Academic librarians report widespread success with course integrated online search instruction. Seminars for special groups prove to be a popular method for teaching search skills. In response to increased interest, Hunter provides valuable advice for librarians who become advisors or consultants to end users,[4] while Halperin and Pagell discuss their point-of-use assistance in a free self-service searching situation.[5]

As part of a large University library system serving over 50,000 students, the Bio-Medical Library has as primary clientele students, staff and faculty from the basic biological and life sciences, as well as dentistry, hospital and health care administration, medicine, mortuary science, nursing, pharmacy, public health, and the University Hospitals. Collections to support the study and research of these disciplines include 270,000 bound volumes and 4,015 active journal subscriptions, with special collections for the Learning Resource Center, the Museum of Natural History, and the Owen H. Wangensteen History of Medicine Library. A staff of twelve professionals and sixteen full-time support staff provides circulation, reference, online bibliographic searches, library instruction, a computer laboratory, and technical services. In addition, the Biomedical Information Service, a fee-for-service program, extends the use of the Library's collections and services to corporate and other non-University clients.

The Bibliographic Search Service of the Bio-Medical Library has been offering computerized database searches since 1972. On the average, more than 5,500 searches per year are processed. Primary databases searched include MEDLINE, HEALTH PLANNING AND ADMINISTRATION, BIOSIS PREVIEWS, PsycINFO, TOXLINE, and ERIC. Approximately 90 percent of the Library's online searches are run on the BRS system. Other database vendors used are the National Library of Medicine and DIALOG.

Although library instruction has received special impetus at the Bio-Medical Library during the past two years, the reference librarians have been teaching seminars and invited classes for many years. Currently, computer database discussions or demonstrations, especially MEDLINE, are included in all classes.

MEDLINE demonstrations and classes have been but one method

of acquainting clients with database searching. Librarians' use of databases as a tool at the reference desk has had an impact as well. The University of Minnesota Libraries are now involved in planning for an online catalog. The online catalog will further expand the computerized information resources available to clients of the Bio-Medical Library, who have been using computer-produced journal holdings, recent acquisitions lists, and a COM (Computer-Output-Microform) catalog for several years. Furthermore, the Learning Resource Center provides instructional access to forty microcomputers, a local area network, and a computer laboratory.

With the advent of the "user-friendly" systems, the reference staff began to receive inquiries from clients, both for information on hardware, software, and access to search systems, and for advice on search strategy formulation, terms, and commands. The librarians felt that it was the right time to provide this help in a more formal way. Thus, the U-Search Program, an effort to provide assistance to end user searchers, was begun.

HISTORY OF THE U-SEARCH PROGRAM

In November 1983, the Bio-Medical Library proposed that the funds from a Health Sciences Faculty Development Grant be used to start a program of instruction in online searching for health sciences faculty, students, and staff at the University of Minnesota. Once funding was received, the planning phase was begun.

The program was called "U-Search" in order to convey the idea of self-service searching to participants in the program. The next step was to obtain hardware. An Apple IIe microcomputer and Epson FX-80 printer were borrowed from the Learning Resources Center, and some of the money from the grant was used to equip the Apple IIe for online searching. This involved purchasing a Hayes Micromodem II with communications software and an 80-column card.

Next came the decision of which user-friendly searching systems to include in the program. Although the initial plan was to offer classes on three systems—BRS/Saunders Colleague, BRS/AFTER DARK, and DIALOG's KNOWLEDGE INDEX—the decision was made to concentrate efforts on one system—Colleague—with occasional classes on the AFTER DARK system. It was felt that the Colleague system, with its primary emphasis on information needs of medical and health sciences professionals, would be the most interesting to library users. Another reason for concentrating on Colleague was the difficulty encountered in obtaining an institutional account for searching KNOWLEDGE INDEX. DIALOG has since changed their policy and has approved the Library's application for an institutional password. A class in KNOWLEDGE INDEX will be offered for the first time this year (1985).

The next phase of the program was the marketing phase, in which the availability of classes in do-it-yourself searching was advertised to library users. Letters describing the U-Search Program and application forms for classes were sent to each of thirty-seven department and program chairs in the various health sciences units at the University. The initial response to this announcement exceeded everyone's expectations. Although the letters had gone out during Christmas vacation, when many University personnel are away, the first two classes were immediately filled. Class size had been originally limited to ten individuals but had to be doubled. Within a month, the waiting list had grown to more than fifty names of users who wanted to register for the classes.

Consistent with the Library's cost-recovery philosophy for database searching, it was decided to charge a registration fee for U-Search classes: $20.00 for Colleague and $10.00 for AFTER DARK. As a marketing gimmick and because support was being received from a Health Sciences Faculty Development Grant, it was determined that classes should be offered at a reduced fee of $10.00 to health sciences faculty. The lower registration fee undoubtedly contributed to the popularity of the class among health sciences faculty.

Since January 1984, a total of eighteen classes in end user searching—fourteen on Colleague and four on AFTER DARK—have been offered. One hundred forty-eight individuals have participated in the U-Search Program. The three largest groups of participants have been faculty (58 percent), staff (26 percent), and graduate students (10 percent). Other groups include residents from the University Hospital, administrators from the Medical School, and several undergraduate students.

More than twenty-six different departments in the health sciences have been represented by U-Search students. The most enthusiasm for end user searching seems to have come from six departments in the Medical School (Surgery, Physical Medicine and Rehabilitation, Obstetrics and Gynecology, Laboratory Medicine and Pathology,

Anatomy, and Physiology), the School of Nursing, and the Dental School. One department in the Dental School—Orthodontics—has even requested a separate class for residents in their department.

CONTENT OF CLASSES

BRS/Saunders Colleague is taught as a two-part course—a two-hour lecture followed by a forty-five-minute individual hands-on training session with each participant. The two-hour lecture session covers the following topics:

1. Definition and general description of the process of online searching.
2. Definition of a database.
3. Bibliographic vs. full-text and other non-bibliographic databases.
4. Description of the MEDLINE database, how it is produced, and the types of information it provides.
5. Characteristics and costs of three major user-friendly online searching systems of interest to the health sciences (BRS/Saunders Colleague, BRS/AFTER DARK, and DIALOG KNOWLEDGE INDEX).
6. Description of the Colleague system and overview of its databases.
7. Basic principles of subject searching (breaking topic down into concepts, finding terms to represent those concepts, and grouping or connecting those terms to form a search strategy).
8. Use of controlled vocabulary, synonyms or freetext, and truncation.
9. Exploding MeSH tree categories.
10. Boolean connectors (AND, OR, and NOT).
11. Positional connectors (ADJ, WITH, and SAME).
12. Working through a sample subject search strategy on the MEDLINE database.
13. Types of searches other than subjects that can be run on the MEDLINE database (author, journal title, author's institutional affiliation, language, year of publication, etc.).
14. Principles of full-text searching and how it differs from searching bibliographic databases.

The second part of the Colleague course is a forty-five-minute individual hands-on training session, scheduled at the convenience of each participant. System commands and the mechanics of searching (how to log on and off, correct typos and input errors, send a break signal, save a search strategy, print, etc.) are covered in the hands-on sessions, instead of in the lecture part of the course, since the terminal mechanics are best learned at the keyboard. Individuals bring their own topics of interest to search. The first few minutes of their training session is spent checking terms against the MeSH vocabulary and going over their search strategy. Then, the student sits down at the terminal and actually runs the search. An instructor sits through the session with each student and uses this time to answer questions, explain system features, and provide individualized assistance. If a student seems to be learning the system fairly easily, the instructor may explain more sophisticated functions, such as command stacking and downloading to disk.

BRS/AFTER DARK is taught in a single three-hour evening period, from approximately 5:30-8:30 p.m. These hours give students and residents an opportunity to attend an online searching class at a time that does not conflict with their daily schedules. The AFTER DARK lecture period is shorter, but covers most of the major topics included in the Colleague course. Hands-on training is conducted immediately after the AFTER DARK lecture in small groups of three to four students. Limiting the class to ten registrants allows each student to spend at least fifteen minutes searching a topic of his or her interest.

EVALUATION OF THE U-SEARCH PROGRAM

Teaching end user searching in the format just described is a relatively labor-intensive experience. Excluding preparation time for lectures, approximately twenty staff hours are spent on each Colleague class, and about five staff hours are devoted to each AFTER DARK class. The program is a team effort on the part of the entire Reference Department. Most Reference Librarians are involved both in teaching the classes and in providing the hands-on training sessions. Other Reference Librarians take extra hours at the reference desk in order to free up time for those involved directly in the end user classes. Although the individual hands-on training sessions are quite time-consuming, plans are to continue teaching end user searching according to the format already tested. A number of trainees have commented that, although the lecture session was interesting and helpful, the individual hands-on training session was the most beneficial part of the course.

Instruction and information on end user searching is now a part of most bibliographic instruction and library use classes offered by the Library. Most of the Colleague lecture and hands-on training in small groups has been incorporated into the credit and selective didactic classes on information retrieval and management presented to medical students.

Typical problems that were encountered during the program in end user searching included the following:

1. Typing ability varied considerably among participants. Individual hands-on training sessions, which were originally planned to last thirty minutes, had to be lengthened to forty-five minutes because of the widespread lack of familiarity with the keyboard.
2. Several individuals exhibited a great deal of difficulty understanding the concepts of Boolean logic. The best approach to teaching Boolean connectors seems to be to incorporate a diagrammatic approach accompanied by oral explanation of Boolean connectors.
3. Many health professionals were frustrated by controlled vocabulary terms, especially when the MeSH term or phrase was different from the term or phrase they commonly used. Extra time devoted to explaining the reasons behind controlled vocabulary and specific-concept indexing was well justified.
4. There seemed to be widespread misconception on the part of novice searchers that the primary goal of constructing a search strategy was to condense it into an absolute minimum number of search statements. As a result, part of the Colleague lecture has been dedicated to explaining the principle of grouping terms together in a search strategy that is both logical and flexible—one that allows for changing the topic or adding emphasis to one or more concepts.

RESULTS OF SURVEY

A survey of participants in the U-Search Program was conducted in September 1984 to determine the extent to which people were actually doing their own online literature searches, how they were using online databases, and whether their level of use of the

Library's Search Service had changed since they had taken a class in end user searching. A total of ninety questionnaires were sent out to U-Search participants. Thirty-one, or 34 percent, were returned. The relatively low rate of return is perhaps due to busy schedules of the health sciences faculty participants in U-Search. In addition, a large number of University faculty are not in their offices until late September.

Of the thirty-one individuals participating in the survey, faculty members comprised the largest group (fifteen, or 48 percent), followed by staff members (eleven, or 35 percent), graduate students (four, or 13 percent), and residents (one, or 3 percent). Most of those surveyed had taken the Colleague class (84 percent), rather than the AFTER DARK class (16 percent).

Almost half of those surveyed (48 percent) were not yet signed up to use Colleague or AFTER DARK. Of the fifteen individuals not yet using any online database search system, eight were faculty, four were staff, and three were graduate students. In other words, 53 percent of the faculty, 36 percent of the staff, and 75 percent of the graduate students surveyed who had taken end user searching classes were not yet doing their own searching. When asked to explain why they were not yet searching, most participants replied that they were still in the process of getting set up to do online searching, i.e., trying to obtain departmental approval to spend the funds, trying to obtain their passwords, and/or purchasing necessary hardware or software for searching.

Of those not yet searching, 44 percent (three faculty and one staff member) indicated that they had decided against doing their own searches. These individuals indicated that they believed the Bio-Medical Library's Search Service could provide them with either better quality, less expensive, or faster searches than they themselves could produce.

When asked what equipment they were using for online searching, most trainees indicated that they were using microcomputers, instead of simple terminals. The two brands of computers being used by most individuals were Apple II series and IBM PC series microcomputers.

The large majority of respondents who were doing their own searching indicated that they were running searches during the day (59 percent), rather than in the evening on weekdays (35 percent) or on weekends (6 percent). The place in which they were doing searching varied. Most individuals were searching on a microcomputer in their department (31 percent) or office (18 percent). The next largest category were those that were searching at home (38 percent).

Those trainees who were now searching indicated that they were processing relatively few searches. More than half (61 percent) were only going online to search once or less than once per month. When asked to estimate how many minutes they spent online doing an average search, most (53 percent) of the respondents who search replied that an average search takes them ten to twenty minutes. No one processed a search in less than five minutes, on the average. Although 18 percent took an average of between twenty and forty-five minutes and 6 percent took an average of between forty-five and sixty minutes per search, no one took more than sixty minutes to process a search.

Although most of the end user searchers were using only the MEDLINE database (63 percent), some individuals had tried BIOSIS PREVIEWS (14 percent) and CHEMICAL ABSTRACTS (8 percent). PsycINFO, ERIC, HEALTH PLANNING AND ADMINISTRATION, DISSERTATION ABSTRACTS, and COMPENDEX had each been used at least once by survey participants.

Although a few trainees were downloading search results to disks, most individuals (76 percent) were printing their references online. Only one person was using the offline print feature of Colleague with any regularity.

One of the primary purposes of this survey was to explore how classes in end user searching might affect the use of the Library's Search Service. Survey participants were asked to estimate, on the average, how often they requested computer searches from the Bio-Medical Library before they took a class in online searching and how often they *now* requested searches from the Bio-Medical Library. Twenty percent indicated they had never requested a search from the Bio-Medical Library, and 64 percent replied that they requested searches less frequently than once a month, prior to taking a class in Colleague or AFTER DARK. Now that they had taken a class in end user searching, 68 percent were no longer requesting searches from the Library and 28 percent were requesting searches from the Library less than once a month. The implication was that, although most end user searchers were now using the Library's Search Service less than once a month or not at all, most of these individuals had never been frequent users of the Bio-Medical Library's Search Service to begin with.

When asked how satisfied they were with Colleague and/or AFTER DARK, most end user searchers replied that they were either very satisfied (60 percent) or somewhat satisfied (27 percent) with these systems. One person indicated he was very dissatisfied with AFTER DARK and had cancelled his account because of the monthly minimum charge, which was levied even when he did not use the system.

CONCLUSION

Staff at the Bio-Medical Library are quite pleased with the results of the U-Search Program. It has proven to be an excellent outreach and public relations mechanism for the Library and has provided the Library with a high level of visibility with respect to do-it-yourself online searching activities within the health sciences departments at the University of Minnesota. Through the U-Search Program, members of the Library staff have also been able to keep in relatively close contact with users who are doing their own online searching. End users seem to have reached a greater appreciation and awareness of the Bio-Medical Library as a multi-dimensional source of support for microcomputer-based information management activities—not just a place to drop off search requests and pick up results.

How will programs such as U-Search affect the traditional search services at the Bio-Medical Library in the years to come? To date, the Library's search statistics continue to increase steadily. It is anticipated that users will continue to call on the Search Service at the Bio-Medical Library to run more in-depth, complex topics or searches on databases with which they are unfamiliar. End users will probably perform their own searches on topics that are relatively simple and straightforward, or whenever they need just a few references. Most of the Library's users will probably never have the time or the need to develop the same high level of searching skill that is available to them through the Bio-Medical Library's Search Service. Therefore, the need for an efficient and well-trained staff of online searchers at the Bio-Medical Library is expected to continue into the foreseeable future.

The future for search intermediaries is reflected in the professional moving industry in the United States. Although a large number of people rent their moving equipment from self-service companies and do most of the work themselves, there are still quite a few individuals who prefer to contract with professional moving companies to do all of the work for them. Just as there is plenty of room in the moving industry for both kinds of services, there will continue to be room in health sciences information management for both do-it-yourself and library-mediated online searching.

REFERENCES

1. Medical Library Association. 85th Annual meeting, New York, N.Y., May 24-30, 1985.
2. Ojala, Marydee. "End User Searching and its Implications for Librarians." *Special Libraries* 76 (Spring 1985):93-9.
3. Wessner, Cecilia. "The Compleat Electronic Researcher." *Personal Computing* 8 (December 1984):125-40.
4. Hunter, Janne A. "When Your Patrons Want to Search: The Library as Advisor to Endusers . . . A Compendium of Advice and Tips." *Online* 8(May 1984):36- 41.
5. Halperin, Michael, and Pagell, Ruth A. "Free 'Do-it-yourself' Online Searching . . . What to Expect." *Online* 9(March 1985):82- 4.

ADDITIONAL SELECTED REFERENCES

Baker, Carole A. "Colleague: A Comprehensive Online Medical Library for the End User." *Medical Reference Services Quarterly* 3 (Winter 1984):13-26.
Broering, Naomi C. "The miniMEDLINE System: A Library-Based End-User Search System." *Bulletin of the Medical Library Association* 73 (April 1985):138- 45.
Freeman, Joan K., and O'Connell, Kathie A. "The Marketing of Biomedical Information at the University of Minnesota: Creative Error Correction." In: Wood, M. Sandra (ed.) *Cost Analysis, Cost Recovery, Marketing, and Fee-Based Services: A Guide for the Health Sciences Librarian.* New York: The Haworth Press, 1985, pp. 159-71.
Friend, Linda. "Independence at the Terminal: Training Student End Users to Do Online Literature Searching." *Journal of Academic Librarianship* 11 (July 1985):136-41.
Haines, Judith S. "Experiences in Training End-User Searchers." *Online* 6 (November 1982):14-23.
Janke, Richard. "Online After Six: End User Searching Comes of Age." *Online* 8 (November 1984):15-29.
Lyon, Sally. "End-User Searching of Online Databases: A Selective Annotated Bibliography." *Library Hi-Tech* 6 (1984):47-50.
Mueller, Mary, and Foreman, Gertrude. "A Credit Course for Medical Students." *Medical Reference Services Quarterly* 4 (Fall 1985):61-6.
Ojala, Marydee. "Knowledge Index: A Review." *Online* 7 (September 1983):31-4.
Snow, Bonnie. "Making the Rough Places Plain: Designing MEDLINE End User Training." *Medical Reference Services Quarterly* 3 (Winter 1984):1-11.
Ward, Sandra N. "Course-Integrated DIALOG Instruction." *Research Strategies* 3 (Spring 1985):52-64.

Implementing End User Systems at the Massachusetts General Hospital Health Sciences Libraries

Rhonda A. Rios Kravitz
Ellen R. Westling

ABSTRACT. During the 1980s, direct end user searching has become a new reality for health sciences libraries. Using the Paper-Chase end user system as a model, this paper discusses the processes used to plan, implement, and manage end user systems at the Massachusetts General Hospital Health Sciences Libraries. Emphasis is placed on managing end user systems on a cost recovery basis.

Strategies to recover costs, end user instruction clinics, marketing programs, document delivery service, and user satisfaction are described as they relate to promoting and selling an end user service.

Librarians at the Massachusetts General Hospital (MGH) Health Sciences Libraries have recently been hearing a new type of question from their users: "I have a computer at home (or in my office)—can I do my own computer searching?" During the 1980s, end user searching has become a new reality for health sciences libraries. This development should not come as a surprise; library searchers have been crucial to the development of the online database market.[1] As Leslie Wykoff recently pointed out: "Librarian searchers have, indeed, preached the good news of online searching. Our own excitement has been inspiring our patrons and now we may be feeling something like the missionary whose congregation 'believes' and wants to 'do it itself'."[2]

Rhonda A. Rios Kravitz is the Assistant Director for Library Consult Services, MGH Health Sciences Libraries, Massachusetts General Hospital, Boston, MA 02114. She received her M.S.L.S. from Simmons College.

Ellen R. Westling is the Assistant Director for Information Services, MGH Health Sciences Libraries, Massachusetts General Hospital, Boston, MA 02114. She received her M.S.L.S. from Simmons College and is currently a part-time M.B.A. student at the Simmons Graduate School of Management.

This trend can be viewed as an opportunity for librarians to expand their roles, to become "information specialists, consultants, and educators."[3] Not only is this an adaptive vision that will help libraries avoid obsolescence, but it will also offer librarians an active role in shaping their professional future.

Traditionally one of the primary functions of librarians has been to serve clients' information needs by providing them with information resources and the skills to use them effectively. The librarian's goal regarding end user online searching can be similar. Given that database vendors are aggressively marketing their products directly to potential end users and have a vested interest in their products, librarians can assist users by critically evaluating these systems, making them available, and improving online searching efficiency.

This paper will review the administrative, marketing, and teaching experiences of the professional library staff of the MGH Health Sciences Libraries in introducing online user-friendly systems to their clientele in the medical community. Although the Libraries are larger than most hospital libraries, many of the implementation and management decisions made about end user systems will be relevant to other hospital libraries, regardless of size, and to academic medical libraries.

BACKGROUND

The Setting

The MGH Health Sciences Libraries serve over 4600 medical professionals. Affiliated with Harvard Medical School, Massachusetts General Hospital is a major teaching, research, and patient care center in Boston, Massachusetts. Its new degree-granting Institute of Health Professions offers academic programs in nursing, physical therapy, social work, and dietetics. This diverse user population has a broad range of bibliographic information needs.

The MGH Health Sciences Libraries, consisting of Treadwell and Palmer-Davis Libraries, are staffed by 8.5 FTE professional librarians and 8 FTE support staff. Computerized literature searching has been an important library service since it was first introduced in 1974. During fiscal year 1984/85, the Libraries' Computer Search Center conducted 1260 comprehensive online searches and 1136 monthly updates on a fee-for-service basis. In addition, the reference personnel have provided free, five-minute, up-to-ten citations MEDLINE quick searches to its users since 1981. During fiscal year 1984/85, over 5000 quick searches were conducted.

Through these services, the Libraries' clientele have become familiar both with the usefulness of computer searching and with the staff's expertise in using online databases. End user systems would allow users access to the computerized literature from off-site locations twenty-four-hours a day, a need which most hospital libraries cannot meet with mediated search services. Thus, the introduction of end user searching was considered a natural extension of the reference and comprehensive computer search services currently offered at the Libraries.

PLANNING

In making a decision to offer user-friendly systems, a library's staff must review the institution's goals and assess its ability to support such a new service. End user systems may require additional staff support, equipment, and funding. Most hospital libraries have small staffs who are already overburdened with responsibilities. Additionally, hospital cost containments have reduced budgets and decreased chances for adding new staff. Although many hospital libraries do not charge for their services, a user-friendly system may be a good place to start. Vendors are marketing their products directly to end users. Libraries, too, can market these systems to their users and work toward recovering all costs.

The planning team for the initial implementation of end user online systems consisted of the Director, the Assistant Director for Library Consult Services, and the Assistant Director for Information Services. Because most services have been offered on a "charge back" basis to their users, the planning team decided to implement user-friendly systems on a fee-for-service basis. Early planning discussions focused on three basic questions: (1) what did the users want, (2) what costs would they be willing to pay, and (3) what support (i.e., equipment and staff) could the library provide? Thus, the selection of specific user-friendly systems needed to consider the best fit between the user population needs and the Libraries' current staffing and budgetary constraints.

As for user needs, assessment of current online searching indicated that, although many databases are used, MEDLINE is the most frequently searched. In addition, users expressed a desire to be able to search from a remote site (office or home) at any time of the day or night. Finally, given the time and energy constraints of the user population in the MGH clinical care setting, any system which was to be provided needed to be easy to learn and use.

From the Libraries' perspective, MGH administrative and cost constraints had to be addressed. Library staff levels have been reduced, and it is very difficult to add new positions. This necessitated the decision to offer end user services as an off-the-operating-budget project on a total cost recovery basis. This decision meant that users would be charged any costs which were incurred each and every time they used the system. The online database system chosen would need to monitor individual access and provide billing information for charge-back purposes, because very little staff time would be available for this function.

In addition, consideration had to be given to what users would be willing to pay for the service. The Libraries needed to charge enough to recover all vendor and support costs, (i.e., all equipment, telecommunications, paper, ribbons, and marketing costs). But the fees had to be kept close to vendor's fees so that users would not choose to subscribe directly to the vendor.

By offering a user-friendly system through the library, the staff essentially does "work" for the vendor. The library promotes and provides access to the system, as well as offers customer support. Most vendors recognize this marketing service and offer volume discounts to high usage customers. The discount is based on the number of hours used on the system. The volume discount plays a key role in allowing libraries to recover their costs. By billing its subscribers the vendor's non-discounted individual rate, the library can use the difference to cover the costs incurred in providing the system. There is also a built-in motivation for the library staff to encourage the use of the system since the volume discount increases with the volume of use.

In early 1984, the Libraries' staff began to review and test the major end user online systems available: BRS/AFTER DARK, BRS/Saunders Colleague, KNOWLEDGE INDEX, Sci-Mate, and PaperChase. Many of the Libraries' users were already familiar with PaperChase because it was developed in Boston at the Beth Israel Hospital in 1979. Other users either had seen advertisements for, or had subscribed to, BRS/AFTER DARK or KNOWLEDGE INDEX. The users' enthusiasm and excitement coupled with the number of questions received reinforced the Libraries' decision to offer and manage user-friendly systems.

After hours of "test trials," user discussions, and staff input, the professional staff decided that more than one end user system for online database searching would be required to meet the diverse information needs of the MGH community. However, it was also felt that implementation of each system would present a unique set of administrative problems to solve and should be phased in over time.

PaperChase was selected as the initial system and was introduced to the Libraries in June 1984. The vendor services and system features that recommended PaperChase to the library staff were: (1) a billing software package that met the Libraries' cost recovery accounting needs, (2) a substantial volume discount to allow recovery of library costs, (3) ease of use for the end user, and (4) twenty-four-hour accessibility.

As of September 1985, Paperchase has been available in the Libraries for sixteen months. The experience gained by the professional staff during this time period has guided the introduction of other end user systems, BRS/Saunders Colleague and MEDIS, and has provided a model for off-the-operating-budget projects.

PAPERCHASE

PaperChase is a computer-based bibliographic retrieval system developed by physicians that enables users with no prior searching experience to search MEDLINE, the National Library of Medicine (NLM) online database.[4] In June 1984, PaperChase became commercially available at selected pilot sites as an end user system accessing the MEDLINE database back to 1979. Since its inception, its user-friendly interface has continued to be refined. Currently it has extended access to the MEDLINE database back to 1975 and is available nationwide.

PaperChase is a menu-driven system with two basic menus: a "LOOK FOR" display and an "OPTIONS" display. A user begins a search at the "LOOK FOR" display and may type in a title word, an author's name, journal title, year, language, Medical Subject Heading (MeSH) or Tree number. The "OPTIONS" menu allows the user to combine lists using Boolean logic, display titles, and print. These two menus make searching the system fairly easy.

Several user benefits and a few limitations of the PaperChase system have been identified. First, PaperChase's program is adapted to the likely search strategies of untrained users. For example, it will accept any entry for an author's name or any reasonable abbreviation of a journal title, and it automatically looks for spelling variants, such as anemia, anemias, anaemia, and anaemias. Second, it points the user to MeSH terms from title words entered in the "LOOK FOR" display, thus providing more appropriate or additional search terms. In addition, putting a slash after a MeSH term will automatically display all the appropriate subheadings for that term. A user may use these subheadings to refine a search. Third, it is the only system that monitors the user's search strategies while the search is in progress by storing MeSH terms which occur most frequently in the retrieved references and presenting them to the user at various strategic points. During the search the user can then opt to expand or refine the search with these terms.

There are a few minor limitations both in the database itself and in the program. First, PaperChase searches only the MEDLINE database, and only back to 1975. However, as stated earlier, MEDLINE is the major database used by the Libraries' users, and meets most of their needs. In the future, the vendor plans to offer the entire MEDLINE database. Second, the PaperChase program searches for words only in the title and not in the abstract. This can be limiting when a user is searching for a method, technique, or rare entity likely to be mentioned in the abstract, but not in the title or Medical Subject Headings. Finally, although online help screens are available, the current list of instructions is not easy to use and system updates/changes occasionally occur without notification to users or institutions.

For a library, PaperChase provides management options which offer flexibility in managing the system. For example, a library can enter its journal holdings in order to allow the user to limit a search to the library's collection or to simply print the library's holdings first. The library staff also has the option to monitor system use and individual search strategies. At the end of each search, the system offers users the opportunity to comment on any problems encountered. The library staff, in turn, can provide online responses.

IMPLEMENTATION

Once the decision had been made to obtain PaperChase, management, marketing, and user support service strategies needed to be developed. A three-month trial period was initiated in June 1984, to allow time to develop and pilot these strategies. During this time,

PaperChase was offered to users free of charge but was not actively marketed.

The first implementation step was to purchase and set up a computer work station with a visual display terminal (VDT), printer, and modem dedicated to PaperChase. It was located in Treadwell Library near the reference desk to facilitate answering users' questions about the system. Equipment maintenance demands are frequently overlooked when planning for the implementation of end user systems. The purchase of equipment, supplies, and maintenance service contracts is relatively easy; unanticipated demands, however, often come from the need to "troubleshoot" equipment failures. Not only does the staff need to become adept at working with computer hardware, but they also have to be available to correct problems. For example, static made the printer sporadically unusable. Identifying and solving this problem took time, yet it was critical that the problem be tackled immediately. Users encountering consistent equipment failures will easily become disillusioned, not only with the hardware, but also with the searching software.

In calculating the cost of operating the system, library staff time for managing the system must be added to hardware and maintenance expenses. Staff time is often the unknown factor in the budget equation. The following PaperChase tasks have been identified: (1) register users, (2) input user data, (3) monitor use and prepare bills, (4) troubleshoot the equipment and system, (5) instruct and demonstrate the system to individual users, (6) develop and present user clinics, (7) communicate with vendors, and (8) pull and photocopy articles electronically selected through the new Copy Order Service.

The other major management task was to operate PaperChase on a cost recovery basis. Initially, the Libraries' income was generated for PaperChase from two sources: (1) a one-time user registration fee of $25.00 for MGH affiliates and $50.00 for outside users, and (2) the vendor's volume discount rate calculated on the total dollar amount of use per month. The vendor's discount rate ranges from 4 percent to 35 percent. The volume discount received at MGH each month has ranged from 9 percent to 20 percent.

The online costs to each user are charged at the vendor's non-discounted individual rates and are not subsidized by the Libraries. The system software keeps track of each user's online time and provides monthly billing information adapted to the Libraries' billing format. The Libraries' staff maintains user files and prepares monthly bills that are sent to the hospital accounting department for collection. Because the PaperChase account is not part of the Libraries' operating budget, the hospital's accounting department deducts an overhead charge for administering the account. The institution overhead rate must be considered as an additional budgetary expense.

Since the introduction of PaperChase, two further income-generating services have been added: a copy order service and user instruction clinics. These will be discussed below. The volume discount, along with other income-generating mechanisms, has allowed the Libraries not only to cover the cost of the equipment and supplies, but also the cost of one twenty-five-hour per week support staff person to handle most of the daily tasks of registering users, maintaining user files, preparing bills, and filling the copy order requests.

Marketing

Marketing of PaperChase to the MGH community was begun slowly due to uncertainty about the potential volume of use and the Libraries' capability to handle the billing and practical administration of the system. During the first three months of use, PaperChase was offered free of charge. No formal promotional activities were initiated until September 1984, when a brochure announcing PaperChase was made available to the Libraries' users. The Assistant Director for Library Consult Services began systematic outreach to MGH departments to explain and promote the service. In October 1984, the Libraries sponsored a computer information fair promoting PaperChase throughout the day. One month later the first user instruction clinic on PaperChase was offered to a hospital department. A letter from the Libraries' director introducing PaperChase was sent to all MGH professional staff in May 1985. Several user instruction clinics were offered in April and September 1985.

In addition, PaperChase users are provided with several sources of information on the Libraries' services. The Libraries' staff has developed a PaperChase newsletter for its users. The format consists of a "What's New" section, "Search Tips," and a section on "When PaperChase Is Not Enough." New services are announced through messages broadcast on the video display terminals when a user signs on. For example, the copy order service and the user instruction clinics have been advertised in this format.

The response of the MGH community to PaperChase can be seen in Figures 1 through 3. Figure 1 shows the rapid and continuing growth in the cumulative number of PaperChase registrations. As of

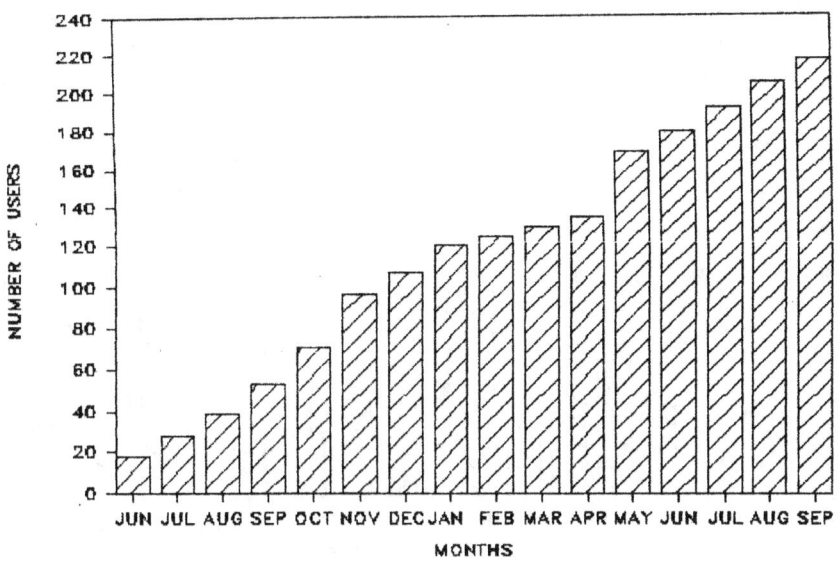

Figure 1
CUMULATIVE NUMBER OF PAPERCHASE REGISTRATIONS
June 1984 - September 1985

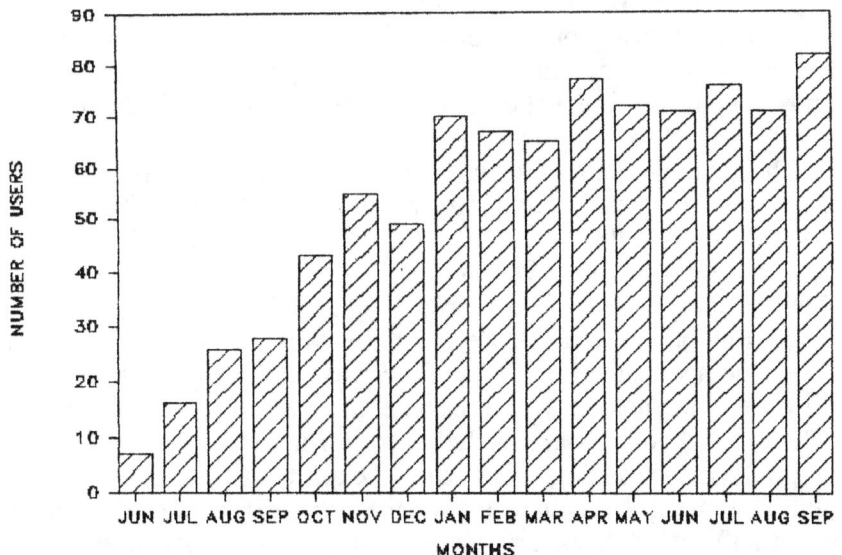

Figure 2
NUMBER OF ACTIVE PAPERCHASE USERS PER MONTH
June 1984 - September 1985

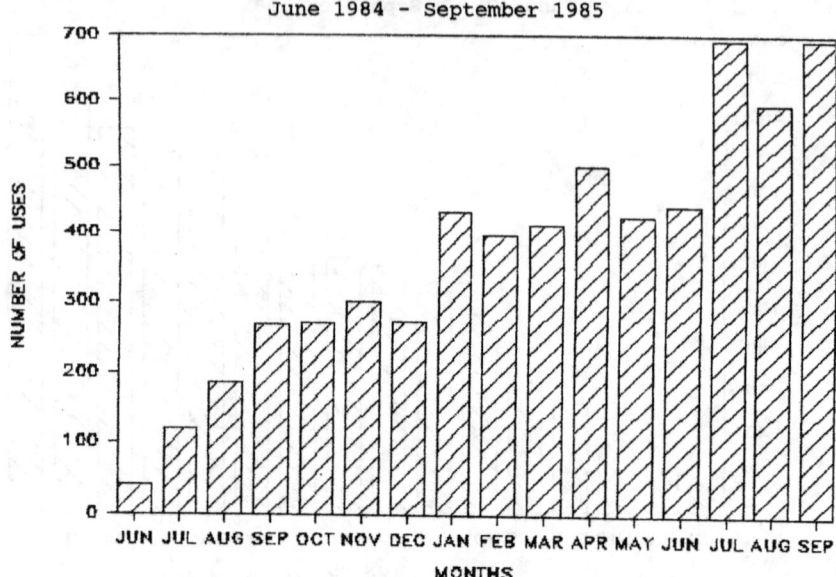

Figure 3
NUMBER OF PAPERCHASE USES PER MONTH*
June 1984 - September 1985

* These monthly totals exclude one unusually heavy user who had a total of 2,590 uses during this period.

September 1985, 217 people have registered as PaperChase users. Figure 2 indicates the actual number of active users each month. Since the Libraries' promotional efforts were begun, the number of active users each month has risen to seventy or more, and since the most recent user instruction clinics in September 1985, the number has increased to eighty-two.

The total number of monthly uses by these users is shown in Figure 3. For these calculations, a "use" simply means that a user has signed-on to the system. The number of uses has increased from less than fifty in June 1984, to nearly seven hundred in September 1985. PaperChase has been used a total of 8600 times during the sixteen-month period. However, there was one unusually heavy user who accounted for a total of 2590 uses, 30 percent of the total. In order to graphically demonstrate the overall pattern of PaperChase use, his totals are excluded from Figure 3.

Increased marketing efforts can be expected to attract new users, thus increasing the volume use and the volume discount. Also, given the Libraries' staff expertise with managing the system, and their development of specialized training clinics, the MGH Libraries are offering to manage the system for other libraries. Two local medical libraries have contracted for the service.

The library literature is filled with concerns over the effect of end user systems on other computer search services offered by librarians. "Will it effect their jobs?" "Will it take business away from them?" The experience at MGH suggests that the number of paid searches in the Computer Search Center has continued to increase by approximately 5 percent per year, while free quick searches have decreased by 9 percent. A recent survey of 166 MGH PaperChase users revealed that only 39 percent (64) had ever requested a paid search. This end user system appears to have reached an additional clientele not attracted to the traditional search services offered. For example, many of the users are busy residents who do not have time to come to the Libraries and prefer to do searches on their own hardware taking advantage of twenty-four-hour accessibility.

User Support Services

Although PaperChase is called a "user-friendly" system that can be used by untrained users, the MGH experience indicates a wide range of user competency. There are some users who, with little or no assistance, function quite well. However, as reported by others in the literature,[5] the majority of users can benefit from additional instruction. From its inception, the staff has provided informal individual demonstrations for PaperChase users.

More formal, user instruction clinics have been offered five times to date. For the clinics offered in September 1985, approximately 180 users were notified, of whom 23 percent (42) registered and 21 percent (38) attended. A $10 fee was charged for these clinics which focused on saving time and money by using PaperChase efficiently. Topics taught included: how to solve equipment problems, how to use the basic menus, how to limit or expand a subject search, how to locate review articles, how to limit by year or language, and how to verify a reference.

To provide document delivery, the Libraries' staff worked with the vendor to develop an online copy order service. As users are reviewing their citations online, they can select the copy option for each article that they would like to have photocopied. The Libraries' staff retrieves the references daily, photocopies the articles and sends them to the users. The charge for each request is $5.00. This service, which has been in operation for six months, has averaged sixty-two requests ($310) per month, and has proved to be especially popular for subscribers working at remote locations. This has provided the Libraries with another opportunity to offer an additional service that reaches beyond the Libraries' walls.

Although no formal user satisfaction surveys have been conducted as yet, there are some indications that users are becoming more efficient searchers with PaperChase. For example, the average number of PaperChase uses by individual users has dropped over the sixteen-month period from twelve to nine per month and the average time spent per use has dropped from sixteen minutes to ten minutes over the same period. These figures suggest an improvement in searcher efficiency. In general, users' response to PaperChase and to the Libraries' support of the system has been very favorable. However, more formal and systematic evaluation efforts are needed and will be undertaken in the future to judge user satisfaction and efficiency.

CONCLUSION

The decision to implement end user systems at the MGH Health Sciences Libraries involved several preliminary stages: identification of user needs, evaluation of existing library services, a review of the availability and capabilities of existing end user systems, and the development of management strategies to implement them. The major management decision was to establish these systems on a cost recovery basis. This decision was based on the reality of the Libraries' budgetary constraints and in recognition of the market value of these services.

The experiences gained in managing, marketing, and teaching PaperChase served as a model for the Libraries' recent introduction of BRS/Saunders Colleague and MEDIS. These experiences indicate that end user systems are a natural extension of a library's information services and that librarians continue to have an active, creative role to play as information management consultants.

REFERENCES

1. Stabler, Karen C. "The Continuation of Libraries as Intermediaries." In: Williams, Martha E., and Hogan, Thomas H., comps. *National ONLINE MEETING PROCEEDINGS-1984, New York, April 10-12, 1984.* Medford, N.J.: Learned Information, Inc., 1984, pp. 375-81.

2. Wykoff, Leslie W. "Teaching Patrons to Search." *Medical Reference Service Quarterly* 4 (Summer 1985): 57-61.
3. Dowlin, Kenneth E. *The Electronic Library, The Promise and the Process*. New York: Neal-Schuman Publishers, Inc., 1984.
4. Horowitz, Gary L., and Bleich, Howard L. "PaperChase: A Computer Program to Search the Medical Literature." *New England Journal of Medicine* 305 (October 1981): 924-30.
5. Snow, Bonnie. "Making the Rough Places Plain: Designing MEDLINE End User raining." *Medical Reference Services Quarterly* 4 (Winter 1984): 1-11.

# The BRS/AFTER DARK Search Service in a Health Sciences Library

Marjorie Simon

ABSTRACT. An end user search service was established by the Health Sciences Library to complement the Library's mediated search service. Initially, Library staff believed that choosing a menu-driven system such as BRS/AFTER DARK would mean that only a minimal amount of librarian assistance would be required. Unfortunately, users' problems resulted from a lack of conceptual understanding of the search process, rather than from problems with search mechanics. Although the best way to train occasional users on a search system is still subject to debate, individualized pre-search assistance from the librarian has proven effective.

INTRODUCTION

The University of Maryland Health Sciences Library serves the Schools of Medicine, Nursing, Pharmacy, Dentistry, Social Work and Community Planning, the Graduate School, and the University of Maryland Medical System. The Library contains more than 240,000 volumes, with 3,100 current periodical subscriptions. The collection size ranks the Library among the fifteen largest health sciences libraries in the United States.

In recent years the Library has utilized new information technology to provide information services to the campus. The Library's online catalog, part of the Health Science Integrated Library Information System (ILIS), offers more searching options than the card catalog, and can be accessed twenty-four hours a day via on-campus terminals linked through the campus computer network and through office or home terminals or microcomputers with dial-up capabilities. Another component of the ILIS, Electronic Access to Ref-

---

Marjorie Simon is Head, Reference Services, University of Maryland Health Sciences Library, 111 S. Greene Street, Baltimore, MD 21201. She holds an M.S.L.S. from Simmons College School of Library and Information Science.

erence Services (EARS), gives members of the campus the ability to request reference services twenty-four hours a day. The service allows requests for online searching from the Library's mediated search service, photocopying of journal articles, and interlibrary loans of books and journal articles not owned by the Library.

The Library has followed closely the development of commercial systems that allow users to do their own database searching. An end user search service established in early 1984 complemented the already existing mediated search service and employed new information technology to meet changing needs.[1]

MEDIATED SEARCH SERVICE

The University of Maryland Health Sciences Library introduced a mediated search service in the early 1970s. The service initially was restricted to databases available through the National Library of Medicine. Soon it was apparent that restricting the search service to the MEDLARS databases ignored the research needs of the School of Social Work and Community Planning and the increasingly interdisciplinary perspective of the other schools on campus. In 1978 the Library began offering access to the DIALOG and BRS systems. Although the MEDLINE file is by far the Library's most frequently searched database (73 percent of all searches in 1984-85), there continues to be strong demand for social sciences databases, especially in the fields of psychology, education, and business.

The mediated search service is a nine-to-five weekday operation. It is run on an appointment basis, and students are required to be present while their searches are run. The reference staff was concerned that the service was not meeting the needs of part-time students who worked during the day, or of those full-time students who, because of field or clinical assignments, only had access to the Library during evenings and weekends. Although there is a professional librarian on duty whenever the Library is open, the evening/weekend librarians' primary responsibilities are supervising the Library and covering the reference desk. The Head of Reference felt that performing computerized literature searches would interfere with their other duties. Thus, to offer an evening search service, an additional librarian had to be scheduled. Although searching hours were extended on a trial basis, the limited usage did not justify the costs.

INITIATING SELF-SERVICE SEARCHING

In the Fall of 1983, the Library hosted a series of demonstrations of selected commercially available end user systems. The demonstrations allowed the reference staff to become familiar with KNOWLEDGE INDEX and BRS/AFTER DARK and led to an awareness of the opportunities that an end user search service could offer the Library. Since the searching would be "self service" and would require limited assistance from the librarian, end user searching seemed to be one way that the Library could provide online reference services during evening and weekend hours without increasing staff.

Instituting an end user search service in the Library was attractive for other reasons as well. It was hoped that making such a service available would demonstrate interest in new developments in information management and would promote the Library staff's potential role as consultants. Observing the successes and problems experienced by patrons doing their own searching would help chart the Library's future direction as both provider and teacher of the end user option. In addition, the staff felt that offering such a service would give interested members of the campus exposure to the service without their going to the expense of initiating a personal subscription.

Once the decision was made to offer end user searching in the Library, selection of the vendor was easily accomplished. Both BRS/AFTER DARK and KNOWLEDGE INDEX offered MEDLINE and appropriate social sciences databases. Thus, either service would meet the needs of all segments of the campus. As a menu-driven system, however, BRS/AFTER DARK was considered better suited to an anticipated audience of new or occasional users. In addition, AFTER DARK did not require libraries to use a credit card for payment, as DIALOG's KNOWLEDGE INDEX did at that time.

Policies and Procedures

The next step was to establish policies and procedures for the new service. The Assistant Director for Public Services decided that the service would be administered by the three evening/weekend librarians under the guidance of the Head of Reference. Policies were written in accordance with those already established for the

Library's mediated search service.[1] Users signed up for thirty-minute appointments. The search forms filled out by the users prior to going online were similar to the search forms filled out by those requesting a mediated search. The basic five-dollar charge was the same for both services, although the five dollars covered more on BRS/AFTER DARK than on the mediated search service. On BRS/AFTER DARK the basic charge covered up to thirty minutes of computer time, regardless of the databases selected. On the mediated search service, however, the basic charge rarely covered more than a simple MEDLINE search.

The procedures for the end user search service were designed to cause minimal interference with the evening/weekend librarians' other duties. A 1200 baud terminal was set up behind the reference desk, within easy access of the librarian. When an appointment for an AFTER DARK search was scheduled, the user was given a search form and a one-page brochure listing basic instructions. After the user completed the search form, the librarian briefly discussed the search request with him or her. The librarian then logged onto the system and advanced to the first menu. Initially, it was thought that once guided to the first menu, searchers would be on their own. Based on the librarians' own observations and discussions with users during informal exit interviews, they soon realized that most new users needed additional guidance to execute a successful search.

THE SURVEY

In order to better determine what aspects of the search process were causing difficulty for the new or inexperienced searcher, the evening/weekend librarians replaced the informal exit interview with a survey they developed for first-time users of the system. The survey (see Figure 1) revealed that approximately two-thirds of the first-time users had never been exposed previously to even a mediated computer search. Thus, it was not surprising that users' problems were related to their lack of a conceptual understanding of the search process rather than problems with mechanics. The BRS/AFTER DARK software simplifies the process of entering terms and printing results, but it is less successful in helping the patron deal with constructing or modifying search strategies.[1,2] Further-

FIGURE 1

The following figures reflect the responses to ninety-six surveys completed between September 1984 and September 1985

BRS/After Dark User's Survey 1984-85

My previous computer experience includes:
(Check one that is applicable.)

32 being present while my computer search was done by the librarian.

10 attending a BRS/After Dark orientation

36 using the Health Sciences Library online catalog.

17 using my home computer.

26 using a computer at work.

8 searching BRS/After Dark.

31 other, please specify. _____

I discovered BRS/After Dark through:
(Check each one that is applicable. Fill in blanks if appropriate.)

31 the Library's brochure. Where did you see it? _____

17 a colleague's recommendation.

24 an orientation to the library.

26 a librarian's suggestion.

4 a poster. Where did you see it? _____

5 other, please specify. _____

I chose to use BRS/After Dark because:
(Check each one that is applicable.)

43 it is affordable.

25 a librarian is not available to do a computer search for me when I need it.

66 it is faster than using a printed index.

14 I am interested in new technology.

18 I prefer to do my own search online.

6 I wanted to try out BRS/After Dark before entering my own subscription.

2 other, please specify. _____

I will use the results of my search:
(Check each one that is applicable.)

58 as the basis of a paper for a class.

6 as the basis of a grant proposal.

16 as the basis of a thesis or dissertation.

13 as a reading list on a subject of interest.

FIGURE 1 (continued)

<u>44</u> as a preliminary search for literature on a subject.
<u>12</u> to update a bibliography.
<u>9</u> to answer a question.
<u>1</u> other, please specify. _____

I encountered these problems while searching:
(Check each one that is applicable.)

<u>15</u> My typing is too slow.
<u>5</u> The menu process was too slow and cumbersome.
<u>8</u> The computer messages were confusing.
<u>21</u> I had trouble correcting errors.
<u>3</u> I had trouble printing the citations I needed.
<u>14</u> I did not know which database was best for my topic.
<u>2</u> I had trouble switching to another database.
<u>24</u> I had trouble selecting search terms for my subject.
<u>6</u> I had trouble finding the right format to locate an author, date, language, or other term.
<u>14</u> I had trouble combining my search terms.
<u>13</u> The citations I found were often not relevant.
<u>14</u> I did not find enough citations.

After using BRS/After Dark,
(Check one and complete the sentence.) - Eight people checked both choices and one person did not complete this section

<u>85</u> I feel satisfied with my results because _____
_____

<u>13</u> I am disappointed with my results because _____
_____

FOR RESULTS OF THIS SECTION SEE FIGURE 2

For further training I prefer:
(Number in order of preference. #1 is your first choice.)
___ learning by using BRS/After Dark.
___ relying on a librarian's assistance before and during my search.
___ reading handouts on particular topics i.e. description of databases, fundamentals of searching strategy.
___ attending a workshop explaining how to search BRS/After Dark.
___ learning about databases and search strategy through computer assisted instruction.

more, although the second edition of the BRS/AFTER DARK manual was far more detailed than the first edition, the documentation was still considered inadequate for some databases. The evening/weekend librarians have spent much time developing supplementary documentation for the most frequently used databases. Appendix A illustrates one of the Library developed search guides.

End User Education

One surprising revelation of the survey of first-time users was that, despite the problems encountered, eighty-five of the ninety-six people surveyed between September 1984 and September 1985 considered their searches at least partially successful. The librarians, however, felt that with instruction the users' searches could improve.

The first formal user education program developed by the evening/weekend librarians consisted of hour-long seminars concentrating on the overall search process and on search strategies. Approximately eleven sessions were held between April and December 1984, with typically only two to three attendees per session. Although the programs were rated highly by those attending, in retrospect it is not surprising that a user group already satisfied with their ability to search would be reluctant to invest an hour in trying to improve those skills.

To determine the kind of training users wanted, a section of the survey for first-time users asked people to rate five kinds of user training. As illustrated in Figure 2, users prefer to "learn by doing," either on their own or with a librarian's assistance. Accordingly, the evening/weekend librarians expanded the initial request form and instruction sheet to provide step-by-step guidance for developing search strategies. These forms are reproduced in Appendixes B, C, D and E. Despite these improved user aids, in-depth reference interviews have proven the major vehicle for user education.

The evening/weekend librarians consider the pre-search assistance given to BRS/AFTER DARK users as basically the same as the individualized guidance routinely offered to anyone starting a manual search of the literature. The librarians screen the search requests first and on that basis refer some users with inappropriate search topics to manual indexes or to the mediated search service. Typically, requests judged to be unsuitable for BRS/AFTER

FIGURE 2

First-Time User Survey - Choices for Further Training

This section of the survey was not completed by all users. In addition, some users checked their choices rather than ranking them. All checked choices were coded as first choices.

	1st Choice	2nd Choice	3rd Choice	4th Choice	5th Choice
LEARN BY USING BRS AFTER DARK	43	14	3	6	1
RELYING ON LIBRARIAN'S ASSISTANCE	24	15	10	7	3
READING HANDOUTS	3	4	13	10	10
ATTENDING WORKSHOP	12	4	4	7	18
COMPUTER ASSISTED INSTRUCTION	12	15	12	9	7

DARK include those where the topic is too broad for a computerized literature search, those subjects requiring strategies too complex to be handled adequately without at least some search training, or topics requiring system capabilities not available on BRS/AFTER DARK. The latter is becoming less of a problem as BRS/AFTER DARK continues to develop.

Once the topic is judged appropriate, the librarian helps the user to select the database(s) to search. After consulting available thesauri and system documentation, the user, with the librarian's guidance, chooses subject headings and/or free-text vocabulary. If necessary, the librarian assists the user in developing a search strategy. Most explanations are limited to Boolean operators and system mechanics, such as narrowing retrieval to English language journals or to specific years. With more experienced searchers the librarian shares advanced search techniques. The librarian then accesses the system and explains the menu concept to the user, going through the menus until reaching search statement one of the selected database. At this point, the user is on his or her own. If any questions arise, he or she is encouraged to ask for additional assistance from the librarian. Since there is usually only one librarian on duty, the amount of assistance the searcher is given depends on how many other Library users have reference questions. BRS/AFTER DARK users do not have priority over other users.

CONCLUSION

Despite the fact that having BRS/AFTER DARK in the Library has required more staff time than originally was anticipated, the Health Sciences Library staff is enthusiastic about the end user search service. Survey results revealed that two-thirds of first-time BRS/AFTER DARK users have never used the Library's mediated search service although both services are publicized during orientations and in the Library's promotional material. There is reason to infer, therefore, that the end user search service meets the need of a previously underserved segment of the campus. Thus, the Library's primary objective in instituting this service has been met.

It is difficult to know if the attraction of BRS/AFTER DARK stems from the evening and weekend hours, the challenge of doing one's own searching, the low prices for accessing the social sciences databases, or a combination of all three factors. Whatever the case, experience with BRS/AFTER DARK has increased the reference librarians' understanding of end user expectations and needs. The librarians are uniquely qualified to represent to the user both the limitations and possibilities of end user searching. This knowledge, coupled with what has been learned from working with BRS/AFTER DARK, will help the reference staff better serve the campus as consultants and trainers for available end user systems.

REFERENCES

1. Slingluff, Deborah; Lev, Yvonne; and Eisan, Andrew. "An End User Search Service in an Academic Health Sciences Library." *Medical Reference Services Quarterly* 4 (Spring 1985): 11-21.
2. Lev, Yvonne. "Instructing the BRS/After Dark End User." Paper presented at the 85th Annual Meeting of the Medical Library Association, New York, New York, 27 May 1985.

```
                      APPENDIX A
                       MEDLINE
                   A DATABASE GUIDE


     LABEL:  MESH--1979 to DATE
             MS78--1975 to 1978
             MS74--1971 to 1974
             MS70--1966 to 1970

     DESCRIPTION:  MEDLINE provides bibliographic information for articles
                   published in biomedical journals throughout the world,
                   plus selected monographs of congresses or symposia.  The
                   file encompasses medicine, nursing, dentistry, pharmacy
                   and allied health as well as the biological and physical
                   sciences, humanities and information science as they
                   relate to medicine and health care.  Abstracts are
                   available for about half of the records.

     YEARS OF COVERAGE:  1966 to DATE

     UPDATED:  Monthly -- approximately 20,000 records added monthly

     PRINTED EQUIVALENTS:  Index Medicus
                           International Nursing Index
                           Index to Dental Literature

     SEARCH AIDS:  Medical Subject Headings--Annotated Alphabetic List
                   Permuted Medical Subject Headings
                   List of Serials and Monographs Indexed for Online Users

     PRODUCER:  National Library of Medicine
                8600 Rockville Pike
                Bethesda, MD 20209
```

APPENDIX A (continued)

GUIDE TO SELECTED SEARCHABLE FIELDS:

Code	Description	Sample Entry	Sample Search	
AU	Author	Shangraw-R-E Turinsky-J	S-- Shangraw-R-E.au. S-- Turinsky-J$.au.	
IN	Author Affiliation	Department of Physiology, Albany Medical College, NY	S-- Albany Medical.in.	
TI	Title	Altered protein kinetics in vivo after single-limb burn injury	S-- protein kinetics.ti. and burn$1.ti. S-- protein kinetics with burn$1.ti.	
SO	Source	Biochem-J. 1984 Nov. 1 223(3). P747-53	S-- Biochem-J.so. and 1984.so. S-- 1 and 1984.so.	*1
LG	Language	EN GE	S--1 and en.lg. S--1 and ge.lg.	*1 *1
DE	Descriptors	BURNS: me. PROTEINS: me. ANIMAL. GROWTH. KINETICS....	S-- burns.de. and kinetics.de. S-- proteins.me.de S-- proteins-me	*2 *3 *3
MJ	Major Descriptors	BURNS:me. PROTEINS:me.	S-- burns.mj. S-- proteins-me.mj.	*3
PN	Personal Name as Subject	Doe-J-Q	S-- Doe-J-Q.pn.	
RN	CAS Registry Number and/or Enzyme Commission	57-92-1-Streptomycin EC-1-9-3-1-Cytochrome Oxidase	S-- 57-92-1.rn. S-- ec-1-9-3-1.rn.	
AB	Abstract	Recovery from burn injury is associated with stimulated whole-body protein turnover...	S-- protein turnover same burn$1.ab.	

HINTS

*1 The 1 refers to a previous search question and its results. Back referencing allows you to use the results of a previous search question without retyping the term. Identify the set of results you want to use by its search question number. The number can then be combined with other terms or qualifiers to yield more precise results.

*2 The Descriptor field includes terms appearing in either major or minor descriptor fields. Use "and" as the connector to search for terms in both fields.

*3 Subheadings may be searched by any of the formats shown. In these examples (*3), -me is used with proteins to indicate proteins-metabolism.

SAMPLE CITATION--The sample citation may include fields that are not identified in the above guide. If you have questions about any of the fields, ask the librarian for assistance.

APPENDIX A (continued)

```
AN  85072039. 8503.
AU  Shangraw-R-E. Turinsky-J.
IN  Department of Physiology, Albany Medical College, NY.
TI  Altered protein kinetics in vivo after single-limb burn injury.
SO  Biochem-J. 1984 Nov 1. 223(3). P 747-53.
LG  EN.
MJ  BURNS: me.  PROTEINS: me.
MN  ANIMAL.  GROWTH.  KINETICS.  LIVER: me.  MALE.  MUSCLE-PROTEINS:
    me.  RATS.  RATS-INBRED-STRAINS.  SUPPORT-U-S-GOVT-P-H-S.
AB  Recovery from burn injury is associated with stimulated whole-body
    protein turnover.  Since skeletal muscle and liver are the ...
```

Prepared by the Reference Staff
UMAB Health Sciences Library
June, 1985

APPENDIX B

University of Maryland
Health Sciences Library
111 South Greene Street
Baltimore, MD 21201

BRS/AFTER DARK RECORD

LAST NAME, FIRST	PHONE NUMBER	DATE
ADDRESS	FUND & BUDGET NUMBER (FACULTY & STAFF)	

UNIVERSITY STATUS: ___ FACULTY ___ STAFF ___ STUDENT ___ NON-UNIVERSITY

UMAB AFFILIATION: ___ Central Administration ___ Dental School ___ HSL
___ Law School ___ Medical School ___ MIEMSS ___ Nursing School
___ Pharmacy School ___ Social Work/Community Planning ___ UMMS/Hospital

If not at UMAB, work or school affiliation: _____

1. Write a summary statement describing what you are researching.
   Example: ARTICLES ON THE EMERGENCY TREATMENT OF BURNS

2. Divide the statement into separate concepts.
   Example: EMERGENCY TREATMENT / BURNS

3. Select an appropriate database. (You may need a different strategy for each database you select.)
   Example: MESH (MEDLINE 1979 to present)

4. List your search terms. Include synonyms and/or subject headings for each concept.
   Example: EMERGENCY TREATMENT   BURNS
             EMERGENCY MEDICAL SERVICE$1   BURN$1
             FIRST AID

APPENDIX B (continued)

5. Broaden your search by combining your search terms describing a concept into OR search statements. Consider truncation.

   Example: $1 - FIRST AID OR EMERGENCY MEDICAL SERVICE$1

   S -➔ _____ OR _____ OR _____
   S -➔ _____ OR _____ OR _____

6. Narrow your search by combining subjects into AND search statements. Consider limiting retrieval by year published, language, age group, sex, review article, human or animal. Also consider the connectors WITH, SAME, NOT.

   Example: S2 - 1 AND BURN$1 AND EN.LG.

   S -➔ _____ AND _____ AND _____
   S -➔ _____ AND _____ AND _____

FOR OFFICE USE ONLY

DATABASES USED:

SESSION NUMBER:

TIME ONLINE: SIGN OFF:
              SIGN ON:
              TOTAL TIME:

TOTAL COST:

APPENDIX C.

HOW TO PREPARE A SEARCH STRATEGY

1. Write a **summary statement** describing your topic. Use the BRS/After Dark Record form.

   Example of author search: STETZER, MAXINE L.
   Example of subject search: EMERGENCY TREATMENT OF BURNS

2. Divide the subject into **concepts**.

   Example of concepts: EMERGENCY TREATMENT / BURNS

3. Select a **database** that covers your topic, covers the time period you wish to search, and covers the materials you wish to search (journals, books, government documents, dissertations etc.). The BRS/After Dark brochures lists the databases most used at HSL and their labels.

   Example of label: MESH (the label for the MEDLINE database which covers biomedical journal literature from 1979 to the present)

4. Select **search terms** to describe each concept of your topic.

   --If doing an author search:

   a. Check a database guide or the BRS/After Dark manual for the author name format used in the database.

      Example of MESH format: STETZER-M-L

APPENDIX C (continued)

    b. Consider truncating the author's name, particularly if multiple author name formats are used in the database. The truncated form will retrieve the author whether the database includes her full name or just her surname and initials. BEWARE: The citations will include all M. Stetzers, Marvin Stetzer as well as Maxine Stetzer.

    Example of truncation: STETZER-M$

--If doing a subject search:

    a. Find out if the database uses subject headings to index each document.

        If it does:

        1. Ask the librarian to assist you in locating the database thesaurus. Check the thesaurus for subject headings describing each concept.

        2. Consider using your own terminology if the thesaurus subject headings are not specific enough.

        If it does not:

        1. Make a list of synonyms to describe each concept. Using more synonyms usually results in retrieving more citations.

--If doing a subject search: (continued)

    b. Check the thesaurus or BRS/After Dark manual to find out if the database allows you to limit your retrieval by date, sex, age group, animal or human, or review article.

    c. Consider truncating the subject terms. Instead of searching several synonyms with the same root, you can truncate the root with a dollar sign and retrieve all the variations of BURN$: BURN, BURNS, BURNED, BURNOUT, BURNISH. Specify the number of letters you will accept after the root to make your retrieval more relevant: BURN$1 will retrieve BURN, BURNS or BURNT.

    Example of subject truncation: BURN$ (any suffix accepted)
                                                    BURN$1 (1 letter suffic only)

    d. Consider limiting your search to one part of the record. Follow the search question with a period, the abbreviation of the record field, and a period. To find the record fields and their abbreviations for a particular database, ask the librarian for the database guide.

    Example of author search: STETZER-M$.AU.
    Example of title search: BURN$1.TI.

5. <u>Combine synonyms</u> to broaden a search.

    Example: FIRST AID OR EMERGENCY MEDICAL SERVICES

This search question finds any records containing EITHER the phrase "first aid" or "emergency medical services" ANYWHERE IN THE RECORD.

6. <u>Combine different concepts</u> to narrow a search. By using AND, SAME, WITH, or NOT connectors, you will limit your retrieval to just those citations which include the concepts you have specified.

    Example of AND: BURNS AND EMERGENCY MEDICAL SERVICES

BOTH the word "burns" and the phrase "emergency medical services" must be present WITHIN THE RECORD.

APPENDIX C (continued)

Example of SAME: BURNS SAME EMERGENCY MEDICAL SERVICES

BOTH the word "burns" and the phrase "emergency medical services" must be present WITHIN THE SAME PARAGRAPH OR FIELD.

Example of WITH: BURNS WITH EMERGENCY MEDICAL SERVICES

BOTH the word "burns" and the phrase "emergency medical services" must be present WITHIN THE SAME SENTENCE.

Example of NOT: EMERGENCY MEDICAL SERVICES NOT FIRST AID

ONLY the phrase "emergency medical services" must be present IN THE RECORD. Any record containing the phrase "first aid" will be eliminated even if "emergency medical services" is present.

APPENDIX D

HOW TO SEARCH BRS/AFTER DARK

The librarian will sign on to the BRS/After Dark computer, connecting the terminal to the BRS/After Dark search service. For new users, the librarian will explain the menus leading to the database the searcher has selected. At the prompt for the first search question, the searcher will take over the terminal to type in the search strategy. Each time a searcher types in a search question or command, the searcher must remember to hit the RETURN KEY. This sends the information to the computer.

1. COMPUTER will indicate the title of the database and years covered. It will prompt the user for the first search question or command.

   BRS / MESH / 1979-1985
   TYPE IN SEARCH TERM, OR ENTER COMMAND:
         M TO RETURN TO MASTER MENU, D TO CHOOSE NEW DATABASE,
                  OR O TO SIGNOFF

   S1 -➔

   SEARCHER will type in first search statement, key word, or command.

   S1 -➔   EMERGENCY MEDICAL SERVICE$1 OR FIRST AID (Hit RETURN key)

2. COMPUTER will indicate how many documents are found, list options for your next step, and prompt you for your next search question or command.

   A1   2458 DOCUMENTS FOUND
   TYPE IN SEARCH TERMS, OR ENTER COMMAND
         P TO PRINT DOCUMENTS FOUND, R TO REVIEW SEARCH QUESTIONS.
         M TO RETURN TO MASTER MENU, D TO CHOOSE NEW DATABASE
         OR O TO SIGN OFF

   S2 -➔

   SEARCHER will either

   (1) continue with search by typing a search question or key word.

   S2 -➔   BURN$1 AND 1 (Hit RETURN key)

   (2) print documents found.

   S2 -➔   P (Hit RETURN key)

APPENDIX D (continued)

(3) choose a new database.

    S2 -➤ D (Hit RETURN key)

(4) sign off the computer.

    S2 -➤ O (Hit RETURN key)

APPENDIX E

HOW TO PRINT CITATIONS

BRS/After Dark offers three formats for citations.

S -- Short form; includes author, title and source
M -- Medium form; includes author, title, source and descriptors
L -- Long form; includes complete record: author, title, source, and anything else available in that database ie. descriptors, abstract, registry number, cited references etc.

<u>BEGINNING METHOD WITH COMPUTER PROMPTS</u>

1. <u>SEARCHER</u> types the P command to print.

    S2 -➤   P (Hit RETURN key)

2. <u>COMPUTER</u> will ask you to identify which search question has the citations you wish to print.

    ENTER A SEARCH QUESTION TO PRINT FROM (I.E. 1 OR 2, ETC.)
    XX-➤

    <u>SEARCHER</u> types search question number.

    XX-➤ 1 (Hit RETURN key)

3. <u>COMPUTER</u> will ask you in which format to print the citations.

    ENTER S FOR SHORT PRINT FORM, M FOR MEDIUM PRINT FORM,
    OR HIT ENTER FOR LONG PRINT FORM.
    XX-➤

    <u>SEARCHER</u> types letter to indicate choice of format.

    XX-➤   S (Hit RETURN key)

4. <u>COMPUTER</u> will ask you to specify the document numbers you wish printed.

    ENTER DOCUMENT NUMBER(S) TO BE PRINTED. USE
    A HYPHEN FOR SEQUENTIAL DOCUMENTS (X-X),
    COMMAS FOR NON-SEQUENTIAL DOCUMENTS (X,X,X),
    OR ENTER INDIVIDUAL NUMBER (X). TYPE ALL TO
    PRINT ALL DOCUMENTS OR HIT ENTER TO PRINT FIRST
    DOCUMENT.
    XX-➤

    <u>SEARCHER</u> types document numbers needed or ALL for a complete list.

    XX-➤   ALL (Hit RETURN key)

<u>SHORTCUT METHOD WITH COMMAND STACKING</u>

1. <u>SEARCHER</u> types P;1;S;ALL (Hit RETURN key)

2. <u>COMPUTER</u> will Print the citations from search question #1 in Short format and print ALL of them.

III. THE END USER'S VIEWPOINT

Ultimately, the final test is whether users do, in fact, make use of online database searching, and whether they find the information that they need. Users have expressed both positive and negative reactions to doing their own searching. Nowacek and Hodge propose a search strategy outline to help occasional users conduct efficient online searches. Myers relates the decision-making process, implementation, and four years' of positive experience of physicians at a small, rural hospital. Neubauer in a "confession," lends a personal view of a medical researcher's experience with online searching. McNabb discusses end user searching in a small hospital environment; her conclusions, some of which are negative, are based on interviews with physicians.

Search Strategy Outline: An Approach to Assist the Occasional End Searcher

George Nowacek
Robert H. Hodge

ABSTRACT. A Search Strategy Outline (SSO) is proposed to help occasional users such as medical residents conduct efficient online searches. The SSO is in outline form, covering all recurring steps from LOGON to LOGOFF. A SSO can be custom-designed for a specific professional group/database(s) combination and further adapted for the individual user's unique searching needs. Two SSOs are presented: one for residents searching for diagnostic and treatment information, and a second for medical educators searching the literature for program development and evaluation purposes.

ONLINE ADVANTAGES FOR MEDICAL PROFESSIONALS

Searching the medical literature is an integral part of hospital residency training programs. Because answers are often needed quickly to assist in patient management, there are many drawbacks to the manual "shelf" search: the time that it takes to search, the possibly limited hours of the library, the selection of journal titles available, and the sometimes distant location of reference tools are but a few of the barriers to finding an answer quickly. Searching databases via telecommunication alleviates many of these problems, particularly since the communication link can be as near as the most convenient phone line, and the hours of service are less restricted.

Dr. George Nowacek is Director, Office of Medical Education and Associate Professor of Medical Education at the University of Virginia School of Medicine. He received his Ph.D. in Educational Psychology from the University of Michigan and an M.A. in Tests and Measurement from Columbia University, Teacher's College.

Dr. Robert Hodge is Medical Director, Ambulatory Care Services and Associate Professor of Medicine at the University of Virginia, Medical Center. He received his M.D. degree from Harvard and completed his internship and residency at the University of Colorado Medical Center.

The benefits of end user searching for housestaff in the medical professions are no doubt similar to those experienced by other professional groups; an interactive search with a database such as MEDLINE will often suggest different keywords and modifications in strategy during the process. Nonmediated contact with a database can also develop a better understanding of its potential use and often a real cost savings in connect time may result.

DRAWBACKS

Because housestaff fall into the "occasional user" category, however, maintaining their status as effective searchers can present problems. Computer search skills will deteriorate rapidly if not used regularly, and time required for relearning can have a negative impact on the future use of an information retrieval system. Housestaff are chronically short of time (evidenced by their long hours and lack of sleep). Any optional activity that becomes too time-consuming will usually be avoided.

Decreasing the relearning time for the occasional user would be desirable. Educational learning theory has clearly demonstrated the advantages of learning aids and reference materials. The existing materials for instruction and reference on DIALOG, for example, cover a wide range of detail and specificity. The full reference manual[1] offers a thorough description of commands and features of the system, and is appropriately updated when changes are made in the system. There is also written material to accompany workshops and other training sessions that is useful not only for instruction but for future reference purposes. DIALOG advanced seminar instructional materials represent an intermediate level of specificity, often including database-specific information and tailored to the searching needs of a targeted group. Finally, the Pocket Guide[2] is a very compact command summary booklet, which summarizes the command syntax and is a good reference source for the experienced searcher.

These three types of vendor publications represent a spectrum of detailed learning aids, from the most specific in the full reference manual to the least specific in the commands summary guide. Nonetheless, it is very difficult for the occasional searcher to relearn effective online strategy from either the full reference manual, workshop manuals, or the command summary reference card.

A "RELEARNING AID"

An alternative approach is a one-page Search Strategy Outline (SSO), developed to assist the occasional searcher in quickly relearning the system and to guide him or her through the search process. Such an outline may even encourage more frequent searching and thus facilitate maintenance of skills. Designed to reduce relearning time, it can also be customized to the unique searching needs of an individual. While the conventional search sequence is much the same for all persons conducting searches, each individual has unique information needs and interests best served by developing a specific search strategy tailored to the database(s) of his or her choice.

A Search Strategy Outline should not exceed one or two pages, ideally guiding the searcher from logon to logoff, with instructions for all of the important intermediate steps. The outline format should include very little extraneous narrative; a worksheet layout will facilitate note-taking. While the outline itself is brief, its design encourages individuals to develop their own set of reference material and to organize an effective search strategy.

Figure 1 is an example of a proposed SSO for residents using MEDLINE. It contains four major sections: pre-search formulation, search 1, keyword check, search 2. In the pre-search section, the searcher writes out the question, identifies relevant keywords and places them in a command statement. Search 1 consists of entering the first strategy in order to locate a citation which may reveal additional keywords, including database-preferred descriptors. In many cases, this first search will be sufficient. However, the "keyword check" phase encourages the searcher to modify a strategy, if necessary, providing a structured approach to browsing. The cycle may be repeated as needed.

Appended References accompany the SSO, offering more detailed information for the accomplishment of each step. This background material is often necessary for efficient searching, yet is too detailed to be recalled easily by the occasional searcher. References appended to the SSO's are all reproductions of selected pages from the *DIALOG Seminar for Medical Professionals* used in initial training on the system. Figure 2 outlines the content of each SSO Appendix with page references to the *Seminar* booklet. Reference materials include: (1) user aids especially adapted for end searchers,[4] modifying those included in *Annotated Alphabetic MeSH*,[5] and (2)

FIGURE 1

DIALOG Search Strategy Outline
For Medline (154,153,152)

Presearch
1. State the question underlying the keywords _____ Appended References
2. Use MeSH subheadings if possible _____ A (Topical Subheadings by Categories)
      B (Topical Subheadings)
3. If there is a key article, use the indexes AU=
   (author(s), publication year, journal name) PY=
      JN=
4. Formulate search command: SS _____ descriptors
      AND OR (W) (L) _____ pre-explosions
      AND OR (W) (L) _____ subheadings
      AND OR (W) (L) _____ (etc.)
      AND OR (W) (L) _____ (etc.)

Search 1
5. Logon, B 154 (153, 152), enter search statement (S)
6. Locate key article or browse (format 6)
7. Type key article (format 5) or references (format 3)
8. Consider Expanding keywords or reviewing zz= for permuted terms   C (On-line Thesaurus)
9. LOGOFF (optional logoff hold for 10 minutes)   D (Permuted MeSH)

Keyword Check
10. Review descriptor field of key article for keywords
11. Check Pre-explosions   E (Pre-Explosions)
12. Reformulate the search command: SS _____ descriptors
      AND OR (W) (L) _____ pre-explosions
      AND OR (W) (L) _____ subheadings
      AND OR (W) (L) _____ (etc.)
      AND OR (W) (L) _____ (etc.)

Search 2
13. Logon and B 154 (153, 152), enter search statement
14. Locate key article or browse (format 6)
15. Type key article (format 7) or references (format 3)
16. Consider Expanding keywords or reviewing zz= for permuted terms
17. LOGOFF (logoff hold for 10 minutes)
18. Optional - Repeat 10, 11, 12 as necessary

NOTES:

Formats: 3 - bibliographic citation 6 - title 7 - bibliographic citation and abstract
T   Set#/Format#/Range e.g. 6/3/1,3,5-6 (PR offline print   PR- cancel offline print)
DS   to display all sets
P   to request another screen of display after the Expand command
?   truncation at end of word, wild card within word

sample searches illustrating online entry format, extensively annotated. The advantage of beginning with the SSO worksheet is that it points out an obvious structure in the search process, reminding the user of the steps that may be taken. The sample SSO is intended for MEDLINE and is designed for the housestaff officer who wants a quick answer to a medical question, rather than an exhaustive bibliography in preparation for a paper or a talk. A reference article on the topic will not usually be available before the search.

A separate Search Strategy Outline is desirable for each professional/database "combination." These "combinations" are roughly equivalent to those addressed in the specialized workshops now offered by DIALOG, but even within these workshop groups, there is a potential for modifying the Outline to address different combinations of databases used by individual "subgroups." In health care, for example, in addition to physicians who need to search for diagnostic and treatment information, there are also medical educators, nurses, and allied health professionals who conduct searches for research and other academic purposes. A sample Search Strategy Outline for medical educators involved in research projects is shown in Figure 3. This SSO assumes a representative publication is known, and the researcher intends to conduct an exhaustive and comprehensive search on a specific topic. Such a SSO is accompanied by more reference material, but appendices are none the less "generic," facilitating use of communications equipment at any location.

CONCLUSION

Search Strategy Outlines are not intended to be used without prior introductory instruction to, and hands-on practice with, DIALOG. A Search Strategy Outline would be incorporated into the initial

FIGURE 2

CONTENTS OF APPENDED REFERENCES FOR SEARCH STRATEGY OUTLINES

```
Appendix A.  Subheadings (p.58-63).*
             1. List of "Topical Subheadings by Category:
                Abbreviations and Year of Entry"
                adapted from Annotated Alphabetic MeSH.
             2. Sample searches illustrating online entry format for
                applying subheadings to both individual main headings
                and "exploded" descriptor codes (Tree Numbers).

Appendix B.  Subheading Scope Notes - an adaptation of the MeSH listing,
             especially designed for end users (p.50-7).*

Appendix C.  Illustration of the Online Thesaurus (p.46-8).*

Appendix D.  Permuted MeSH Online (p.110-11).*

Appendix E.  Pre-Explosions (p.41-5).*
             1. A list of 138 pre-exploded descriptor codes (Trees)
                available on DIALOG, replacing MeSH's shorter list.
             2. Sample searches illustrating entry format.

Appendix F.  DIALINDEX (p.90-3).*

Appendix G.  Special Indexing Features.
             1. LIMITing descriptors to "MAJOR" emphasis (p.27-8).
             2. Check Tags (p.64-6).*
             3. Author Searching (p.70-1).*
             4. Language (p.72).*
             5. Journal Name Searching (p.73).*
             6. Document Types (p.74-5).*
             7. Publication Year (p.76).*

Appendix H.  Time-Saving Techniques (p.85-8).*
             1. Sample search using Temporary Search-Save.
             2. Logoff Hold.
```

*Page number references for DIALOG Seminar for Medical Professionals.[3]

FIGURE 3

DIALOG Search Strategy Outline
For Medical Educators

```
Presearch                                                          Appended References
  1. Select primary subject descriptors (keywords)  _____
  2. Select MeSH subheadings                        _____  A (Topical Subheadings
                                                                         by Categories)
                                                                     B (Topical Subheadings)
  3. Identify key article representative of search question  AU=
     (author(s), publication year, journal name)             PY=
                                                             JN=
Connect to DIALOG
  4. Begin 154 (or other file)
  5. Locate key article. (e.g., SS AU=THOMAS? AND PY=1981
     Print full article (Format 5 in Medline)
  6. Expand (keywords) to review descriptors with related terms ____  C (On-line Thesaurus)
  7. Expand with zz - for permuted terms                        ____  D (Permuted MeSH)
Disconnect from DIALOG (optional: end/savetemp or logoff hold)
  8. Review descriptor field of key article for keywords
  9. Check pre-explosions for descriptors           _____   E (Pre-Explosions)
 10. Construct search statement(s)   SS                              descriptors
                                     AND OR (W) (L) _____  pre-explosions
                                     AND OR (W) (L) _____  subheadings
                                     AND OR (W) (L) _____  (etc.)
                                     AND OR (W) (L) _____  (etc.)
Reconnect to DIALOG
 [optional: begin 411 (DIALINDEX) to search multiple files if
            uncertain of file to use]                                F (DIALINDEX)
 11. Begin (file#) and conduct search      FILES: _____
     (pre-explosions),
     [optional: reduce excessive number of hits]
                - LIMIT MAJOR or HUMAN
                - checktags                                          G (Indexing Features)
                - AUTHOR/JOURNAL/DOCUMENT/LANGUAGE
 12. Print hits (online/offline)  (remember LIFO)
 13. If finished, LOGOFF
     If search other files with same search statements:              H (Time-Saving
        END/SAVETEMP      (write-down savesearch #)                      Techniques)
        Begin (file#)
        .EXS (save search #)

NOTES:
        Medline Formats:  3-basic citation; 6-title; 7-citation + abstract; 5-full record
     T    set#/format#/range e.g. 6/3/1,3,5-8  (PR offline print   PR- to cancel offline print)
     DS   display all sets
     P    next screen after Expand
     ?    truncation at end of word, wild card within word
```

training materials to encourage its use and to help individuals to customize instruction for their specific needs while still in the classroom (e.g., identify databases likely to be used, record abbreviations of journals of most interest, etc.).

The Search Strategy Outlines can be viewed as the next "level" of instructional material after a workshop. The full DIALOG reference manual is perhaps the first level of instructional material for the system. The workshops represent the second level of instruction and are designed to highlight those features of DIALOG for groups with common interests and searching needs. These proposed Search Strategy Outlines are a possible third level of instructional material, customizing system features for individuals within a group. But this customizing must be done by the individual user. The proposed

Search Strategy Outlines will, hopefully, encourage the development of a structured strategy. It is anticipated that the use of SSOs, by promoting more efficient and cost-effective use of an online system, will increase the number of searches performed by individual medical professionals and thus decrease the need for relearning.

REFERENCES

1. *Guide to DIALOG Searching*. Palo Alto, CA: DIALOG Information Services, 1979.
2. *Pocket Guide to DIALOG Version 2*. Palo Alto, CA: DIALOG Information Services, 1985.
3. Snow, Bonnie. *DIALOG Seminar for Medical Professionals*. Palo Alto, CA: DIALOG Information Services, 1984.
4. Snow, Bonnie. "Making the Rough Places Plain: Designing MEDLINE End User Training." *Medical Reference Services Quarterly* 3(Winter 1984):1-11.
5. *Medical Subject Headings—Annotated Alphabetic List*. Bethesda, MD: National Library of Medicine, 1985.

Physician Searching:
A Rural Hospital Experience

Frederick J. Myers

ABSTRACT. Online searching by physician end users serves the bibliographic search needs of a small, rural hospital. With little knowledge of search mechanics, a vendor was chosen, equipment and user aids assembled, and needed skills obtained. During the first four years' experience, an average of one hour per month was spent online, one-half using the MEDLINE database. A search often gives an immediate answer to a clinical question through online abstracts, but obtaining the complete article remains a problem to the rural practitioner.

In order to arrive at what you do not know
You must go by the way which is the way of ignorance.

T. S. Elliot

Online bibliographic searching by practicing physicians has become practical and valuable at a small, 85-bed rural hospital serving the medical needs of Woodbury, a middle-Tennessee town with a population of about 3000 people.

A NEED

In 1981, the construction and equipping of a new facility, Stones River Hospital, provided an opportunity to develop a new medical library. The nearest reference library with the services of a professional librarian was about sixty miles away at Vanderbilt Univer-

---

Frederick J. Myers, M.D., F.A.C.S., is a staff physician at Stones River Hospital in Woodbury, Tennessee. He is a graduate of Loma Linda University, Loma Linda, California, and took postgraduate training at Kettering Memorial Hospital, Kettering, Ohio. His practice experience has included two years in a remote mission hospital in central Ethiopia.

sity. It was felt that a local collection of standard reference books and bibliographic search tools were needed by the staff of four general practitioners and one general surgeon. Little library space was available and funds were limited.

A POSSIBLE SOLUTION

Online searching was the resource suggested by the most widely read member of the medical group, who had come across the concept in the medical literature. This idea seemed to offer the solution to several problems. Little physical space would be needed, requiring only a small desktop and some shelf space for searching aids. There would be an initial investment in a terminal, but minimal ongoing expense was anticipated. With limited usage projected, online charges were expected to be considerably less than subscription costs for *Index Medicus*. Searches could be made more quickly, and the appeal of this new technology was undeniable. Some disadvantages were not as apparent at the time: new skills would have to be developed, successful searches would depend upon the development of these skills, and no one was familiar with the equipment or databases available. The hospital staff decided to study in detail the concept and how it could be applied to their situation.

Three major database vendors were considered: BRS, DIALOG, and MEDLARS. MEDLARS, a service of the National Library of Medicine, was not readily available to end users at that time (1981). BRS was offered as a subscription service, charging a yearly fee for a specified number of connect hours. The minimum, one-year subscription was $750 for twenty-five connect hours. Access hours were from 8:00 a.m. until 8:00 p.m., Monday through Friday, DIALOG charges were based on connect time alone with no minimum usage fee; the service was available twenty-two hours a day. At the time, there was no means of evaluating ease of usage of the latter two commercially available systems.

Evaluation of equipment also was difficult. When the search for equipment led to the hospital's corporate headquarters, Hospital Corporation of America, and their information specialist, a Texas Instruments 787 terminal was borrowed. A feeling of cautious optimism for the success of the project pervaded. Advice from other information specialists was less helpful, and little encouragement was forthcoming. Equipment was said to be sophisticated and expensive, and extensive professional training was considered mandatory. The message from the information industry seemed to be: "Searching is for searchers, not physicians."

Computer stores were even less helpful. In early 1981, salespeople often were unfamiliar with the idea of remote databases. Not infrequently, as experience grew, a physician would demonstrate simple online searching on the salesman's equipment in his computer showroom.

A COMMITMENT

DIALOG was finally chosen as the vendor to be used, a decision based on availability and cost considerations. Usage was expected to be less than the minimum BRS subscription, and it was available more hours each day.

Equipment options ranged from an inexpensive ($400) video terminal to more sophisticated printing terminals. Data transmission speed was an important issue. The higher speed machines were more expensive, but a cost savings of online time was anticipated. Identical searches performed at 30 characters-per-second (cps) and at 120 cps were compared. Depending somewhat on the nature of the search, the lower speed took from 1.3 to 2.3 times the online time of the faster communication speed. At an estimated two hours usage each month, savings of $204 to $564 yearly would be realized through the use of the higher transmission speed. The hospital staff, when presented with these options, elected to purchase at a cost of $2000 a used Texas Instruments 787 printing terminal capable of communicating at either 30 or 120 cps. Hospital administration agreed to contribute one-half of the cost of the terminal, with staff members contributing the other half. Long distance phone charges, necessitated by the absence of a local network node, in addition to paper and other supplies, would be financed from the hospital budget. Connect time to the databases would be paid by the physician user. A small area of the physician lounge/library was set aside for the terminal search station and a collection of user aids was purchased by the physicians (see Figure 1). Finally, a dedicated telephone line was installed. Initial use of the terminal was characterized by indefinable logon difficulties: at times, logon would occur without problems, but at other times, things would simply not work.

For no logical reason, consistent proper function finally began and has continued.

Because of their personal interest, two of the staff physicians attended training seminars on general use of the DIALOG system and on the specific medical databases, MEDLINE and Excerpta Medica (EMBASE). Although these training sessions were offered in nearby cities, they required two and one-half days away from practice. The seminars were extremely well-planned and were found, in retrospect, to have provided skills indispensable to satisfactory searching. The information specialists were correct in this regard: special training *was* essential. Concepts of Boolean logic were familiar, however, and search strategy paralleled previous experience with the medical literature.

FIGURE 1

USER AIDS

Medical Subject Headings, Annotated Alphabetic List, 1982. National Library of Medicine, Bethesda, Maryland, 20209.
Medical Subject Headings, Tree Structures, 1982. National Library of Medicine, Bethesda, Maryland, 20209.
List of Serials and Monographs Indexed for Online Users, 1981. National Library of Medicine, Bethesda, Maryland, 20209.
Permuted Medical Subject Headings, 1982. National Library of Medicine, Bethesda, Maryland, 20209.
Excerpta Medica List of Journals Abstracted 1980. Excerpta Medica, Princeton, New Jersey, 08540.
Guide to the Excerpta Medica Classification and Indexing System, 1978. Excerpta Medica, Princeton, New Jersey, 08540.

ONLINE USAGE

Searches were demonstrated to the entire staff and enthusiasm grew for the project. This initial enthusiasm for database searching resulted in a single month's online charge of over $1000! Usage has been quite variable (see Figure 2). Online time has averaged fifty-seven minutes each month over the four-year hospital experience.

Fifty-three percent of searching has been on the MEDLINE database. Time spent online to perform a search on a single topic averages twelve minutes. Search topics have usually been directly related to patient care, with the attending physician seeking answers to current treatment problems. Figure 3 lists typical search topics found in one physician's personal log. As might be expected, the only physicians continuing to use the system are those who received formal training.

The hospital library includes no journal subscriptions. While each staff physician subscribes to several journals, many references found in a search are not readily available. Early experiences with online ordering were disappointing; several weeks were required to receive an "expedited" order. Lending libraries have become more restrictive in their services to individuals by telephone and mail. Fortunately, the increased availability of abstracts online can often answer specific questions. Oftentimes, however, the physician must travel to the regional library to obtain the needed paper.

FIGURE 2

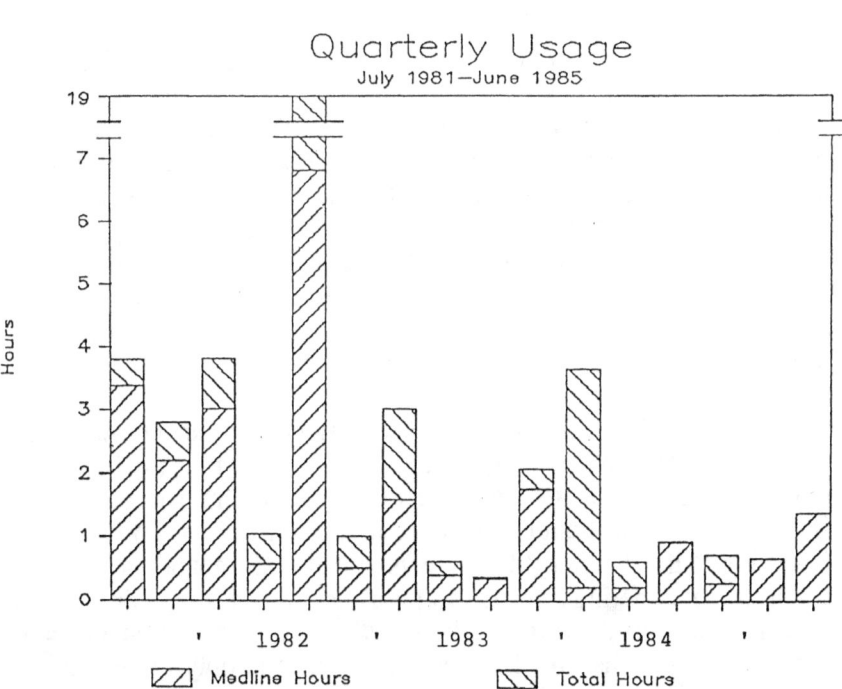

FIGURE 3

SELECTED SEARCH TOPICS

Recurrent hiatal hernia
Lymphadenopathy
Hematoma, soft tissue
Rectal perforation
Fecal incontinence
Gastric polyps
Gynecomastia
Aberrant breast
Occult primary malignancy
Breast carcinoma and carcinoembryonic antigen (CEA)
Aberrant pancreas
Dermatofibrosarcoma protruberans
Doberman pincer (canine)
The "Quickcode" computer program
Suture line recurrence
Doxepin and peptic ulcer disease

As searching has become a regular, though small part of hospital activity, a few changes have been made. The dedicated phone line has been replaced without incident by a simple extension line. Also, the hospital has begun paying all search costs. While the original terminal has functioned flawlessly, the thermal print paper has been difficult to work with. As a result, more searches are being done outside the hospital on personal computers. Information can then be stored on floppy disk, edited, and printed on standard paper. The novelty has also worn off. While still recreational and fun, online searching has settled into its niche as a small but important instrument in the clinical armamentarium.

Online searching has certainly been effective in answering questions in an efficient and timely manner. While recall is probably less than that achieved by an active search specialist, precision and specificity seem to be better.[1] When online, staff can follow up new leads immediately, and blind alleys are quickly abandoned. Minimum usage sometimes results in poor techniques, extending search time and expense, but the ability to scan the literature at virtually any time outweighs this disadvantage. With the only other alternatives being a half-day trip to the nearest regional library, or relaying search requests by telephone or mail, most questions would go unanswered. Indeed, it has been shown that a minority of physicians go to literature to meet their information needs. Lack of time is given as the most common reason for going elsewhere or doing without the information altogether.[2]

SPREADING THE WORD

Overall satisfaction with end user searching at this hospital has resulted in a staff member's "Scientific Exhibit" presentation of the concept at the American College of Surgeons' Clinical Congress in Chicago in October 1982. His exhibit demonstrating "live" online searching was visited by hundreds of surgeons, and over five hundred pieces of descriptive literature were taken by attendees. Many surgeons had no idea that this type of service was available to "private individuals." For some, two days of formal training was too high a price to pay for a service already available to them through libraries. For others, the convenience of searching at any time and virtually any place was of considerable value. Several were already satisfied end users.

Yet, end user searching is rarely mentioned in the medical literature. It seems to have been "discovered" for the most part, by physicians interested in computers, and is seen as an additional application or rationalization for computer equipment. While helpful articles are found in the popular computing journals,[3] discussing equipment and databases, and pointing out special advantages to physicians, the medical journals seem virtually silent on the topic. Physicians are aware of the benefits of online searching through intermediaries. A recent New England MEDLARS utilization study showed physicians to be the largest single group requesting searches.[4] Regrettably, end user searching, free of the constraints of time, institutions, and personnel, has not been presented to the medical profession as the valuable aid to patient care and current awareness that it is. This hospital's experience has, perhaps, exposed the ignorance necessary to lead to further learning.

> Attempt the end and never stand to doubt.
> Nothing's so hard but search will find it out.

Robert Herrick

BIBLIOGRAPHY

1. Barber, A. S.; Barraclough, E. D.; and Gray, W. A. "On-line Information Retrieval as a Scientist's Tool." *Information Storage and Retrieval* 9 (August 1973):429- 40.
2. Mosley, I. J. "Computer-based Information Services in Medicine." *New Zealand Medical Journal* 23 (July 1980):60-3.
3. Zarley, Craig. "Dialing Into Databases." *Personal Computing* 7 (December 1983): 135-9, 234.
4. Fazzone, Nancy, and DeSimone, Mary G. "MEDLARS Utilization Profile in New England." *Bulletin of the Medical Library Association* 72 (January 1984):6-11.

Confessions of an End User

David N. Neubauer

ABSTRACT. The author offers a personal account of one medical researcher's experience and perspective on end user searching. Particular attention is given to the role of the microcomputer in the search process. The discussion includes the significant advantages of storing references in a disk file, thereby allowing easy editing and reorganization of data.

There are a number of ways that I identify myself. At times I consider myself a clinician, an academician, or a researcher. At other times I am a computer enthusiast, a musician, or a photographer. Never do I consider myself to be an "end user," however. Frankly, I don't even know what it is that I am supposed to be using the end of. There must be a better word than this peculiar appellation coined by database vendors and reference librarians to designate those of us who do our own database searching. I, for one, would welcome suggestions.

In spite of my difficulty with the name of this activity, I am a strong advocate and active user of online databases. For a number of years I have been involved in a variety of academic pursuits and have worked with computers during much of that time. I have observed the popularization of information technology with great delight. When I decided to pursue online searching, I saw a chance to combine my dual interests of computers and research. Of course, computer-based information resources have been available for a long time through trained search intermediaries and reference librarians.

The first step identified in many studies on end user searching begins with submitting a search request at the library. It sometimes

---

Dr. Neubauer is a member of the Department of Psychiatry of the Johns Hopkins University School of Medicine, Baltimore, MD 21218. He received his M.D. degree from the University of Miami School of Medicine and completed his residency at Johns Hopkins. His research interests include chronobiology and sleep disorders.

would take several searches, each of varying lag time, for the searcher to produce the desired references. Even then, one didn't necessarily understand by what magic they appeared, nor what else might be out there. The mystique of online searching was at least, in part, a result of user passivity and ignorance. A more active role for the end user in the process of online searching has some impressive advantages. Speed and economy are obvious attractions. It's very gratifying to have the desired references instantly—whether they are for a particular project or simply the result of online explorations. And, with one of the discounted evening and weekend services, a few searches per month will make the service pay for itself.

The inexpensive hourly rates allow users to browse or wander through the databases. The privacy of working online alone lets the end user consider search questions that might be too trivial, ridiculous, or potentially embarrassing to present as formal library requests. Certainly, the number of searches that I do now is much greater than the number that I would have requested through an intermediary.

It is also possible to do a fair amount of research while online. I research a topic by reviewing many short form citations that have just been printed, and then returning online to get selected items with abstracts. Reviewing abstracts can cut down significantly on library time, and in itself offers precise data.

Another useful application is doing searches on the publications of certain individuals that I will be meeting in the future. I can easily find information about their interests and accomplishments before we meet. This tactic can also help to prepare for an interview with someone.

Although doing a traditional MEDLINE search was my stimulus for going online in the first place, I have since then discovered many other reasons and conditions for accessing other databases as well. So far, my online searching has been through BRS/AFTER DARK, and I believe that I have already experimented with all of that service's databases. Admittedly, I spend most of my time searching MEDLINE. BIOSIS, PsycINFO, SOCIAL SCISEARCH, and BOOKS IN PRINT have been valuable from time to time, also.

While the above advantages pertain mostly to convenience, there are aspects that make doing one's own searching qualitatively different from relaying the search request to someone else. Already mentioned is the process of assessing how databases are structured and how they represent individual specialty areas. Increased familiarity with thesauri and other ways in which a database treats a particular discipline enhances search results. In addition, examining descriptors in relevant citations and searching for particular authors, journals, years, or languages renders online searching a powerful research tool.

It must be emphasized that the skills necessary for effective and efficient online searching are never as automatic as the log-on procedures. The vendors are somewhat misleading in promising easy access to vast reserves of information upon receipt of a password. The inexperienced online searcher is apt to obtain either too few relevant citation or too many irrelevant citations. The sophisticated searcher needs to know what databases are available, when to use them, how their fields are categorized and coded, and how to use Boolean operators. I have to thank the reference staff at the Welch Medical Library for their help and training in such important concepts that go beyond the mechanical aspects of using computers.

Another consideration that sets end user searching apart from reliance on the reference librarian is the ability to download references. Once again, economy is a distinct advantage. It makes a lot more sense to store references onto a disk and print them later when compared to using valuable online time for a slow printer. When one's product is a disk file, as opposed to a pile of paper, references can be used as data for post-search processing. To me, this is what makes online searching on a microcomputer most distinctive. There is a vast difference between searching on a dumb terminal versus a programmable machine.

In order to employ fully the power of a disk reference file, I have developed a series of interconnected BASIC programs that perform several valuable tasks. I call the package Bibliographic File Utilities (BFU), which is used to produce a neatly formatted listing of references for all searches run (see Figure 1). A few libraries are also using BFU.

BFU offers the user a number of options. It can place a heading at the top of each listing. Headings could include the database searched, the exact search question, and the search date. BFU can also display individual references on the screen before deciding whether or not to transfer them to a more specialized file. The user can therefore weed out the obviously irrelevant references that sometimes find their way into any retrieval. The result is a tailored printout of useful references. As an additional aid in locating library journal articles, the program can also provide an alphabetized list of source

FIGURE 1

DATABASE: MESH
SEARCH: REM LATENCY AND DEPRESSION.DE.
SEARCH DATE: 7/2/85

1
Sitaram-N. Dube-S. Jones-D. Pohl-R. Gershon-S.
Acetylcholine and alpha 1-adrenergic sensitivity in the separation of depression and anxiety.
Psychopathology. 1984. 17 Suppl 3. P 24-39.

2
Akiskal-H-S. Lemmi-H. Dickson-H. King-D. Yerevanian-B. Van-Valkenburg-C.
Chronic depressions. Part 2. Sleep EEG differentiation of primary dysthymic disorders from anxious depressions.
J-Affective-Disord. 1984 Jun. 6(3-4). P 287-95.

3
Akiskal-H-S.
Diagnosis and classification of affective disorders: new insights from clinical and laboratory approaches.
Psychiatr-Dev. 1983 Summer. 1(2). P 123-60. (REVIEW).

4
Kupfer-D-J. Hanin-I. Coble-P-A. Spiker-D-G. Sorisio-D. Grau-T-G.
EEG sleep and tricyclic blood levels: acute and chronic administration in depression.
J-Clin-Psychopharmacol. 1982 Feb. 2(1). P 8-13.

5
Reynolds-C-F-3d. Coble-P-A. Kupfer-D-J. Holzer-B-C.
Application of the multiple sleep latency test in disorders of excessive sleepiness.
Electroencephalogr-Clin-Neurophysiol. 1982 Apr. 53(4). P 443-52.

6
Gillin-J-C. Sitaram-N. Duncan-W-C.
Muscarinic supersensitivity: a possible model for the sleep disturbance of primary depression?.
Psychiatry-Res. 1979 Jul. 1(1). P 17-22.

7
Shimizu-A. Hiyama-H. Yagasaki-A. Takashashi-H. Fujiki-A. Yoshida-I.
Sleep of depressed patients with hypersomnia: a 24-h polygraphic study.
Waking-Sleeping. 1979 Sep-Dec. 3(4). P 335-9.

8
Vogel-G-W. Vogel-F. McAbee-R-S. Thurmond-A-J.
Improvement of depression by REM sleep deprivation. New findings and a theory.
Arch-Gen-Psychiatry. 1980 Mar. 37(3). P 247-53.

9
Hippius-H. Ruther-E.
[Sleep problems and their treatment in psychosis (author's transl)].
Wien-Klin-Wochenschr [Suppl]. 1979. 91(106). P 6-10.

10
Gillin-J-C. Duncan-W. Pettigrew-K-D. Frankel-B-L. Snyder-F.
Successful separation of depressed, normal, and insomniac subjects by EEG sleep data.
Arch-Gen-Psychiatry. 1979 Jan. 36(1). P 85-90.

FIGURE 1 (continued)

```
    11
Gillin-J-C.  Wyatt-R-J.  Fram-D.  Snyder-F.
The relationship between changes in REM sleep and clinical
improvement in depressed patients treated with amitriptyline.
Psychopharmacology (Berlin). 1978 Dec 8. 59(3). P 267-72.

    12
Post-R-M.  Gerner-R-H.  Carman-J-S.  Gillin-J-C.  Jimerson-D-C.
Goodwin-F-K.  Bunney-W-E-Jr.
Effects of a dopamine agonist piribedil in depressed patients:
relationship of pretreatment homovanillic acid to antidepressant
response.
Arch-Gen-Psychiatry. 1978 May. 35(5). P 609-15.

    13
Reite-M.  Short-R-A.
Nocturnal sleep in separated monkey infants.
Arch-Gen-Psychiatry. 1978 Oct. 35(10). P 1247-53.
```

items (see Figure 2). The source listing also is automatically indexed to the original listing. Finally, the program can offer a directory of files already stored on the disk.

After downloading the retrieval, the system editor can delete the extraneous lines before and after the references themselves. BFU then takes over. The program has limitations, nevertheless. It is dependent on the two-letter field indicators being part of the search output. Without the field labels, it would be impossible to isolate the individual lines. Thus, this approach works only with systems that have the two-letter field codes.

There are many other potential advantages to having the references in a data file. One is that a separate personal database can be created, edited, expanded, and most importantly, searched. Information from different online sessions on various databases can be easily linked in a series. The user could download all references on a particular topic and later search by author, journal or other parameters. Even relatively primitive system editors, such as the IBM PC's EDLIN, incorporate some search function. A more sophisticated and more readily searchable personal database can be developed by using one of the popular database managers now on the market. Creating and maintaining a personal database requires substantial advance planning and a time commitment, even with an automated system.

There are a few products currently advertised which claim to simplify the search process. The user can express the topic of interest and the program will automatically dial up and sign on, choose the appropriate database, present the search questions, and store the

FIGURE 2

REM LATENCY AND DEPRESSION.DE.

```
Arch-Gen-Psychiatry 1978 Oct. 35(10). P 1247-53. # 13
Arch-Gen-Psychiatry 1980 Mar. 37(3). P 247-53. # 8
Arch-Gen-Psychiatry 1978 May. 35(5). P 609-15. # 12
Arch-Gen-Psychiatry 1979 Jan. 36(1). P 85-90. # 10
Electroencephalogr-Clin-Neurophysiol 1982 Apr. 53(4). P 443-52. # 5
J-Affective-Disord 1984 Jun. 6(3-4). P 287-95. # 2
J-Clin-Psychopharmacol 1982 Feb. 2(1). P 8-13. # 4
Psychiatr-Dev 1983 Summer. 1(2). P 123-60. (REVIEW). # 3
Psychiatry-Res 1979 Jul. 1(1). P 17-22. # 6
Psychopathology 1984. 17 Suppl 3. P 24-39. # 1

Psychopharmacology (Berlin) 1978 Dec 8. 59(3). P 267-72. # 11
Waking-Sleeping 1979 Sep-Dec. 3(4). P 335-9. # 7
Wien-Klin-Wochenschr [Suppl] 1979. 91(106). P 6-10. # 9
```

results. The producers make the process sound as dubious as it sounds grand! This user feels much safer directing the complete search process. I want to know exactly where I have looked and what was there.

An appealing new service is being offered by some of the online gateway systems which allows the user to access a very wide variety of databases and other information utilities. The gateway services can provide a cost savings and remarkable flexibility. The Business Computer Network (BCN), for example, can offer access not only to DIALOG and BRS, but also to various financial, legal, news, sports, weather, and entertainment services. Except for the service's nominal monthly minimum, billing costs are limited to the services actually used. The cost of individual memberships and monthly minimums for all of the services available can therefore be circumvented.

Finally, I should say a few words about equipment. Hardware requirements are minimal. Any personal computer with a printer, disk storage capacity and modem will suffice. My equipment includes an IBM PC with 256K internal memory on two 360K disk drives. A hard disk system, now relatively affordable, would be preferable because of its memory capacity. I also use a Hayes 1200 Smartmodem. The accompanying Smartcom II communications software accomodates all of my applications. With a few keystrokes, the program will automatically dial and sign on to a specified vendor. Any output to the screen can be simultaneously stored on the disk faster than it can be read. It is possible also to pre-store search questions prior to going online and then bring them up later with a single maneuver. Though not done too often, the process could be useful for regularly inputting a particularly long search strategy. While my own equipment and software configuration has worked well, many other microcomputers and telecommunications packages will operate as effectively.

Online searching is a powerful and fairly straightforward process, but undoubtably not for everyone. Online searching has something to offer a variety of professionals in many fields. I don't think that we're far from the time when developing online searching skills will be requisite to academics and research. Librarians will play a key role in educating the end user and in serving as resource consultants. Tremendous changes have taken place during the last few years which suggest that we are still in a transitional phase of information management. The roles and relationships between online searchers, database vendors, producers and librarians have yet to solidify. With continued communication and cooperation among professionals in interrelated fields, even more efficient systems are likely in the future.

End User Searching in the Small Hospital Setting

Corrine R. McNabb

ABSTRACT. With many physicians leaving urban areas to practice in smaller communities, the need for end user searching becomes particularly significant. End user searching in geographically remote areas can to some extent surmount the problem of inaccessibility to large academic health science centers. With lower physician-patient ratios, physicians in non-metropolitan areas are sometimes so busy with patient care that little time remains for research. These physicians are quick to accept computerized systems that make practice management more efficient, but might be less likely to engage in doing their own online searching. Full-text databases have the most potential for physicians in non-metropolitan areas because of the possibility of immediate, concrete data.

The medical profession is undergoing a great deal of flux, as are most occupations that are feeling the direct effects of changing information technologies. What's more, physicians seem to be drowning in more paperwork than ever, due to the administrative pressures of DRGs and the attending need to defend and document all practice decisions. Competition is also affecting the traditional practice of medicine in both metropolitan and rural communities. High technology comes eventually to even geographically remote, medically underserved areas that are far removed from state-of-the-art practice as defined by the academic health science centers. There are still many hospital libraries that do not offer mediated online services; is it any wonder, then, that end user searching in such areas has not thrived to the extent that many national conferences have implied?

Recent evidence indicates that physicians—both specialists and

---

Corrine R. McNabb was recently Director of Library Services at the Carbondale General Hospital, Carbondale, Pennsylvania. She was an Associate of the National Library of Medicine for 1982-1983, and graduated from the Drexel University School of Library Science.

those that provide primary care—are settling outside major cities to a greater degree than in past years.[1] Board-certified specialists have appeared in many non-metropolitan areas for the first time. The number of rural physicians increased 23 percent between 1974 and 1978 and is still increasing. Physicians are migrating in rapid numbers away from urban or densely-populated areas to locations that might be far away from any major medical center. There are implications for rural hospital library services, which, for the most part, have been successfully implemented and greatly welcomed. It can be argued that it is easier to be creative and innovative in a smaller operation where the bureaucratic structure is less developed.

One innovation that is only slowly catching on, however, is end user searching. Even though it would seem that a busy private practice in a non-metropolitan area would offer great potential for end user searching, several factors might offset user interest. Possible factors include the traditional dichotomy between an academic versus clinical orientation, fear of computers, readily available hospital library services, and finally, ignorance of computers or telecommunications. Each one of these elements will be explored separately as follows.

ACADEMIC ORIENTATION VERSUS CLINICAL PRACTICE

Many physicians practicing in non-metropolitan areas are office-based. That is, unlike house officers contracted by the hospital, they maintain their own privately administered service. Private practitioners in non-metropolitan areas are generally not engaged in research as much as health professionals based at academic institutions. Herein lies a major discrepancy. End user searching might be most beneficial to researchers who like to browse serendipitously and who also prefer comprehensive retrieval. End user searching is apt to be less successful for the family physician or internist who, for example, discovers the need for a few key articles on bullous dermatitis in an elderly patient about to be discharged from the hospital.

With 127 medical schools in the United States, there are a great number of physicians who practice in areas that are several hours away from any major medical center. It has been shown that these rural physicians see 22 percent more patients each week than their urban counterparts.[2] Even though many physicians are automating their practice management, in many instances the office assistants actually operate the systems in place. Similarly, it is possible that physicians who subscribe to an online search service might assign the mechanics of logging in or printing retrieval to the office assistant. It is likely, however, that the office-based physician simply does not have the luxury of finding time to learn or undertake his or her own searching, especially if library services are accessible. There is an important distinction between residents and practitioners in this regard. Environments that sponsor residency programs might be more academically oriented and more likely to foster fertile ground for practicing end user searching.

COMPUTER LITERACY

The media has widely heralded the arrival of the computer age, which has affected the routine tasks of many professions. The information industry has expanded dramatically within the last few years and is promoting its wares even to schoolchildren. Effective and maximal use of systems does not automatically proceed from exposure, let alone experience.

Medical school curricula in the 1980s address computer applications in medicine more so than in past decades. Accordingly, medical school libraries are developing and implementing bibliographic instruction courses that address the use of microcomputers.[3,4,5] Residency programs are also featuring computer applications in their curricula.[6] Perhaps as a result of new information skills, physicians now coming into practice will be more likely interested in end user searching than older physicians who might have had fewer dealings with computers. It is interesting to consider whether or not newly graduated physicians will choose private practice or full-time academic appointments. Recent surveys indicate that just under two-thirds will seek a career in private practice, bringing a certain measure of computer literacy away from the teaching environment and out into the field.[7]

It would seem, however, that medical students and residents might not be as familiar with online systems as their program directors and librarians might suppose.[8] Even student attitudes might militate against learning about computer systems. Some medical schools have made attempts to influence student interest in computer applications. One program established a pilot project that required first-year medical students enrolled in the Microbiology course to create personal filing systems; the program ultimately concluded that lack of student interest had to do with students aspiring to primary practice instead of research medicine in the academic setting.[9]

Another concern is that the use of home computers, which have been a large portion of the potential end user market, has lessened. The popular literature speculates that the home computer might actually be the first indicator of a downslide in computer sales.[10] There is evidence that many personal computers have been purchased by people who already owned outmoded machines. Home computer use might have reached its saturation point. The future growth of end user searching in the medical professions might eventually depend upon further development and expanded use of office-based computer systems. This possibility raises the question of whether or not a need for end user searching might ever gain attention in a community practice setting.

HOSPITAL LIBRARY SERVICES

As previously stated, physicians in private practice are primarily busy with patient care. In addition to their appointment schedules, they must make daily rounds of their hospitalized patients and brace themselves for any possible emergencies. In a sense, primary care providers, such as family practitioners, internists, and pediatricians, must extend and diversify their services in communities with few specialists. To such primary care providers, time is likely to be a very limited commodity. While access to medical information is critical, it is difficult to justify time spent away from an already heavy patient care load when a local hospital librarian can provide a tailored literature search of key citations.

A case in point would be the Wilkes-Barre and Scranton area of northeastern Pennsylvania. The community has about fifteen hospitals, averaging approximately 250 beds. Seven of the hospitals have residency programs, and all of them have established library services. The hospital libraries have an average of 2000 volumes, about 200 journal subscriptions, and most offer online search services. The libraries have developed an active resource-sharing network to offset the geographic barriers to major health sciences centers in New York or Philadelphia. It is possible that this network typifies consortia arrangements in other rural areas nationwide. Librarians in the area are aware of few physicians who do their own online searching. In a recent survey of 251 staff members conducted by one of the larger hospital's libraries, it was found that physicians' interest in end user searching was a close second to practice management computer applications.[11] Results also showed a significant gap between expressed interest and actual use.[12]

One reason that end user searching has not attracted many physicians who responded to the survey could be the high calibre of their institutions' libraries. In most instances, a physician need only drop by the library or request a search by phone or mail. Photocopy service promises twenty-four-hour turnaround time if references are from libraries within the network. The service is subsidized by the hospitals and extended free of charge to staff physicians. Such tailored service diminishes user incentive for online searching. Ironically, it is as if hospital librarians have done their jobs too well. In a different vein, lack of interest in end user searching can indicate little need.[13]

BIBLIOGRAPHIC REFERENCES VERSUS FULL-TEXT RETRIEVAL

When physicians raise patient care questions, quick search results are highly valued. Since patient problems can arise unexpectedly, libraries can hardly predict usage patterns. This can pose a problem for smaller hospital libraries without extensive journal collections. Even a delay of a few days to process an interlibrary loan request can fail to serve user needs. Unfortunately, end user searching cannot transcend the problem of document delivery for rural hospital library users.

It is apparent that the information needs of primary care physicians in a community hospital setting differ from the research needs of the physician based in a university's basic science department. The implication of full-text searching of entire journals by end users is one way of closing the gap between resources and services available to different types of physicians—regardless of their unique needs. This is especially significant for physicians in smaller hospital settings who are looking for actual data instead of bibliographic references. User enthusiasm for full-text searching has already been widely reported in the literature.[14,15] A related issue concerns access to clinical information databanks, such as those offered by AMA/NET. Since private enterprise in the information world carefully guards figures on the market share, however, it is difficult to estimate the demographics on physician use.[16] Such data would undoubtably prove useful to studies on end user searching in the health sciences.

It would appear likely that end user searching lends itself best to urban or academic health care environments because end user searching is a research activity that conflicts with the time demands of primary care providers. Physicians in non-metropolitan areas, whose numbers are increasing, seem to lack the time or inclination to explore end user searching as it is currently practiced.[17] The popularization and marketing of full-text databases and clinical information databanks might offer the greatest potential for these users. Even though physicians have been quick to employ the latest technology to automate and streamline their practice management, they have not demonstrated equal interest in online literature searching. As described earlier, this might be a backward compliment to their library services. It has been suggested that most people, including physicians, are not yet able to identify instances when they might need access to online searching.[18] Meanwhile, librarians must, as user advocates, question the viability and effectiveness of the commercial sector's promotional claims.

Librarians must look beyond the confines of medical schools and teaching hospitals to gauge the need for new information technologies by staying close to their users. Finally, search intermediaries might consider that the library itself is a system, which no less than the microcomputer, deserves coverage and promotion among users.

REFERENCES

1. Schwartz, W.B. et al. "The Changing Geographic Distribution of Board-Certified Physicians." *New England Journal of Medicine* 303 (October 30, 1980):1032-38.

2. "City vs. Country Practice: Which Pays Off Best Today?" *Medical Economics* 61 (March 5, 1984):256-68.

3. Calabretta, Nancy. "End User Searching—Whither Goest Thou?" *The Chronicle: Newsletter of the Philadelphia Regional Chapter of the Medical Library Association* Spring (1985).

4. Foreman, Gertrude E., and Mueller, Mary H. "A Credit Course for Medical Students." *Medical Reference Services Quarterly* 4 (Fall 1985):61-6.

5. McGowan, Anna T. "Information Management Education in the Academic Health Sciences Library." Paper presented at the Mid-Atlantic Health Congress, Atlantic City, New Jersey, May 22, 1985.

6. Interview with Glen Morgan, United Health and Hospital Services, Family Practice Residency Program, Kingston, Pennsylvania, June 1985.

7. Project Panel on the General Professional Education of the Physician and College Preparation for Medicine. "Physicians for the 21st Century." *Journal of Medical Education* 59 (November 1984): Part 2.

8. Boilard, David W. et al. "Profile of the Physician as Potential End User." Paper presented at the Annual Meeting of the Medical Library Association, New York, May 24-30, 1985.

9. Interview with Anna T. McGowan, Health Sciences Library, University of North Carolina, Chapel Hill, North Carolina, October 17, 1985.

10. Gelman, Eric et al. "Hard Times in High Tech." *Newsweek* (April 22, 1985):50-1.

11. Wilkes-Barre General Hospital, Library User's Survey, January 1985.

12. Poisson, Ellen H. "The Present Status of End-User Searching in Medicine." Paper presented at the Annual Meeting of the Medical Library Association, New York, May 24-30, 1985.

13. Batson, Eric. "Microcomputers for MD's." *Postgraduate Medicine* 77 (April 1985):95-6.

14. Tenopir, Carol. "Dialog's Knowledge Index and BRS/After Dark: Database Searching on Personal Computers." *Library Journal* 108 (March 1, 1983):471-4.

15. Ojala, Marydee. "Knowledge Index: A Review." *Online* 7 (September 1983):31-4.

16. "Searching the Databanks." *Medicine & Computer* 2 (January/February 1985): 31-4.

17. Tenopir, Carol. "Systems for End Users: Are There End Users for the Systems?" *Library Journal* 110 (June 15, 1985):40-1.

18. Janke, Richard V. "BRS/After Dark: The Birth of Online Self-Service." *Online* 7 (September 1983):12-29.

IV. BIBLIOGRAPHY AND GLOSSARY

End User Searching: A Selected Annotated Bibliography

M. Sandra Wood

The literature on end user searching has literally exploded over the past three years. High interest in end user searching, both on the part of the librarian, or search intermediary, and the end user, has been fueled by a number of simultaneous developments: the proliferation of new "user-friendly" systems, both menu-driven and command-driven; the introduction of front-end processors or gateway systems; the markedly increased sales of microcomputers and modems; and aggressive marketing on the part of database vendors directly to the end user. This focus on the end user has caused librarians, who have functioned as search intermediaries since the advent of online systems in the early 1970s, to reevaluate their roles.

Keeping up with the literature in this fast-growing field has become almost impossible; in fact, from the time that this bibliography is completed until it is published, it will be significantly out-of-date. Nonetheless, it is hoped that this bibliography will provide a "core list" of references from which the researcher can move forward. Several excellent bibliographies already exist;[1,2] however, they are not annotated. Others, while annotated[3] or presented as a review,[4] are not extensive enough to be useful, or are outdated by several years. While it is not possible nor desirable for this annotated bibliography to be complete, it is hoped that the key literature is included. The focus of the bibliography is end user searching in the health sciences; a secondary focus is on end user educational programs in academic, corporate, or other settings. References to computer interfaces, front ends, and gateway systems are included

---

M. Sandra Wood is Head, Reference, The George T. Harrell Library, The Milton S. Hershey Medical Center, The Pennsylvania State University, Hershey, PA 17033. She received an M.L.S. from Indiana University and an M.B.A. from the University of Maryland. Ms. Wood edits *Medical Reference Services Quarterly*. The author would like to acknowledge the editorial comments of Virginia Lingle.

since they provide user-friendly access to databases. Information on the librarian's evolving role from search intermediary to consultant and educator is also a part of the bibliography because this change is a direct result of end user searching. Online access has recently become popularized in the computer literature and in periodicals intended for the general public. It is important for librarians to know what the public is being told about online bibliographic searching; therefore, popular literature is included to "balance" the view.

All of the references in this bibliography were personally examined by the author. Certain materials have been purposely excluded, including: news items or vendors' announcements of new products; dissertations; government documents; directories of online databases; and international meeting proceedings. Selectively included are meeting proceedings from the United States. For example, the *Online Conference Proceeding* (e.g., *Online '85, Online '84*) are known to contain papers on end user searching; however, these *Proceedings* were not readily available when the bibliography was compiled and so were not included. Conversely, the *National Online Meeting Proceedings* for 1983 through 1985 were available, and are therefore included. Readers are encouraged to consult the *Online Conference Proceedings* and earlier *National Online Meeting Proceedings* for additional references. Also of interest is a new monthly magazine, *Database End-User* (Vol. 1, no. 1, July/August 1985, Meckler Publishing, ISSN 0882-326x), which will be expected to carry information relevant to both the professional online searcher and the searching professional.

The following bibliography is divided into eight sections: General Sources, which includes both overviews and citations which didn't fit into other categories; the Role of the Librarian, as related to end user searching; End User Searching in the Health Sciences; End User Searching in Academic Institutions; End User Searching in Corporations; Other End User Education, which includes studies which complement the previous three categories; Computer Interfaces, including front ends and gateways; and the Popular Literature, including articles in the professional literature which discuss end user systems for the general public.

REFERENCES

1. Janke, Richard V. "Online After Six: End User Searching Comes of Age." *Online* 8 (November 1984):15-29.

2. Janke, Richard V. "Presearch Counseling for Client Searchers (End-Users)." *Online* 9 (September 1985):13-26.
3. Lyon, Sally. "End-User Searching of Online Databases: A Selective Annotated Bibliography." *Library Hi Tech* 2 (September 1984):47-50.
4. Lowry, Glenn R. "Training of Users of Online Services: A Survey of the Literature." *Science & Technology Libraries* 1 (Spring 1981):27-40.

GENERAL SOURCES

Burton, Hilary D. "The Changing Environment of Personal Information Systems." *Journal of the American Society for Information Science* 36 (January 1985):48-52.

Technological developments are changing the context of personal information systems. Growing commercial service support, increasing microcomputer support, and downloading capabilities will all have an effect on efforts to standardize system interfaces, and may change "the ways an individual develops and uses his personal information system." An appendix lists fifteen representative personal file managers.

Butler, Brett. "Online Public Access: The Sleeping Beast Awakens." *ASIS Bulletin* 10 (December 1983):6-10.

Libraries have difficulty coping with success. Online reference systems and online public access systems are becoming so successful that libraries are having difficulty adapting to and finding funding for such systems. Users are accessing these systems in increasing numbers; however, "the success of public access creates an increasing budget obligation for the library which is totally beyond its control." Online reference systems will become increasingly operated without staff assistance. In coping with its newfound success, libraries can handle the costs through four paths: budget transfers, budget increases, subsidies, and user fees.

Cleverdon, Cyril. "Optimizing Convenient Online Access to Bibliographic Databases." *Information Service & Use* 4 (April 1985): 37-47.

Present bibliographic services are inefficient, overpriced, and "hostile to end-users." Although the article jumps through a variety of topics, the author has some interesting suggestions: that Boolean logic has serious disadvantages and should be replaced by a quorum function search and the use of natural language; and that the natural sciences and technology literature (with the exception of chemical literature) should be combined into one large database which is restricted to papers from the more important journals. Such changes would make online searching less intimidating to end users.

Cochrane, Pauline. "Improving the Quality of Information Retrieval-Online to a Library Catalog or Other Access Service . . . Or . . . Where Do We Go From Here?" *Online* 5 (July 1981):30-42.

Cochrane predicts that by 1985, "we will have a majority of users who are occasional but serious users of several systems and multiple databases who will not always be using the assistance of an information professional." In order to ensure that we are doing better searching by 1990, we must better understand the information seeker, since individual user behavior may be the greatest variable in a successful search. "Search strategy may be the real key to improvement in information retrieval quality."

Des Chene, Dorice. "Online Searching by End Users." *RQ* 25 (Fall 1985):89-95.

Trends and new developments in end user searching are overviewed. From initial unsuccessful attempts to train end users in the 1970s to the advent of intelligent front ends or gateway systems in the 1980s, online information systems have made, and will continue to make, great strides in making information more available to the end user. Librarians will adjust to new roles as consultants and instructors. An extensive list of references is included.

Dolan, Donna R. "Offlines: Databases for Everyman." *Database* 6 (December 1983):101-4.

Dolan accuses the database vendors of providing "tempting systems with enticing menus when the information in them may be unpalatable." The Source and CompuServe were both begun with the general public in mind, whereas KNOWLEDGE INDEX and BRS/AFTER DARK now offer "scaled down" versions of their parent systems which are intended for the end user. Dolan makes a fairly detailed comparison between the two types of systems and the databases that each offer for the lay person. A major error is in the premise that the two types of systems are being marketed for the same users. While the end users for The Source and CompuServe are in fact the general public, it seems that KNOWLEDGE INDEX and AFTER DARK may be intended for a highly educated professional market.

Fenichel, Carol Hansen. "Online Communications Publications for End-Users." *Online* 9 (May 1985):129-32.

Fenichel has compiled a bibliography of "how-to" publications intended "to help end-users utilize online communications systems." Excluded are highly technical publications, basic and advanced works for librarians, and expensive directories. A majority of the publications would be found at a local bookstore or computer store. Also included is a list of newsletters and journals. The microcomputer buff will find the list highly useful, as will the librarian who needs technical knowledge to set up an end user workstation.

Hansen, Carol. *The Microcomputer User's Guide to Information Online*. Hasbrouck Heights, NJ: Hayden, 1984.

Intended for the novice, Hansen has provided an excellent basic guide to accessing online databases. Basic information is given, from describing what information is available online and from whom, to the hardware and software necessary to connect with online services. The search process, including Boolean logic, is briefly discussed. Although some information (ie., games, entertainment) is included for the general public, this book would be more useful for the subject specialist or professional who might be looking for another use for their microcomputer.

Howitt, Doran, and Weinberger, Marvin I. *Inc. Magazine's DATA-BASICS; Your Guide to Online Business Information.* New York: Garland Publishing, 1984.

Aimed at the business world and the general public, this book contains literally "everything you always wanted to know about business databases." The book is divided into five parts: part 1 describes the information industry; part 2 is a guide to selected databases, divided into "subject groupings"; part three discusses database vendors; part four discusses communications; and part five discusses the future (some of which is already here!). Appendices list information brokers and hardware. Information contained in the book will need to be updated frequently to remain relevant.

Hunter, Janne A. "What Did You Say the End User Was Going to do at the Terminal and How Much is It Going to Cost?" *National Online Meeting Proceedings* (1983):223-9.

End user searching has increased in popularity over the past several years. The advent of full-text databases is extending the "vision" that the end user can use his terminal to find anything in five minutes. Barriers to end users doing their own searches include: the lack of standardization in search systems, requiring different commands for each system; and the problem of subject indexing and retrieval, which may be partially remedied by full-text databases. New user-friendly systems such as KNOWLEDGE INDEX and AFTER DARK will be a good way to introduce end users to online systems at a reasonable cost. Users who wish to do their own searching should be encouraged; users who do not show interest should not be encouraged or forced to do so, as their resultant product is likely to be "sketchy, if not downright bad."

Hunter, Janne A. "When Your Patrons Want to Search—The Library as Advisor to Endusers . . . A Compendium of Advice and Tips." *Online* 8 (May 1984):36-41.

Hunter gives some "grass roots" advice on what to do and how to handle the library patron who wishes to do his own searching. The article is filled with a wealth of tips from training needs and advice regarding database structure, to advice on hardware and software and letting the patron use the library's terminal to "get a feel" for doing online searching before he commits himself. Overall, the article can be summarized by the statement, "Be as helpful as you can," because in the long run, the patron and the librarian must work together to gain access to information.

Kaplan, Robin. "Knowledge Index: A Review." *Database* 8 (June 1985):122-8.

KNOWLEDGE INDEX is an abbreviated, simplified version of DIALOG. It is a low-cost (40¢ a minute), "after hours" information service that was developed for end users. Kaplan reviews the database coverage, costs of the system, and basic commands. KNOWLEDGE INDEX is compared to DIALOG, and receives a favorable review from the author.

Kesselman, Martin. "Online Update: BRS After Dark." *Wilson Library Bulletin* 58 (May 1984):652-3, 687.

The "Online Update" column describes the "basics" of BRS/AFTER DARK, including menu choices, availability, and cost. Also mentioned are other BRS menu-driven systems: Medical Colleague, Educator Colleague, and EXEC INFO. At this point in time, much of the information is a bit dated.

Lowry, Glenn R. "Training of Users of Online Services: A Survey of the Literature." *Science & Technology Libraries* 1 (Spring 1981):27-40.

Lowry does an excellent job of synthesizing the literature of the training of end users of online services from 1976 to 1979. Issues include what techniques should be used and initiative of end users to learn the systems. End users vary in their need and desire to use online services. Training should include "hands-on" practice; computer-assisted instruction is one method which has been utilized successfully for training.

Lyon, Sally. "End-User Searching of Online Databases: A Selective Annotated Bibliography." *Library Hi Tech* 2 (September 1984):47-50.

Lyon has selected citations from the literature which discuss end user search services and systems, the role of the intermediary, and training for the end user. The list covers twenty-six articles and conference papers from 1981-84. More comprehensive bibliographies are available in the two Janke articles (*Online* 8 (November 1984):15-29, and *Online* 9 (September 1985):13-26).

Mount, Ellis, editor. *Serving End-Users in Sci-Tech Libraries.* New York: The Haworth Press, 1984. (*Science & Technology Libraries,* Volume 5, Number 1, Fall 1984.)

This thematic issue of *Science & Technology Libraries* focuses on the end user in both corporate and academic situations. Separate entries for two of the six major articles (the remaining deal with public relations, machine-aided indexing, and audiovisuals) are found under: Lescohier, R.S.; and Ward, Sandra N.

Ojala, Marydee. "Knowledge Index: A Review." *Online* 7 (September 1983):31-4.

KNOWLEDGE INDEX receives a favorable review by the author. In this user-friendly system, DIALOG has retained all of the power and flexibility of its full search service, but has simplified commands for the inexperienced end user. In fact, experienced DIALOG searchers have more trouble adjusting to KNOWLEDGE INDEX than would the beginning end user. Also reviewed in the article is BRS/AFTER DARK, a menu-driven service. Ojala prefers KNOWLEDGE INDEX.

Shedlock, James. "Looking Down the Road: End User Searching." *Medical Reference Services Quarterly* 1 (Fall 1982):61-5.

Shedlock examines the future of online searching from the role of the search intermediary to that of the end user. The trend toward end users doing their own searching has philosophical, educational and "role" connotations for librarians. End user searching is viewed by Shedlock as evolutionary—the search intermediary will become a search counselor.

Shuman, Bruce A. "Who's User-Friendly? A Comparative Appraisal of DIALOG, ORBIT, and BRS." *National Online Meeting Proceedings* (1983):491-8.

New users are frequently intimidated by online search systems. The author has undertaken an evaluation of the "user-friendliness" of the three major systems: DIALOG, ORBIT and BRS. The evaluation was based on ten subjective criteria: number of files, convenience of logging on/off and changing files, detail of search components, security coding, browsability, searching mode, easiness of reading, error correction, online tutorials and "most human." ORBIT received the highest marks both on a simple summary of scores, and on a weighted evaluation of the scores.

Summit, Roger K., and Meadow, Charles T. "Emerging Trends in the Online Industry." *Special Libraries* 76 (Spring 1985):88-92.

Trends include more source data, greater subject variety, better communications, and more powerful user language. The advent of the microcomputer has greatly increased the number of database end users. PCs offer greater searching capabilities than earlier terminals, allowing the user more control over the data. "Users of all classes are becoming dependent on on-line systems," and the demand continues to increase.

Tenopir, Carol. "Dialog's Knowledge Index and BRS/After Dark: Database Searching on Personal Computers." *Library Journal* 108 (March 1, 1983):471-4.

Tenopir's column, "Online Databases," introduces and compares DIALOG's KNOWLEDGE INDEX and BRS/AFTER DARK, two new entries into the end user market. Both systems are organized via a subject focus. KNOWLEDGE INDEX is command-driven, while AFTER DARK is menu-driven. On both systems, searching is greatly simplified; thus these user-friendly systems are less powerful than their parent services. The potential for such systems is great, but improvements are needed for the end user to achieve results equivalent to those of a search intermediary.

Tenopir, Carol. "Systems for End Users: Are There End Users for the Systems?" *Library Journal* 110 (June 15, 1985):40-1.

Tenopir's column is a reaction to, and summary of, the Sixth National Online Meeting in New York, which had as its focus end user searching. Tenopir defines three types of "transparent" systems: front-ends (ex.: In-Search); intermediary systems (ex.: MicroDisclosure and Search Helper); and gateway systems (ex.: Easynet). After a digression to discuss BRS/BRKTHRU and Easynet, the column focuses on whether there really is an end user market. Based on the presentations at the National Online Meeting, it seems that end users really don't know that they are "end users," that the market really has not yet been targeted (librarians have a role here), and that many people don't yet know why online information may be important to them.

Thompson, Benna Brodsky. "Future Direct Users of Sci-Tech Electronic Databases." *Database* 6 (June 1983):6-9.

In an editorial, Thompson envisions the future with end user searching. Using scenarios that depict different levels of, and enthusiasm for, end user searching, her conclusions are not as "optimistic" as others. The final picture is similar to that of manual literature searching, with some users doing their own searching with help from the librarians and others still preferring librarians to do their searching.

Trautman, Rodes, and Graham, Deborah L. "Three-Party Telecommunications to Facilitate Public Use of Interactive Systems." *Proceedings of the 48th Annual Meeting of the American Society for Information Science* 22 (1985):258-61.

The configuration described here, with two telephone circuits and two modems, allows a single terminal to interact with two different computers at the same time. Two major applications are suggested: a trained intermediary has the equipment and a patron calls "requesting information that can be obtained online," "or an end user searcher has the equipment and contacts the librarian, while on line, for help with a search." Several potential applications and practical examples are given for each category.

Williams, Martha E. "Electronic Databases." *Science* 228 (April 26, 1985):445-56.

This is a fine overview of online databases. After a general introduction, databases are discussed in three groups: bibliographic, full-text, and numeric; specific examples are given of each, along with brief information on coverage and producer. Database vendors are discussed, along with new user-friendly front ends and the role of artificial intelligence as related to online databases. Issues and trends discussed include copyright and downloading, transborder data flow, and optical disks. Although end user searching is not the focus of the article, the fact that it was published in a journal which is widely read by basic scientists makes it relevant to searching by end users.

Williams, Phil W. "How Do We Help the End User?" *National Online Meeting Proceedings* (1985):495-505.

The information retrieval market has saturated the professional searcher/intermediary market and is now moving attention to the general professional. Access in Europe is made much more difficult than in the United States because of the billing structure. Features needed to attract new users include: marketing, minimizing barriers, simple accounting, assistance with search formulation, and ease of use. System features which will assist the end user include automated communications, single station access, and assistance in database selection. "The advantages of implementation on microcomputers . . ., on minicomputers . . . and on the host mainframe are described." The focus of the article is on making it easy for end users to access the systems, from simplified billing to simplified system mechanics.

ROLE OF THE LIBRARIAN

Berry, John. "Intermediaries: Our Tough, New Job." *Library Journal* 109 (May 1, 1984):834.

In his *LJ* editorial column, Berry discusses the search intermediary's new role as consultant and educator. He points out that "new knowledge, skills, and a new critical literature" will be needed to ensure that the end user gets the "most, best information for the time and money."

Dalrymple, Prudence W. "Closing the Gap: The Role of the Librarian in Online Searching." *RQ* 24 (Winter 1984):177-85.

The librarian's role in online searching is changing and evolving, as discussed and explored by Dalrymple. The reference interview, online search evaluation, user training and information service management all are discussed in light of the new trend toward end user searching. While the intermediary may be viewed only as a tool or means of access, the librarian-intermediary serves as a source of information and counsel, exercising professional judgement about online systems and services.

Duckitt, Pauline. "The Intermediary Today and Tomorrow." *ASLIB Proceedings* 36 (February 1984):79-86.

The intermediary, or "middleman," is a service position, and only those who excel and are flexible will survive. The intermediary role, especially that of online searcher, is changing. The intermediary of tomorrow will become more of a consultant and educator, and there will be a need for fewer search intermediaries. The training needs for information intermediaries will need to change, also, to include: keyboarding and online skills, programming and file design, interpersonal skills, business skills, and knowledge of mass communication.

Faibisoff, Sylvia G., and Hurych, Jitka. "Is There a Future for the End User in Online Bibliographic Searching?" *Special Libraries* 72 (October 1981):347-55.

In the four short years since this question was raised, the answer is "yes, there is a future for end user searching." The roles of the intermediary searcher and the end user are discussed, along with problems and obstacles faced by end users. Differences in approach between the two groups yield different results. The intermediary uses thesauri and tends to think in terms of exhaustive searching, whereas the end user lacks sophistication and knowledge of indexing techniques but in reality may be after only a few good articles. There will always be a need for search intermediaries, although their role and the types of searching they do may change.

Girard, Anne, and Moureau, Magdeleine. "An Examination of the Role of the Intermediary in the Online Searching of Chemical Literature." *Online Review* 5 (1981):217-25.

There are three knowledge areas necessary to search an online database: knowledge of the database itself, knowledge of the search system, and knowledge of the subject involved. The intermediary and the end user will differ in their expertise of these areas, and therefore in their ability to search. Five sample searches are illustrated, along with the differences in approach taken by an end user versus the intermediary. Some searches can be done by either the skilled online expert or the end user, while others require the skilled intermediary.

Jackson, Angela R. Haygarth. "Online Information Handling— The User Perspective." *Online Review* 7 (January 1983):25-32.

After reviewing a decade of online searching covering both European and United States systems, the author looks to the future which includes end user searching. Three reasons might motivate research scientists to do their own online searching: direct access to the literature, generation and development of ideas, and access to factual information. The role of the information scientist will change as a result of end user searching, but there will always be a need for an intermediary. End users will expect information scientists to provide training and search expertise on online searching.

Meadow, Charles T. "Online Searching and Computer Programming: Some Behavioral Similarities (Or . . . Why End Users Will Eventually Take Over the Terminal)." *Online* 3 (January 1979):49-52.

This "early" article on end user searching draws valid parallels with the development of computer programming. Just as computer programmers resisted development of higher-order languages and the advent of amateur programmers, so librarian search analysts are resisting the move to end user searching. The change is inevitable, and librarians will learn to accept their new role of handling "top of the line" searches. Training of reference librarians must change to meet the need for a higher level reference interview.

Nielsen, Brian. "Teacher or Intermediary: Alternative Professional Models in the Information Age." *College & Research Libraries* 43 (May 1982):183-91.

Reference service has been considered a "core professional task" for librarianship. The "information versus instruction" debate is based on opposite premises. The information side claims it is the librarians' role to deliver information "in as complete and digested a manner as possible," whereas the instruction side argues that users should be taught to find answers for themselves. The growth of online searching has reopened this debate, as database vendors begin to market searching directly to the end user. "Forging a new role model for reference librarianship requires first the disabusing of the idea that reference must be a 'core task' of a status-seeking profession." The librarian's new role will move toward the instruction side as end user searching increases in popularity.

Ojala, Marydee. "End User Searching and its Implications for Librarians." *Special Libraries* 76 (Spring 1985):93-9.

Some corporate librarians view end user searching as a threat, while others view it as a promise. Librarians are going through a difficult time of change; this, coupled with perceptions of diminished status, make some librarians fear the advent of end user searching. Ojala recommends that librarians set policies about end user searching before others set policies for them, and that librarians manage all passwords in the institution so as to maintain their coordinator's role. The author also suggests that "coexistence with end users is the best survival tactic."

O'Reilly, James C. "The Future Role of the Intermediary." *National Online Meeting Proceedings* (1984):259-64.

In May/June 1983, the Library and Information Services unit of the Electricity Supply Board, Ireland, conducted a survey of 1480 engineers and management, to evaluate patterns of information transfer in the organization. It was determined that there were serious barriers to information flow, that the library was underutilized, and that users were aware of newer technologies and preferred them to an intermediary. Conclusions were that the librarian's role is evolving to that of a consultant and trainer.

Peart, Peter A. "Online Retrieval: Intermediaries vs. End Users." *National Online Meeting Proceedings* (1985):357-63.

In an opinion paper, Peart states the case for the trained, experienced search intermediary. Mastering the retrieval process and the voluminous number of databases cannot be done overnight; what's more, keeping updated with new search techniques and databases is a full-time job. Despite the advent of the new user-friendly systems, the end user will continue to see the value of the search intermediary in saving the user time and money. "Besides, who can be more user-friendly than an intermediary professional?"

Somerville, Arleen N. "Evolving Roles of End-Users and Librarians in Academic Computer Searching." *Science & Technology Libraries* 5 (Winter 1984):45-50.

The results of a survey of twenty-two chemistry librarians at colleges and universities are presented. Librarians were asked questions related to their roles as search intermediaries and that of end users in searching online databases. Librarians see a continued role both as search intermediaries and as teachers and resource persons.

Stabler, Karen Chittick. "The Continuation of Librarians as Intermediaries." *National Online Meeting Proceedings* (1984):375-81.

Stabler contends that "librarians will continue to perform the key intermediary role in most online searching." The history of research in the U.S. is traced from the eighteenth century, through the development of indexing and abstracting services, to the librarian's role in providing bibliographic assistance with manual and online searching. While some research end users will do their own online searching, librarians will continue to provide the primary access to online databases because of the extensive knowledge needed to perform sophisticated searches and because of their experience with a variety of systems.

Wykoff, Leslie W. "Teaching Patrons to Search." *Medical Reference Services Quarterly* 4 (Summer 1985):57-61.

According to Wykoff, the issue regarding end user searching "is not whether patrons will search, but whether they will do 'good' searches." The term "patron searching" is used in this article rather than "end user searching" since the searchers are all patrons of the library. The librarian's new role will be to help patrons learn to search.

END USER SEARCHING IN THE HEALTH SCIENCES

Baker, Carole A. "COLLEAGUE: A Comprehensive Online Medical Library for the End User." *Medical Reference Services Quarterly* 3 (Winter 1984):13-26.

BRS/Saunders Colleague is an online information retrieval service intended for use by health professonals. Baker describes the various search capabilities and databases that can be searched via Colleague, and compares the system with BRS/AFTER DARK and the regular BRS SEARCH System. The article ends by discussing the role of the librarian in end user searching.

Barber, A. Stephanie; Barraclough, Elizabeth D.; and Gray, W. Alexander. "On-Line Information Retrieval as a Scientists Tool." *Information Storage and Retrieval* 9 (August 1973):429-40.

MEDUSA was a program "designed to allow physicians to interrogate the MEDLARS database." Physicians were able to interrogate five months of MEDLARS online; then, the search formulation was combined with that of a librarian and together, run in batch mode against the full database. Results, evaluated for recall and precision, showed "that physicians can use an on-line system effectively." This study, conducted before the advent of MEDLINE, shows early concern for the involvement of the end user in searching.

Beckley, Robert F., and Bleich, Howard L. "Paper Chase: A Computer-Based Reprint Storage and Retrieval System." *Computers and Biomedical Research* 10 (1977):423-30.

The system described here is the "forerunner" of the current commercially available PaperChase. The authors describe a computer program which is designed to store and retrieve citations from reprint collections. Each document is assigned subject words in addition to title words; these, along with the authors and journal, become keys to its retrieval. The program, written in MUMPS, runs on a PDP-15, PDP-11, Nova or ECLIPSE computer, uses Boolean logic, and can serve over twenty users simultaneously. Storage capacity allows up to four billion documents resulting in a 50 percent loss in search speed. The authors compare the system with MEDLINE.

Bleich, Howard L.; Jackson, Jerome D.; and Rosenberg, Howard A. "PaperChase: A Program to Search the Medical Literature." *MD Computing* 2 (March/April 1985):54-9.

PaperChase, a user-friendly, menu-driven computer program that allows the physician to access MEDLINE directly, has been used at Beth Israel Hospital, Boston, and Mount Auburn Hospital, Cambridge, Massachusetts, for over four years. PaperChase allows access to the literature by title word, MeSH, subheading, author's name, journal title, year of publication, or language of publication. Sample searches are presented, and detailed instructions for use of the system are given. An important feature of PaperChase allows the creation of a subset in which the library can specify institutional journal holdings.

Branden, Shirley, and Wehmeyer, Jeffrey M. "Do-it-Yourself Computer Searching: Launching an Educational Program for the End User Searcher." *Medical Reference Services Quarterly* 4 (Summer 1985):11-14.

Staff at the J. Hillis Miller Health Center Library, University of Florida, developed a course for users on how to get started doing their own searching. Information was provided on MEDLARS, DIALOG, and BRS, with emphasis on MEDLINE and the use of MeSH. Twenty-five participants attended the initial two-hour session. Librarians must be familiar with all health-related databases and all major search systems, whether or not they are available in the library, since end users will expect the librarian to be knowledgeable in these areas.

Broering, Naomi C. "The Georgetown University Library Information System (LIS): A Minicomputer-Based Integrated Library System." *Bulletin of the Medical Library Association* 71 (July 1984):317-23.

As of 1982, the Georgetown University Library Information System (LIS) "consisted of eight on-line components: the public catalog, circulation, serials control . . ., computer-assisted instruction (CAI), and bibliographic management, including a special feature called 'Mini-MEDLINE.' " System hardware and functional components of LIS are discussed. Of special interest is miniMEDLINE, which is discussed in more detail in a later article also by Broering.

Broering, Naomi C. "The Georgetown University Minicomputer and Microcomputer Versions of Library Information Systems (LIS)." *National Online Meeting Proceedings* (1984):37.

Of interest to end users is the miniMEDLINE system, a special component of the Library Information System (LIS). The special program "allows users to execute a bibliographic search of a selected portion of the MEDLINE database." Stand-alone versions of miniMEDLINE are also available. Only the abstract of the full paper is printed in the meeting proceedings.

Broering, Naomi C. "The miniMEDLINE SYSTEM: A Library-Based End-User Search System." *Bulletin of the Medical Library Association* 73 (April 1985):138-45.

The miniMEDLINE SYSTEM was developed in 1981 at the Georgetown University Medical Center. The database is a subset of MEDLINE, containing citations to articles in over 160 journals for the past three years. This user-friendly system is maintained on Georgetown's minicomputer and is directly searchable by end users through the Library Information System (LIS). This article discusses system planning and design, creation of the database through downloading, and use of the system over a two-year period. Eight other medical centers have subscribed to miniMEDLINE.

Clancy, Stephen. "BRS/Saunders Colleague: An Information Service for Medical Professionals." *Database* 8 (June 1985):108-21.

Aimed at the health professional, BRS/Saunders Colleague is a joint effort between BRS and Saunders Publishing. It is a menu-driven system that provides less expensive access to the full complement of databases available from the standard BRS SEARCH Service. Files are grouped into subject libraries, whose division appears linked to database royalty requirements. The mechanics of the system—command structure, print commands and formats, non-menu commands, command stacking, and other features—are presented with a description of the files on the Medical Search Service, the core of Colleague. The menus are presented, along with a sample MEDLINE search and a list of full-text materials in the Comprehensive Core Medical Library. An Appendix lists the Colleague Libraries and Databases.

Collen, Morris F., and Flagle, Charles D. "Full-Text Medical Literature Retrieved by Computer, a Pilot Test." *JAMA* 254 (November 15, 1985):2768-74.

A pilot test of MEDIS, a full-text medical literature retrieval service, was conducted for three months in 1984 at seven sites. Over 500 health care professionals conducted 9,377 searches; the purposes of the searches were for education and teaching, patient care, research, and browsing, in that order. About half the users indicated that they had found relevant documents despite the objective of the test being to evaluate the system's capabilities rather than the database's comprehensiveness. (At that time only 13 publications were available full text; MEDIS now has over 70 publications full text and is adding MEDLINE to its database). A majority (76 percent) said they would continue to use the system; of the 24 percent who said they would not continue to use MEDIS, "only one user preferred to use the library." The pilot test of full-text searching was considered successful. The only service limitation is the current inability to retrieve graphs and images.

Bader, Shelley; Harbert, Cathy; and Linton, Anne. "Searching Computer Databases from Your Office." *Internist* (October 1985): 23-4.

Sound advice is provided for internists who are planning to go online with their microcomputer. Hardware needs, databases, and online systems are described along with basic search mechanics. Physicians are given some parameters with which to evaluate systems, and a table outlines specifics on five vendors: AMA/NET, BRS/Saunders Colleague, PaperChase, KNOWLEDGE INDEX, and AMNET.

Doszkocs, Tamas E.; Rapp, Barbara A.; and Schoolman, Harold M. "Automated Information Retrieval in Science and Technology." *Science* 208 (April 1980):25-30.

The development over the past fifteen years of online databases, particularly those of the National Library of Medicine, is overviewed. Focus, of course, is on MEDLINE, although most of the NLM bibliographic and factual databases are mentioned. Limitations of retrieval systems are discussed, along with the need for a natural language-user interface. CITE, developed at NLM, is a prototype English-language interface to MEDLINE.

Givens, Mary King, and McDonell, W. Ellen. "End User Instructions for Searching MEDLARS." *Medical Reference Services Quarterly* 4 (Summer 1985):63-7.

The University of Tennessee Center for the Health Sciences Library, through a special project grant, developed a course to teach end users to search MEDLINE on the NLM system. Introductory reading of a *Mini-Manual* was required before a one and one-half hour lecture. Following the lecture, users were asked to schedule online practice time. During this hands-on session, searching mechanics and the conceptual aspects of search strategies were reinforced. Tips offered to others planning a similar project were to include evening or weekend hours because of scheduling conflicts and to consider staffing requirements.

Haynes, R. Bryan et al. "Computer Searching of the Medical Literature: An Evaluation of MEDLINE Search Systems." *Annals of Internal Medicine* 103 (November 1985):812-6.

Fourteen access routes to MEDLINE "were compared for retrieval quantity and quality, user and online search time, and cost for randomly ordered, standardized searches on common clinical problems." Librarians performed the searches, as the intent was not to evaluate searching expertise, but the systems. While all routes produced the articles that had been judged to be the most definitive, routes differed significantly with respect to online time, cost, and proportion of articles relevant to the topic. "The results showed that the higher the cost the worse the product," i.e., "systems with low specificity generally had much higher search costs and times." MEDLINE accessed directly from NLM on non-prime time performed the best, i.e., lowest cost and online time and highest relevance, while PaperChase accessed at night had the highest cost and online time with lowest relevance. Rated next to NLM "at night" was BRS/AFTER DARK. Users who anticipate searching MEDLINE frequently were advised to learn the NLM system directly. This study should provide valuable and practical advice for end users who are still deciding on a method of access to MEDLINE.

Henderson, Brian. "Computers and Medicine: The Physician On Line." *Canadian Medical Association Journal* 131 (November 15, 1984):1286, 1288-9, 1292.

Physicians are now using computers for office management and record keeping, but through interactive databases, they can expand their information resources. The article focuses on vendors such as CompuServe and The Source, but also mentions AMA/NET. A list of portable computers with built-in modems is given.

Hewison, Nancy S. "Whatever Shall We Do About User-Friendly Online?" *Medical Reference Services Quarterly* 2 (Winter 1983): 67-70.

Librarians may wonder why users want to do their own searches when "we have done such a good job of it for them." A variety of explanations, from the need for privacy to the fact that online searching is fun, can be postulated to explain the growing demand for user-friendly systems. Librarians can respond with a variety of approaches, from ignoring it and hoping that "it will go away," to actively seeking information about user-friendly systems and disseminating this information to their patrons. The latter role, of active participation and self-education, will place the librarian in a prominent position as information provider, consultant, and educator. Librarians who ignore the trend to end user searching do so at their own peril.

Hildenbrand, Suzanne. "End User Satisfaction With Computerized Bibliographic Searches in Women's Studies: Preliminary Report of an Investigation." *National Online Meeting Proceedings* (1985): 215-9.

Free online searches in the area of women's studies were performed for researchers at SUNY at Buffalo. In this case, "end user satisfaction" would be more properly termed "user satisfaction," since searches were actually performed by the search intermediary. Persons requesting the searches were asked to evaluate results by means of a questionnaire. In an analysis of variance in levels of satisfaction, only 32 percent of satisfaction levels could be accounted for by two variables: number of citations retrieved and percent of relevant citations retrieved.

Horowitz, Gary L., and Bleich, Howard L. "PaperChase: A Computer Program to Search the Medical Literature." *New England Journal of Medicine* 305 (October 15, 1981):924-30.

Horowitz and Bleich describe PaperChase, a user-friendly computer program developed at Beth Israel Hospital in Boston. The program permits searching MEDLINE by author, title word, or medical subject heading. The mechanics of the system are discussed, and sample searches used to illustrate the capabilities of the program. A unique feature of PaperChase is that it is built on a subset of MEDLINE, based on the library's subscription holdings. The database contains 400,000 references covering eight years. Search statistics (1032 users, 8459 searches) are analyzed for the first year of operation, and user reactions are discussed. Searches are available free of charge.

Horowitz, Gary L.; Jackson, Jerome D.; and Bleich, Howard L. "PaperChase; Self-Service Bibliographic Retrieval." *JAMA* 250 (November 11, 1983):2494-9.

Use of PaperChase at Beth Israel Hospital over the past three years has shown a steady, dramatic increase. Users (3,654 individuals) have taken advantage of the free searching by performing 39,022 searches. This article builds on an earlier article published in the *New England Journal of Medicine*, describing advances and modifications of the system and how the program helps the user select appropriate terms. For example, the program matches a user's entry to an author's name, journal name, title word or MeSH term; interprets spelling variants; points from title words to MeSH terms; and finds MeSH terms of further interest.

Ifshin, Steven L., and Hull, Deborah M. "CAI Plus: A Strategy for Colleague Training." *National Online Meeting Proceedings* (1985): 233-40.

BRS/Saunders Colleague is a user-friendly menu-driven system designed for the health professional. Colleague staff have taken a user-oriented training approach for their system. The program was geared to five planning criteria: flexibility, accessibility, consistency, relevance, and modular design. "Self-instructional materials meet all of the above planning criteria." The two formats chosen were computer-assisted instruction (CAI) and workbooks. For group training, slides provide a third format. The CAI programs are available on diskettes and online. The initial diskette, Colleague Basics, consists of six modules which all relate to an initial "Case module." Beta-testing at eleven sites resulted in positive feedback.

Kirby, Martha, and Miller, Naomi. "MEDLINE Searching on BRS Colleague: Search Success of Untrained End Users in a Medical School and Hospital." *National Online Meeting Proceedings* (1985):255-63.

BRS Colleague was used experimentally at the Medical College of Pennsylvania and Hospital to evaluate relevance of retrieval by end users versus search intermediaries. End users were given no prior training. Users were not asked to evaluate precision and recall, but to determine whether the intermediary's search added essential information. The "bottom line" was that in 42 percent of the fifty-two searches, the untrained user felt that nothing was added; however, 60 percent felt that the second search, produced by the intermediary, was better. Users focused on the Colleague "Biomedical Library" files. Generally, users found Colleague to be easy to use. The full questionnaire, with responses, is presented.

Lancaster, F. Wilfrid. "Evaluation of On-Line Searching in MEDLARS (AIM-TWX) by Biomedical Practitioners." *University of Illinois Graduate School of Library Science Occasional Papers* No. 101, February 1972. 20pp.

A test was conducted at four MEDLARS centers from November 1970 to February 1971 of the National Library of Medicine's new online ELHILL system, AIM-TWX. Health practitioners were asked to conduct their own searches, which were later compared for precision and recall to those of a trained analyst. Librarians could offer help only on the mechanical aspects of the search; users had to determine vocabulary and search strategies themselves. A detailed analysis, including personal observations by the author, indicated that most users "were able to conduct productive searches," and that good documentation for using the system is needed. AIM-TWX fills a definite need, but system improvements are needed. Overall, this is a classic study of the forerunner of MEDLINE.

Olson, Paul E. "Mechanization of Library Procedures in the Medium-Sized Medical Library: XV. A Study of the Interaction of Nonlibrarian Searchers with the MEDLINE Retrieval System." *Bulletin of the Medical Library Association* 63 (January 1975):35-41.

A study of sixteen nonlibrarian searches on MEDLINE was conducted at Washington University School of Medicine. The searchers averaged 5.7 modifications per search, which allowed the null hypothesis (that the number of modifications would be greater than three) to be accepted. The conclusion was that nonlibrarians "can and do use the interactive capabilities of MEDLINE."

Sewell, Winifred, and Bevan, Alice. "Nonmediated Use of MEDLINE and TOXLINE by Pathologists and Pharmacists." *Bulletin of the Medical Library Association* 64 (October 1976):382-91.

In one of the earlier end user studies, Sewell and Bevan describe the use of MEDLINE and TOXLINE by pathologists and pharmacists at the University of Maryland Health Sciences Center. While the results are preliminary, nonmediated use is divided into "intensive" and "occasional" use by the scientists. Concepts discussed include use of a controlled vocabulary, training needs, and system design. The authors have developed a minimanual as a quick reference tool.

Sewell, Winifred, and Teitelbaum, Sandra. "Preliminary Observations of Nonmediated Search Behavior of Pathologists and Pharmacists." *Proceedings of the 45th Annual Meeting of the American Society for Information Science* 19 (1982):276-8.

Pathologists and pharmacists at the University of Maryland Health Sciences Center have performed nearly 4,000 searches on NLM databases (primarily on MEDLINE) at terminals in their work areas from 1976 to 1980. A 10 percent sample and a longitudinal study of "heavy" users was done; searches were analyzed in six areas: complexity, sophistication, printing patterns, author searches, subject areas, and individual databases. Complexity was studied through the use of Boolean operators and the explode command, and sophistication was measured by success or failure with system commands. The most common error was the "missed opportunity," or failure to use the EXPLODE command. "Preliminary conclusions are that end users do very well with searching NLM databases by themselves if the terminals are readily available to them and they understand a few basic conventions." System improvements will have a positive effect on nonmediated searching.

Slingluff, Deborah; Lev, Yvonne, and Eisan, Andrew. "An End User Search Service in an Academic Health Sciences Library." *Medical Reference Services Quarterly* 4 (Spring 1985):11-21.

The University of Maryland Health Sciences Library added BRS/ AFTER DARK to complement its mediated search service. The decision to add the service is documented, along with policy and procedure decisions, publicity, and the development of instructional areas. AFTER DARK users used primarily MEDLINE (50 percent of searches), with SOCIAL SCISEARCH, PsychINFO and ERIC, being the next most popular databases. Problems were either mechanical, i.e., related to the terminal, or intellectual, e.g. conceptual problems such as understanding database structure or Boolean logic.

Snow, Bonnie. "DIALOG Seminar for Medical Professionals." *National Online Meeting Proceedings* (1984):367-74.

The "DIALOG Seminar for Medical Professionals" was developed specifically to train health sciences end users to search MEDLINE on DIALOG. Condensed into a one-day session because of the limited time available to health professionals, the seminar covers basic DIALOG commands and searching essentials for the MEDLINE file. Information contained in the *MeSH* tools have been modified, enhanced, and adapted for use by the end user. Course materials are modular and are designed to encourage the health professional to use printed search tools to plan his search strategy. Explosions and subheadings are among the more difficult concepts for the end user to comprehend. Problems initially identified in developing the course were: "barriers in vocabulary, time investment, credibility (product- versus people-orientation), and philosophy/ motivation (vocational versus avocational use)."

Snow, Bonnie. "Making the Rough Places Plain: Designing MEDLINE End User Training." *Medical Reference Services Quarterly* 3 (Winter 1984):1-11.

Snow discusses the need for designing appropriate educational materials for training the end user. Examples are taken from DIALOG's Seminar for Medical Professionals. Materials designed for the search intermediary may not be appropriate for the end user, and modifications may be necessary. The author encourages teaching MeSH and all of its capabilities, including tree structure, explosions, and subheadings. Modular training materials are recommended. This article is useful for those searchers who are faced with in-house development of training materials.

Soben, Phyllis, and Tidball, Charles S. "***MEDLEARN***: An Orientation to MEDLINE." *Bulletin of the Medical Library Association* 62 (April 1974):92-4.

MEDLEARN was developed to help the biomedical community learn to use MEDLINE. The orientation program has four objectives: the student must understand program cues and responses, must be able to issue commands, must be able to use *MeSH*, and must be able to handle the mechanical aspects of interaction with the system. ***MEDLEARN*** is designed with plenty of user participation. Tests at five centers have resulted in positive reaction to the program.

Teitelbaum, Sandra, and Sewell, Winifred. "Survey of Attitudes of Pathologists and Pharmacists Toward Nonmediated Online Searching." *Proceedings of the Annual Meeting of the American Society for Information Science* 19 (1982):298-300.

A questionnaire was sent to pathologists and pharmacists who perform their own online searching at the University of Maryland at Baltimore. Results indicated that the primary use was for a few good recent references. Other uses included author searches, keeping up-to-date, and searching for general reviews. Most users learned to search from colleagues and by trial and error, rather than through formal instruction. In response to why they preferred searching for themselves, convenience was the primary reason, followed by "faster, cheaper and more enjoyable," in that order. Respondents indicated that library searches were preferable for comprehensive bibliographies.

Tousignant, Dwight R. "Online Literature-Retrieval Systems: How to Get Started." *American Journal of Hospital Pharmacy* 40 (February 1983):230-9.

Tousignant has synthesized all of the basic information needed for a pharmacist to understand the concept of online searching and to evaluate the possibility of going online for himself. "The equipment, expense involved, and training necessary to perform online searching efficiently is described." The four major vendors (DIALOG, BRS, SDC, and NLM) are compared, and step-by-step procedures of logging in and searching are presented. The International Pharmaceutical Abstracts database is used as an example of searching online versus using its printed counterpart. While the pharmacist could apply the information supplied here to accessing online systems through an intermediary, the intent is obviously to encourage direct, end user access of the systems.

END USER SEARCHING IN ACADEMIC INSTITUTIONS

Bodtke-Roberts, Alice. "Faculty End User Searching of BIOSIS." *National Online Meeting Proceedings* (1983):45-56.

Ten science faculty at the University of California, Riverside, participated in a library research project on end user searching. The faculty were trained by staff of DIALOG and BIOSIS. Free search time was offered for four months, after which the faculty had to pay for searching. The library staff observed the searching (directly or via the printouts) and interviewed the involved faculty. Use significantly dropped off after the initial four months. The most influential factor in use versus non-use of online searching was the "existing patterns of organizing work of their labs . . ." Researchers who did not see the "added value" of online searching over their already existing methods were less inclined to search.

Corcoran, Maureen; Copeland, Richard; and Clayton, Dennis. "Subject Specialists Searching Chemical Abstracts on SDC." *Proceedings of the 43rd Annual Meeting of the American Society for Information Science* 17 (1980):345-7.

This study was concerned with the quality of searches performed by an end user or occasional searcher. "Twelve chemistry researchers with three levels of background in online searching . . . were tested to determine what might help the occasional searcher get optimum results." As a result of the controlled experiment, the decision was made to focus on search strategy construction and vocabulary development. The intent is to use the findings to design a computerized prompting system to help search Chemical Abstracts on SDC.

Crooks, James E. "End User Searching at the University of Michigan Library." *National Online Meeting Proceedings* (1985): 99-110.

The University of Michigan Library conducted a study on end user searching of BRS/AFTER DARK. During the Fall term of 1984, faculty, staff and students were offered use of BRS/AFTER DARK at no cost in three of the campus libraries. Most users received no instruction prior to their search session, although help was available from librarians during the session. All users were asked to complete a questionnaire. In addition to the questionnaires, data came from the appointment schedule, monitors' diaries, and notes by the reference librarian. Data analysis was not completed in time for publication.

Davidson, Lloyd A., and Hurd, Julie M. "Characteristics of CAS-Online Academic Plan Endusers: A Comparative Study Between Academic Institutions and Between Groups Within the Same Institution." *Proceedings of the 48th Annual Meeting of the American Society for Information Science* 22 (1985):225-8.

At Northwestern University, the Chemistry Department, in cooperation with the Library, contracted for the CAS-Online Academic Plan, which provides unlimited searching for a reduced, flat rate. Librarians provided training to end users, consisting of one and one-half hours of lecture and forty-five minutes of online demonstration. Because of initial high demand, only a general, brief introduction was given, with users expected to obtain more specific and advanced information from the manuals. In comparing types of searching at Northwestern (NU) versus four other schools, the low utilization of substructure searching at NU was evident. This was attributed to the general teaching methods used at NU. Almost all of the end user searchers at NU were graduate students. Although the data are still incomplete, one major conclusion is "that training should be aimed at specific subdisciplines of chemistry rather than giving all chemists the same general introduction."

Ensor, Pat, and Curtis, Richard A. "Search Helper: Low-Cost Online Searching in an Academic Library." *RQ* 23 (Spring 1984): 327-31.

Search Helper is a user-friendly software package that can be used to search Information Access Company databases on DIALOG. The software allows construction of the search prior to logging on to the system, thus saving line time and communications charges. At California State University Long Beach (CSULB), librarians are using the package to perform low-cost searches for undergraduates. Future plans at CSULB are to make the system available to the end user. Search Helper has greatest potential in academic and public libraries because of the databases available through the service.

Evans, Nancy, and Pisciotta, Henry. "Search Helper: Testing Acceptance of a Gateway Software System." *National Online Meeting Proceedings* (1985):131-6.

Search Helper, a gateway program that accesses Information Access Company databases on DIALOG, was made available free of charge on a test basis at the Carnegie-Mellon University Libraries. Little or no assistance was given to the users. A simple questionnaire was used to evaluate user satisfaction. Results showed a high level of satisfaction with the system. Users indicated that they would use the system again. On a scale of 0 to $250, users would be willing to pay $1.00 for a search. Interestingly, 33 percent retrieved more than twenty hits (Search Helper allows only twenty hits, so this group had to "reconnect" to the database to retrieve over twenty hits), and 30 percent found no citations at all. Both of these groups probably would have benefitted from assistance. Nearly two-thirds of the users "reported that less than half or none of the citations looked useful"; despite this, they were still satisfied with Search Helper. System users strongly preferred "online help to printed manuals or other sources of assistance," thus indicating that the system should be self-documenting.

Fjällbrant, Nancy; Kihlén, Elisabeth; and Malmgren, Margareta. "End-User Training in the Use of a Small Swedish Database." *College & Research Libraries* 44 (March 1983):161-7.

Librarians at the Chalmers University of Technology taught a group of engineering undergraduates to carry out online searching on BYGGDOK, a bibliographic database containing references in fields such as architecture, building, civil engineering, and environmental technology. The goals and teaching methods are discussed, along with an evaluation of the results of a questionnaire. Search results of the end users were compared to those of a search intermediary. Recall for the end users was high, but not as good as for the intermediary, while precision for the end users was considerably lower than that of the intermediary.

Friend, Linda. "Independence at the Terminal: Training Student End Users to Do Online Literature Searching." *Journal of Academic Librarianship* 11 (July 1985):136-41.

An experimental program, training twenty-five graduate-level educational psychology students in searching BRS/AFTER DARK, was conducted at the Pennsylvania State University. The program was begun in July 1984 and was underwritten by the academic department. Students were given an introductory lecture and presearch counseling before accessing BRS/AFTER DARK. A post-session questionnaire documented the students' positive reaction to all aspects of the program: training, BRS/AFTER DARK system features, and potential for future use of the system. The role of the librarian as search consultant is discussed.

Garman, Nancy J., and Pask, Judith M. "End User Searching in Business and Management." *National Online Meeting Proceedings* (1985):161-5.

Librarians at Purdue University trained a small group of finance students, as part of an investment class, to search Dow Jones News/Retrieval Service. A group of twenty students from the larger class was selected to participate in special assignments using computers for investment analysis. The assignment given to the students required them to access four databases on Dow Jones. Two students working together were allowed forty-five minutes to complete their assignment. Students expressed satisfaction with the system and indicated that handouts and the class textbook had adequately prepared them for their search. Teaching online searching skills to business students is consistent with the business school's mission statement that emphasizes "computers as an integral part of today's management environment."

Goold, Karla Pearce. "Old (and Young) Dogs Learn New Tricks: A CAS-Online Academic Program Case Study." *Proceedings of the 48th Annual Meeting of the American Society for Information Science* 22 (1985):255-7.

CAS-Online had not been well received by faculty at the University of Notre Dame. In the fall of 1984, "a twelve-week course to students and faculty in chemistry and chemical engineering" was successfully offered using a "second chance" offer from the CAS-Online Academic Program. The specific course content, results of searching by the course participants, and costs are all presented. After the course, a 90 percent discount from CAS allowed the library to continue to offer the service to end users. The course will be offered again jointly by the library and the Chemistry Department.

Grotophorst, Clyde W. "Training University Faculty as End-Use Searchers: A CAI Approach." *National Online Meeting Proceedings* (1984):77-82.

Librarians at the Fenwick Library, George Mason University, have developed a computer-assisted program, "Search Trainer," which is designed to train end users to search DIALOG or BRS. The package, written in BASIC for the IBM PC, consists of seven modules: what is online searching, search strategy, DIALOG commands, BRS/AFTER DARK commands, databases by subject area, and logging on. Consultation services plus availability of BRS/AFTER DARK passwords to end users are also part of the training.

Halperin, Michael, and Pagell, Ruth A. "Free 'Do-It Yourself' Online Searching . . . What to Expect." *Online* 9 (March 1985): 82-4.

The Lippincott Library of the Wharton School, University of Pennsylvania, offers free online searching to end users. Two systems, Executive Information Service and BRS/AFTER DARK, are used. Over 1,200 searches were done in eight months. Despite the service being "do-it-yourself," a great deal of staff time is needed for logging on, signing up, providing documentation, and conceptual help. Students responded favorably to a questionnaire, indicating that they had received adequate assistance, were satisfied with usefulness of the results, and found the system easy to use. End users felt that a trained analyst could not have retrieved more useful information. Most users (62 percent) were willing to pay from $1 to $5 for their search.

Holloway, Clark, and Meadows, Nolan R. "Searching the Business Literature by Computer." *Business and Economic Review* 28 (December 1981):31-8.

The basics of online searching in the business literature are presented. The searching technique, including use of Boolean operators, is illustrated with a sample formulation on ABI/INFORM. Advantages and disadvantages of online retrieval are discussed from the authors' personal experience. Since only a few universities "train their graduate students to do their own searches," researchers may wish to consult the library. A selected list of business files, including subject coverage and size, is given.

Hurt, C.S. "Intermediaries, Self-Searching and Satisfaction." *National Online Meeting Proceedings* (1983):231-8.

Data were collected from two academic libraries to determine user preferences for searches done by search intermediaries versus searches done by self searchers. The hypothesis, that the intermediaries performed better searches, could not be rejected. The analysis presented is highly statistical; the conclusion was that there was a statistically significant difference in the search satisfaction of the intermediary versus the other methods tested. The preference for a search intermediary appeared to be related to the self searcher's problems in handling the search system protocols.

Janke, Richard V. "BRS/After Dark: The Birth of Online Self-Service." *Online* 7 (September 1983):12-29.

The initial part of this article is a description and comparison of BRS/AFTER DARK and DIALOG's KNOWLEDGE INDEX. The major part of the article discusses a pilot project survey of end users using BRS/AFTER DARK at the University of Ottawa. While the results must be viewed as preliminary, the overwhelmingly positive and enthusiastic response of the end users "points to a new era in online searching." One major conclusion of the survey was that most users are looking only for "a few key references on their topic." The full questionnaire and results are presented in appendices. Janke predicts that by 1986 the "electronic home library will very likely be fully established."

Janke, Richard V. "Online After Six: End User Searching Comes of Age." *Online* 8 (November 1984):15-29.

Janke discusses the rapid expansion of end user searching, in particular BRS/AFTER DARK, and details the implementation of "Online After Six," as the service is called at the University of Ottawa. Preparation for the service included a cost study, detailing of regulations for use, training of the librarians, and publicity. A survey evaluated user satisfaction, and implications for libraries are discussed. This study found that a pre- and/or post-search counseling service is essential to aid the end user in constructing his search, Boolean logic, and search mechanics. An extensive bibliography on end user searching is appended.

Janke, Richard V. "Presearch Counseling for Client Searchers (End-Users)." *Online* 9 (September 1985):13-26.

Presearch counseling for end users has both similarities to and differences from the reference interview, which are outlined in this article. Janke guides the reader through thirteen steps in a presearch counseling session, including: explaining regulations or policies applying to online self-service, explaining costs, explaining Boolean logic, and using a pathfinder to illustrate the search process. An appended bibliography updates an earlier bibliography on end user searching.

Kleiner, Jane P. "User Searching: A Public Access Approach to Search Helper." *RQ* 24 (Summer 1985):442-51.

The reference department at Louisiana State University made Search Helper available for direct access by users. The user-friendly information retrieval system provides access via DIALOG to six Information Access Company databases. Over an eleven-month period from April 1983 to February 1984 the system was accessed 287 times, with users paying a $2.00 fee. In March 1984, to use up the subscription, free searching was offered, resulting in 337 subject searches. Several barriers to use were cited, including software problems and staff attitude. In fact, lack of staff support appeared to be a major factor in this study. This system is geared more to public and academic libraries.

Lucia, Joseph, and Roysdon, Christine. "Online Searching as an Educational Technology: Teaching Computer-Wise End Users." *National Online Meeting Proceedings* (1984):187-93.

Librarians at Lehigh University conducted a one-week, one-credit workshop in online searching for end users in July 1983. Participants were trained to search on BRS, with emphasis on education files. After the course, the eight students expressed no hesitancy about conducting searches in the future should the need arise. Six months after the course, students had not run any searches themselves. Barriers to searching were determined to be lack of a password and lack of the necessary equipment.

Schwerzel, Sharon W.; Emerson, Susan V.; and Johnson, David L. "Self-Evaluation of Competencies in Online Searching by End-Users after Basic Training." *Proceedings of the 45th Annual Meeting of the American Society for Information Science* 19 (1982):272-5.

Twelve graduate students were taught both online and manual bibliographic search skills. A focused group interview and questionnaires were used to evaluate their skill level. Of the three competency areas, highest confidence was expressed by the students in their ability to perform the search mechanics. They were less confident in selecting databases, and least confident in the formulation of searches. Unfortunately, the search design is marred by the overall teaching methods, lack of a control group, and lack of a follow-up.

Smith, Rita H., and Phillips, Linda L. "Search Helper: An Online Service for Undergraduates." *Reference Services Review* 12 (Fall 1984):31-4.

Search Helper, a user-friendly, menu-driven program which provides access to six IAC databases on DIALOG, was offered as a routine reference service to undergraduates at the University of Tennessee, Knoxville. Initially, librarians performed the searches, but after four months, students were allowed to run their own searches aided by printed instructions and advice from the reference staff. Limiting factors were that only one search could be conducted at one time, using only one database at a time (thus, multiple database searching yielded a higher cost to the student); that the Boolean operations "or" and "not" could not be used; that citations printed were limited to the most recent fifteen (modified on a newer version); and the fact that it was limited to only six databases. Overall, however, the program was successful. "Search Helper is one of the first products designed to make online database searching feasible for undergraduate students. . ."

Struminger, Leny. "Teaching Information Science Students Using an Electronic Classroom." *National Online Meeting Proceedings* (1985):451-6.

An electronic classroom is used at Rutgers University's School of Communication, Information and Library Studies to teach the basics of "Information and Communication Technology, and "Computer-based Information Systems." In the first course, a DIALOG simulation program is used, along with the Ontap ERIC file on DIALOG to demonstrate online searching. In the second course, various programs are used (Wordstar, Dbase II, and Personal Bibliographic System), along with In-Search. While these are future information professionals who are being trained, similar methods could be used to train end users.

Trzebiatowski, Elaine. "End User Study on BRS/After Dark." *RQ* 23 (Summer 1984):446-50.

This is a limited experiment with twenty first-time end users to evaluate their reactions to searching BRS/AFTER DARK. Questionnaires were used to gather background information on skills such as computer expertise and typing ability, and to evaluate their reactions to performing online searches. Reactions to the BRS/AFTER DARK system were positive; an analysis of the end user's performance on the system included both mechanical and conceptual problems. Librarians can anticipate an increased role as consultants to end users.

Ward, Sandra N. "Course-Integrated DIALOG Instruction." *Research Strategies* 3 (Spring 1985):52-64.

Hands-on DIALOG labs were integrated into three different Stanford University courses for undergraduates: Library 1, a library-oriented course; HB112, a Human Biology Seminar which included two hands-on labs during class time; and HB40, a Health Biology course for which one 50-minute out-of-class lab was developed. The article focuses on the practical aspects of organizing the fifty-minute laboratory for the latter course. The lab course is outlined. Students and faculty were pleased with the results. Repetition of the course will be affected by funding, changes in faculty, and DIALOG 2. While the fifty-minute course is "do-able," the author prefers the two-lab model used in HB112.

Ward, Sandra N., and Osegueda, Laura M. "Teaching University End-Users About Online Searching." *Science & Technology Libraries* 5 (Fall 1984):17-31.

Librarians at Stanford University and San Jose State University describe end user programs at each of their institutions. At Stanford, searching is taught as part of a formal library course and also as part of two Human Biology courses. At San Jose State, searching is taught in Biology and Psychology courses. The objectives of the instruction include: to teach about online searching in general, rather than specifics; to use databases as examples without expecting future use of the specific database; *not* to produce self-sufficient end users; to use online searching to attract interest in other reference tools; and to make the course modular for use in other courses. Specific course descriptions are given, along with details of implementation, such as funding and facilities.

Wiggins, Gary. "The Indiana University Chemical Information Specialist Program: Training the Library User and the Librarian." *Science & Technology* 1 (Spring 1981):5-11.
    Students at the Indiana University School of Library and Information Science, in cooperation with the Chemistry Department, can obtain an MLS with a specialization in chemical information. Online searching is taught as part of the program. Students must formulate an SDI profile in CA Search. Chemistry undergraduate students, eventual "end users," can enroll in the course.

Wilson, John H., Jr. "Transportable Courses to Train Undergraduate Scientists and Engineers the Skills of Online Retrieval." *National Online Meeting Proceedings* (1984):453-6.
    Southern University and the University of Southwestern Louisiana will be jointly undertaking a project suggested by NASA to develop a "set of transportable courses: a full semester course, a mini course (6 weeks), and a brief, intensive workshop (2 or 3 days)." The database to be used for the course assignments is NASA/RECON.

END USER SEARCHING IN CORPORATIONS

Arnold, Stephen. "Hard Lessons About End Users." *National Online Meeting Proceedings* (1985):11-8.
    The term "end user" has been in use since 1971, but has only been popularized over the past five years. The online industry talks about end users, but the group "has not been identified and many in the information industry are not yet communicating effectively with this important market." Three major business information providers, Dow Jones News/Retrieval, Dun's Marketing Services, and Data Courier decided to investigate the end user market by sponsoring a two-hour program, which would provide a two-way exchange of information. Some lessons learned were: "end users

don't recognize themselves by this name," "information-consumers are tough to locate," overheads and handouts wouldn't suffice for the level of professionals attending these workshops, and "getting attendees costs lots of money." In many cases, the "end user" ended up sending the librarian to these sessions, since the librarian is a powerful figure in many corporations. "The lesson is to never forget the intermediary and corporate library."

Dagoni, Ron. "On-Line Literature Searching Catches on Among Researchers." *Chemical and Engineering News* 62 (May 7, 1984): 29-30.

This brief news report gets at the fundamentals of end user searching, from training to benefits. Information specialists at corporations across the U.S. are quoted about their training programs and the benefits of end user searching. One company offers basic training which includes "terminal operations, system commands, Boolean logic, and database organization within the computer." According to another information specialist, "learning the search system itself is a piece of cake"; the real problem is understanding the database, i.e., *Chemical Abstracts*. The need for constant practice to avoid relearning is mentioned.

Fogel, Laurence D., and Zigmund, Claire F. "End User vs. Intermediary: A Personal Perspective." *National Online Meeting Proceedings* (1985):153-9.

A situation is described at the American Cyanamid Company, where a member of the Chemical Research Division was assigned to work on a special project with the Technical Information Services Department. The assignment gradually evolved into a liaison between these two departments and the Patent Law Department. This liaison, or "end user," is now viewed as an Information Consultant, whereas the intermediary is the Information Specialist. Unfortunately, the "end user" reported here is not a true end user, as he is interpreting information for others; it appears that another "layer" has been added to the information management process.

Haines, Judith S. "Experiences in Training End-User Searchers." *Online* 6 (November 1982):14-23.

The Department of Information Services of the Kodak Research Laboratories in Rochester initiated an end user searching program in 1979 at the request of the Organic Research Laboratory. The searching was done on DIALOG, primarily on CA Search, and the most frequent use was to find references on the preparation or use of specific compounds. End users averaged more time and expense online than did the information staff. Recommendations from the pilot project include working with volunteers rather than "draftees," obtaining appropriate equipment prior to training, locating the equipment in the end user's office or laboratory, and holding several short training sessions rather than a full day workshop.

Leipzig, Nancy; Kozak, Marlene Galante; and Schwartz, Ronald D. "Experiences with End User Searching at a Pharmaceutical Company." *National Online Meeting Proceedings* (1983):325-32.

Searching at American Critical Care, a pharmaceutical division of the American Hospital Supply Corporation, began as end user searching. Users search three systems: NLM; AMANDA, an in-house, user-friendly document storage and retrieval system; and Derwent's Chemical Reactions Document Service database. Experience with end users indicates that they "prefer to 'think' online, resist use of a thesaurus, dislike typing, have trouble remembering commands, and prefer to delegate complicated and comprehensive searches to information professionals." For end user searching to be more popular, system enhancements are needed. To make searching easier, more full-text files would assure answers online rather than just references, and microcomputers will need to be commonplace equipment.

Lescohier, R.S.; Lavin, M.A.; and Landsberg, M.K. "Database Development and End-User Searching, Exxon Research and Engineering Company. *Science & Technology Libraries* 5 (Fall 1984): 1-15.

Although Research & Engineering Information Services (REIS) at Exxon have been involved in teaching online bibliographic searching to their chemists, this article describes their "experiences with providing local access to proprietary information for end users at our engineering facility." In Phase I, identifying user needs and databases, REIS made three recommendations: "(1) implementation of a customized online bibliographic database, (2) less dependency upon the engineers to maintain the system, and (3) more detailed indexing of documents in the collection." A fairly detailed description is given of the system which was implemented. Phase II involved end user training for the in-house system. Searching tools were prepared, including a manual, a quick-reference guide, and customized searching aids. Training took place in three parts: a thirty-minute oral presentation, followed by a thirty-minute online demonstration, and an hour-long hands-on practice session. Over 90 percent of the department participated in the classes.

Neelameghan, A., and Pascua-Cruz, Ma. Divina. "Online Access to Remote Data Bases: An Experiment in User Sensitization." *Journal of Information Science; Principles and Practice* 7 (October 1983):105-15.

The role of the user of online information services is discussed in reference to developing countries. While searching by the end user is mentioned, the actual focus is on making the user aware of online systems. A three-week series of lectures by experts in the online field on a variety of systems (most from the United States) was presented to forty-five information specialists and subject specialists from twelve developing countries. Responding to a questionnaire, scientists were quite positive in their reaction to the online systems.

Pritcher, Pamela N. "Strategies for Training the Information End User: Training the Manager How to Use Information." *National Online Meeting Proceedings* (1985):365-76.

The MARS (Market Analysis Research System) Information Management System is a database "designed to monitor the changing telecommunications industry and its market." Developed by Bell Communications Research, it supports the information needs of marketing and research strategy professionals within the company. Training tools include printed workbooks, overheads, and hands-on exercises. Training is modular, moving from an introduction to MARS to advanced concepts, covering everything from conceptual aspects of information retrieval to database structure to searching commands.

Richardson, Robert J. "End-User Online Searching in a High-Technology Engineering Environment." *Online* 5 (October 1981): 44-57.

A limited, initial study of end user searching in a high technology industrial environment was conducted by Raytheon Company and DIALOG Information Services, Inc. The purpose was to see if engineers and scientists will use online searching to support their daily work. During the one-year experiment, the majority of expenses were subsidized by the database producers, NTIS, COMPENDEX and the INSPEC group. Use throughout the study was much lower than expected; after the experiment, only six of the original twenty participants continued to search directly. The overall study design was not intended to be comprehensive or statistically significant; many of the conclusions are based on assumptions and speculation.

Rudin, Joan; Hausele, Nancy; Stollak, Jay; and Sonk, Joseph. "Comparison of In-Search, Scimate and an Intelligent Terminal Emulator in Biomedical Literature Searching." *National Online Meeting Proceedings* (1985):403-8.

Librarians at Smith Kline and Beckman evaluated three "gateway" software packages: In-Search, Sci-Mate, and SoftermPC. The first two are menu-driven, commercially-produced packages; the latter is an intelligent terminal emulator into which some gateway functions can be programmed. All three packages were evaluated based on: ease of use, support available, cost-effectiveness, and suitability for both library professionals and end users. Sci-Mate was by far the most flexible. Since the three programs were generally comparable in other features, "the final decision then becomes cost."

Shelton, Anita L., and Scharf, Davida. "Online Database Documentation for End User Training." *National Online Meeting Proceedings* (1985):415-9.

With the advent of user searching, there is an increased need for enhanced documentation. A survey of end users in business and research organizations revealed that they are task- or goal-oriented, that they usually lack formal training in searching, that they usually search a small number of databases, and that they tend to use databases sporadically. "Formal documentation can be neither eliminated nor replaced by flashcards, pocket guides, and online tutorials, but access will be simplified and enhanced by new instructional devices."

Stewart, Concetta M., and Usenko, Lydia. "Videotex: Addressing the Information Needs of the Corporate End User." *Proceedings of the 48th Annual Meeting of the American Society for Information Science* 22 (1985):73-6.

Information is a strategic resource in the corporate world, and end user searching appears "to be a reasonable answer to the problems of timeliness, accuracy, availability, and quantity." End user searching in the corporate world is briefly overviewed. Videotex is suggested as a user-friendly database management system. The technology of videotex is discussed along with its use in the corporation.

Tatalias, Jean. "Attitudes and Expectations of Potential End User Online Searchers." *National Online Meeting* (1985):457-62.

Attitudes and expectations toward end user searching were assessed by a survey of one hundred end users of online searching in a corporate environment. Based on the survey, an end user program would be well-received "because of the high level of interest in end user searching, the high level of familiarity with Boolean logic, and the high level of availability of computer equipment and systems." Also rated as high were user needs for menu options, database selection and thesauri.

Walton, Kenneth R., and Dedert, Patricia L. "Experiences at Exxon in Training End-Users to Search Terminal Databases Online." *Online* 7 (September 1983):42-50.

Librarians at Exxon devised a training course to teach staff of two divisions to search CA Search on SDC ORBIT. The course consisted of three lectures, covering system commands, database content, and conceptual aspects of searching. Classes were small (ten in one case, and five in the other), and results were mixed. Of the first group, one year later, only three were active searchers. The result was not surprising because only four of the participants had indicated that performing searches was their primary reason for taking the course. The authors suggest a two-part program for training end users, giving basic searching concepts and allowing for adequate supervised online practice time. The necessity of practice for maintaining searching skills is discussed. This is a fairly good "early" article, which discusses practical aspects of course content for training subject specialists on a command-driven system.

OTHER END USER EDUCATION

Caputo, Anne S. "Online Goes to School: Instruction and Use of Online Systems in Secondary and Elementary Education." *National Online Meeting Proceedings* (1985):85-90.

Instruction in online searching in secondary and elementary schools is examined. Benefits to the students include increased understanding of both print and online formats, increased problem-solving skills and logical conceptualization of problems, library/classroom cooperation, and enjoyment of research. Problems include the lack of teaching materials and lack of librarians at the secondary and elementary school level who are trained in online searching. Despite a lowered vendor fee, start up and continuing costs are potential barriers.

Caruso, Elaine. "TRAINER." *Online* 5 (January 1981):36-8.

A preliminary report of TRAINER was published in 1977 (*Online* 1 (October 1977):28-34). TRAINER is a computer-assisted system designed to aid individuals (both end users and librarians) in learning the basic skills necessary to use DIALOG and ORBIT. It consists of seven tutorial modules, and a system emulator for each vendor. It is designed for independent use, and has been implemented at Carnegie-Mellon University for internal use and as a resource for EDUNET.

Caruso, Elaine, and Griffiths, John. "A TRAINER for Online Systems." *Online* 1 (October 1977):28-34.

TRAINER, developed at the University of Pittsburgh, "contains a specially-prepared system of programs which emulate, or behave like the large-scale systems." The program is set up to instruct trainees in the use of DIALOG and ORBIT. Using this local program, online training charges can be avoided. Thus far, three files are available: Paper Chemistry, NTIS and GEOREF.

Caruso, Nicholas, and Caruso, Elaine. "TRAINER—A Computer Tutorial for End Users of Database Services: Context, Content, and Results of Use." *Information Services & Use* 3 (August 1983):191-8.

TRAINER is a "computer-mediated learning aid for users of DIALOG or ORBIT retrieval services," which is available from Carnegie-Mellon University via TELENET or EDUNET. By emulating DIALOG, the program allows students to practice and refine search skills without going online. An experiment involving sixty-one graduate students at the University of Pittsburgh Graduate School of Public and International Affairs showed that skill levels and training time were positively correlated, and that age and typing skills were correlated with success.

Elias, Arthur W.; Vaupel, Nancy; and Lingwood, David. "End User Education: A Design Study." *Online Review* 4 (June 1980): 153-62.

The education and training function of BIOSIS, a non-profit database producer, is traced. User groups are divided into market segments that include educators, students and managers; scenarios for end user education are presented. The article is highly theoretical.

Klausmeier, Jane A. "Microcomputer Based System for End User Training." *National Online Meeting Proceedings* (1985):265-71.

MICROsearch is a self-contained microcomputer-based search system that is designed to teach the ERIC database. The program is available for Apple microcomputers. Users of the program include library schools, academic libraries, and secondary schools. Primary use of MICROsearch includes teaching online searching, use as a reference tool, and use for end user searching.

Mancall, Jacqueline C. "Training Students to Search Online: Rationale, Process, and Implications." *Drexel Library Quarterly* 20 (Winter 1984):64-84.

Students must be taught the necessary skills for information retrieval, not only using manual sources, but also using online bibliographic databases. The overall search process is outlined, from Boolean logic through selection of appropriate subject headings and refining the search to determine final retrieval. Used as a search example is the subject of the cost of solar power for residential use. The search was performed by a ninth-grade honors student. School library media centers must adapt to the newer technologies.

Moghdam, Dineh. "User Training for On-Line Information Retrieval Systems." *Journal of the American Society for Information Science* 26 (May-June 1975):184-8.

The need for training for online information retrieval systems is as important as systems design, hardware, and the database itself. Three categories of training problems are: training devices, motivation, and training methods. This article focuses on training methods, and discusses utilization of printed manuals, guides or visual displays; personal instruction; audiovisual presentations; and computer-assisted instruction (CAI). Recent literature on the successful use of CAI in online training is reviewed. CAI is viewed as an "ideal alternative or back-up to live help."

Ostrum, G. Kenneth, and Yoder, Diane K. "Training in CAS Online for End Users." *National Online Meeting Proceedings* (1985):343-9.

As more capabilities have been added to make online searching more powerful for the professional searcher, the systems have become more intimidating for end users. Chemical Abstracts Services staff were asked to develop a workshop to teach the CA file to end users. The resultant product, the CA File for Chemists Workshop, was designed with a modular approach so that it could be adapted for three target market groups: large chemical companies, academia, and small chemical companies. The complete outline of the course is presented at the end of the article; not all sections are presented to all groups. The workshop contains extensive online practice time, an essential for end users. In 1985, 323 end users in corporations and universities were trained at twenty-six locations; data from these workshops were not yet analyzed when the paper was submitted, but will be available at the oral presentation of the paper. Also at that time, concerns about end user training, such as maintenance of search skills and levels of technical assistance needed, will be discussed.

Pruitt, Ellen, and Dowling, Karen. "Searching for Current Information Online . . . How High School Library Media Centers in Montgomery County, Maryland are Solving an Information Problem by Using DIALOG." *Online* 9 (March 1985):47-60.

In 1982, the library media centers in twenty-two senior high schools of Montgomery County, Maryland, initiated a program of online searching for their students. Students were to exhaust print and nonprint resources before turning to online databases. An analysis of database use over two years (1982-83 and 1983-84) showed heaviest use at "mid-term," when students would be working on term papers. Highest use was made of MAGAZINE INDEX, ERIC, and MEDLINE. A discussion focuses on curriculum needs, problems with print sources, and solutions offered by online sources; sample searches show the advantage of online searching versus retrieval from printed sources.

Queens Borough Central Library Staff. "Search Helper: The Queens Borough Experience." *Online* 9 (November 1985):53-6.

In November 1982, Queens Borough Public Library added Search Helper to its other search services (DIALOG, BRS, and NEXIS). Search Helper provides low-cost access to six Information Access Company databases, all of major interest to the general public. Unfortunately, the service is being used by librarians rather than by end users, as it is ultimately intended.

Vigil, Peter J. "End-User Training: The Systems Approach." *National Online Meeting Proceedings* (1984):419-24.

Based on previous studies, major problems with end user searching have been that online retrieval services are underutilized due to poor strategy, and that few end users continue to search after training or after subsidized computer time ends. Vigil feels that it takes more than institutional commitment—initiative on the part of the end user is the key. A "systems" approach to training is described, which provides introductory information at one session (search systems available, system options, communications, search mechanics, etc.), followed by a more advanced session on database selection and search strategy.

Wozny, Lucy Anne. "Online Bibliographic Searching and Student Use of Information: An Innovative Teaching Approach." *School Library Media Quarterly* 11 (Fall 1982):35-42.

Ninth-grade honors students in science used online bibliographic and conventional searching as part of an independent research assignment. A detailed analysis of the bibliographies of the student assignments was conducted to determine the sources of the information. Although online searching led to the inclusion of few references in the bibliographies, it represented a new method for obtaining references, and helped students in the conceptualization of their search strategies.

COMPUTER INTERFACES—FRONT ENDS

Cole, Elliot, and Trauth, Eileen M. "User Friendly and the User: Applying the Information Systems Model to the Design of User Interfaces." *Proceedings of the 47th Annual Meeting of the American Society for Information Science* 21 (1984):148-52.

In a highly theoretical article, the authors argue "that the concept of 'user friendly' should be applied at the level of the complete information system, rather than at the subsystem level of hardware and software." An online search service is used to show the applicability to the approach.

Crawford, R.G., and Becker, H.S. "Toward the Development of Interfaces for Untrained Users." *Proceedings of the 48th Annual Meeting of the American Society for Information Science* 22 (1985):236-9.

A variety of human factors must be considered in making design decisions for user-friendly interfaces for information retrieval systems. "Some features being tested for modes of command entry include: menus, fill-in-the-blank, and the use of a mouse." Display windowing and the use of multi-level online help features are other considerations. Two interfaces are described: FIRSTUSER is "a combined menu and fill-in-the-blank style of command entry," which interfaces with online bibliographic retrieval systems; and "Drug-Interface" "provides access to four databases containing drug related information on the DIALOG retrieval system."

Crystal, Maurice I., and Jakobson, Dr. Gabriel E. "FRED, A Front End for Databases." *Online* 6 (September 1982):27-30.

End users who attempt to access online databases run into a variety of problems, from selecting a database to coping with command language and indexing methods. FRED was developed as a "hardware/software layer that can be interposed between users and database systems." It makes necessary translations so that "different databases all have uniform appearance to the user." FRED has three major subsystems: user-interface, database-interface, and a knowledge base.

Doszkocs, Tamas E. "CITE NLM: Natural-Language Searching in an Online Catalog." *Information Technology and Libraries* 2 (December 1983):364-80.

The National Library of Medicine's CITE is used in NLM's reading room, providing access to CATLINE, NLM's public access online catalog. Users enter queries in free form, natural language English. CITE suggests potentially relevant keywords and Medical Subject Headings, looks for spelling errors, and assigns weights to the search terms. After the resulting records are displayed in ranked sequence, CITE can apply feedback from the user to find other relevant materials. A detailed description of CITE's capabilities is enhanced by sample screens and several illustrative searches.

Doszkocs, Tamas E., and Rapp, Barbara A. "Searching MEDLINE in English: A Prototype User Interface with Natural Language Query, Ranked Output, and Relevance Feedback." *Proceedings of the 42nd Annual Meeting of the American Society for Information Science* 16 (1979):131-9.

CITE (Current Information Transfer in English) is an English sentence (natural language) query system which interfaces with MEDLINE. Developed at the National Library of Medicine, the design of CITE focuses on: "identification of search terms; combinatorial searching; weighting and ranked output; relevance feedback; and automatic query modification." Discussed in this article are the MEDLINE environment, functional and technical design features of CITE, and the prototype implementation.

Eager, Virginia W. "MicroDISCLOSURE—Software for the IBM PC/XT Enduser." *Database* 7 (June 1984):79-84.

After a brief description of the DISCLOSURE II databases, microDISCLOSURE, a menu-driven system designed for the inexperienced searcher or end user, is presented. Menus are shown in several figures. Basic information on operating costs, the user manual, and system description (i.e., price, and equipment information) are given.

Goldstein, Charles M., and Ford, William H. "The User-Cordial Interface." *Online Review* 2 (1978):269-75.

The term "user-oriented interface" (UOI) indicates a "concern for optimizing the interface for the end user. Several configurations of user models are illustrated using intelligent terminals, front end processors, or software modules. At the National Library of Medicine, an intelligent terminal provides the necessary interface to allow the users of the public card catalog to utilize CATLINE in a "friendly" fashion.

Hawkins, Donald T., and Levy, Louise R. "Front End Software for Online Database Searching. Part 1: Definitions, System Features, and Evaluation." *Online* 9 (November 1985):30-7.

The first of a series of three articles on front end software, this article defines "front end software" and differentiates it from a "gateway" (front ends enhance "the features of a gateway by simplifying and performing some of the steps in the search process"). Barriers to the use of online systems are discussed as some of the reasons why gateways and front ends are needed. Some features of front ends are: access to several databanks, automatic dialing and logon, help features, pre-search editing and uploading, downloading, post-processing the search results, and the user interface (i.e., the menus that are displayed). Front end systems can be located on a personal computer, a host mainframe, or the user's mainframe. Currently no front end software has all of the features mentioned.

Hunt, Richard K.; Fisher, H. Leonard; Hampel, Viktor E. et al. "The 'TIS' Intelligent Gateway Computer, An Alternative to the 'Doomsday Scenario.'" *National Online Meeting Proceedings* (1983):211-21.

Experience with the Technology Information System (TIS) at the Lawrence Livermore National Laboratory (LLNL) is described. End users at LLNL have shown interest in doing their own searches, but "prefer the information specialist to provide the routine and complex searches required for . . . their work." The information specialists have started to use TIS, an intelligent gateway that permits access to major information sources, downloading, and post-processing.

Lamb, M.R.; Auster, E.W.; and Westel, E.R. "A Friendly Front End for Bibliographic Retrieval: The Implementation of a Flexible Interface." *Proceedings of the 48th Annual Meeting of the American Society for Information Science* 22 (1985):229-35.

The authors present a new, user-friendly front end designed for online bibliographic information retrieval. The software is designed as a CAN/OLE interface. It operates in three modes: "a menu-driven mode to guide and instruct beginners; a command language mode for more experienced users; and a transparent mode in which users may communicate directly with the retrieval system in its own query language." Users may freely switch from one mode to the other in the same search session. The program is transportable, and can be adapted to other systems.

Levy, Louise R. "Gateway Software: Is It For You?" *Online* 8 (November 1984):67-79.

This extremely practical article first defines gateway software and discusses available features: communication, interface, and auxiliary program features. Four programs are compared: In-Search, ISI's Universal Online Searcher, microDISCLOSURE, and SEARCH HELPER. In addition to discussing positive and negative features of each program, charts are supplied which compare everything from level of interface to documentation and tutorials to downloading capabilities across all four systems. The material is practical and valuable for end users or libraries considering purchase of one of the software packages.

Marcus, Richard S. "An Experimental Comparison of the Effectiveness of Computers and Humans as Search Intermediaries." *Journal of the American Society for Information Science* 34 (November 1983):381-404.

CONIT is an experimental computer intermediary system "that assists users in accessing and searching heterogeneous retrieval systems." CONIT connects to NLM, ELHILL, SDC ORBIT, and DIALOG. An enhanced version of CONIT was compared with search intermediaries to evaluate recall in online searches. This extensive, detailed research study concluded that natural English language interfaces are, indeed, effective in searching "across a wide variety of subject topics, disciplines, databases, and retrieval systems." Current and future prospects of intermediary systems are explored.

Marcus, Richard S., and Reintjes, J. Francis. "A Translating Computer Interface for End-User Operation of Heterogeneous Retrieval Systems. I. Design." *Journal of the American Society for Information Science* 32 (July 1981):287-317.

Translating computer interfaces are designed to "simplify access to, and operation of, heterogeneous bibliographic retrieval systems and databases." The ultimate goal is to make online retrieval systems easy to use. Users can query the system in common language, which is translated into the appropriate format by the interface. This paper discusses the philosophy, design, and implementation of CONIT, an experimental interface. While the paper is fairly technical, it does provide insight into the complexities of designing a computer interface. A second part of this article discusses evaluation.

Meadow, Charles T. "The Computer as a Search Intermediary." *Online* 3 (July 1979):54-9.

IIDA, Individualized Instruction for Data Access, is being developed at Drexel University. It is "intended to assist people in performing online bibliographic searches." IIDA operates in two modes: an exercise mode, which has three exercises (a "canned" exercise, limited search, and advanced commands and strategy); and the assistance mode. IIDA is dependent on the user inputting something and then reacts to the input. IIDA looks for errors such as null sets, repetition of commands, and unused sets.

Meadow, Charles T.; Hewett, Thomas T.; and Aversa, Elizabeth S. "A Computer Intermediary for Interactive Database Searching. I. Design." *Journal of The American Society for Information Science* 33 (September 1982):325-32.

Individualized Instruction for Data Access (IIDA) is a computer software system that "was designed to encourage end users of information retrieval systems to perform their own searches by (1) instructing them how to search, using computer-assisted instruction, and (2) assisting with the performance of the search by providing diagnostic analyses of the users' performance as well as answering their questions about how to use system commands." IIDA therefore serves as an intermediary between the end user and the system. IIDA consists of two modes, the instructional mode and the assistance mode. The software is designed to interface with DIALOG. This first of a two-part article overviews the system design: the instruction mode, the assistance mode, help facilities, and software components.

Meadow, Charles T.; Hewett, Thomas T.; and Aversa, Elizabeth S. "A Computer Intermediary for Interactive Database Searching. II. Evaluation." *Journal of the American Society for Information Science* 33 (November 1982):357-64.

Part two of this series "describes the development, testing, and evaluation of IIDA." The system was first treated internally by three undergraduate computer science students, and three graduate students and two faculty members of Drexel's School of Library and Information Science. A second-stage evaluation consisted of volunteers from the masters' level library school at Drexel. Third-stage evaluation was done at two Exxon Company sites in New Jersey. Results indicated that end users could indeed perform relevant searches using IIDA. "IIDA clearly represents a viable alternative to gaining direct database access for those end users who cannot or will not do more conventional forms of online searching."

Newlin, Barbara B. "In-Search: The Design and Evolution of An End User Interface to DIALOG." *National Online Meeting Proceedings* (1985):313-9.

Newlin discusses the "inside view" of Menlo Corporation's design and development of In-Search, a user-friendly interface to DIALOG. In-Search was released in Spring of 1984 to "universal acclaim." The major market was expected to be the business professional. Major marketing problems, including training dealers, supporting a sales force, and advertising; DIALOG support for In-Search customers; and changes to the DIALOG system all created barriers to Menlo's entry into the end user market. The realization that the end user market was not ready for In-Search led to drastic cutbacks in the sales and marketing staff, and the development of a new product, Pro-Search, which is designed for information professionals.

O'Leary, Mick. "EasyNet: Doing It All for the End-User." *Online* 9 (July 1985):106-13.

EasyNet, a gateway service which provides access to databases on several major databanks, was developed for nonprofessional searchers by Telebase Systems, Inc. of Narberth, PA. EasyNet provides an effortless pathway to the "appropriate" database based on a complicated series of decisions which are made "behind the scenes." Through EasyNet I, less than 100 databases on DIALOG, BRS, SDC, and four other databanks can be accessed; EasyNet II is a full gateway which allows experienced searchers to bypass the predetermined selection and access all files on seven databanks. Search mechanics, menus, and search statements; search modifications; and displaying results are discussed. A limiting factor is the ten record batch display. Search expenses ($6.00 per batch), plus other fees and surcharges, make EasyNet more expensive than searching on the host databank, as would be expected because of the "value-added" service which is provided.

Pollett, A.S. "A 'Front-End' System: An Expert System as an Online Search Intermediary." *ASLIB Proceedings* 36 (May 1984): 229-34.

Expert Systems are defined and "presented in the context of the computer-based information systems . . ." CANSEARCH, an Expert System, allows users to perform searches for cancer therapy literature on MEDLINE, by translating terms into appropriate search statements.

Shepherd, Michael A., and Watters, Carolyn. "PSI: A Portable Self-Contained Intermediary for Access to Bibliographic Database Systems." *Online Review* 8 (October 1984):451-63.

PSI is a "portable self-contained intermediary which provides the non-expert user a single command language to access multiple bibliographic database systems." Under development at the University of Nova Scotia, PSI is "intended to be self-contained on a specially designed single board computer which fits conveniently under a desktop telephone." It will also operate on a microcomputer. Currently, CAN/OLE and DIALOG can be accessed. The screen is formatted into three windows "which allows the user to view citations in one window while keeping a history of the search strategy in a second window." The third window allows data entry. PSI is intended for end users of the technical literature who are aware of specialized vocabulary, would be infrequent searchers, and would prefer to perform their own searches. Specifics on the system design, screen configurations, and software development are given.

Smith, Linda C. "Implications of Artificial Intelligence for End User Use of Online Systems." *Online Review* 4 (December 1980):383-91.

Artificial intelligence (AI) is a branch of computer science that attempts to develop programs that allow more fluent communication with computer systems. AI is especially appliable to "the design of end user-oriented interfaces to existing online systems as well as in the development of future generations of online systems intended for the end user." Two prototype systems mentioned as examples of these interfaces are: CITE, developed at the National Library of Medicine to help end users search MEDLINE; and IIDA, developed at Drexel University to provide access to DIALOG.

Stout, Catheryne, and Marcinko, Thomas. "SCI-MATEtm: A Menu-Driven Universal Online Searcher and Personal Data Manager." *Online* 7 (September 1983):112-6.

ISI's SCI-MATE was created as a means for librarians and scientists to manage "the flood of reprints that they use in their daily work." The microcomputer package consists of two major components: the "Universal Online Searcher" is a menu-driven system that allows access to several commercially available vendors, while the "Personal Data Manager" organizes the reprint collection into a "mini database." Examples of search screens are displayed.

Tenopir, Carol. "Database Access Software." *Library Journal* 109 (October 1, 1984):1828-9.

Database access software (gateways, front end processors) will have great impact in the next year or so in the end user market. These software packages, coupled with increased sales of microcomputers and modems, greatly increase the researcher's likelihood of searching online. In-Search, a package for accessing DIALOG, is evaluated critically, and a list of database access software is given.

Vickery, A. "An Intelligent Interface for Online Interaction." *Journal of Information Science; Principles and Practice* 9 (August 1984):7-18.

Discussed are "ways of improving the performance of online retrieval systems by introducing an automated interface between the enquirer and the system." Work in artificial intelligence has included natural language interfaces, assembling knowledge structures, and search formulation.

Wible, Joseph G. "Searching Made Easy: Front-End Systems for Medical Databases." *Medical Reference Services Quarterly* 5 (Summer 1986): in press.

Wible "compares microcomputer and mainframe-based front-end software which can be used for accessing medical databases." Described in detail are: Sci-Mate Universal Online Searcher, Pro-Search, PC/Net-Link, Searchmaster, and Easynet.

Williams, Phil. "User Trials of the OASIS Search System." *National Online Meeting Proceedings—1984*. Medford, NJ: Learned Information, 1984, pp. 437-52.

OASIS is a type of "expert system," which serves as an interface system between the end user and the host system. Developed by the British Library, OASIS is designed to formulate a search, log in, run the search (masking the search mechanics from the user), and retrieve results. A detailed evaluation of the project was conducted via a questionnaire. Results showed that: 96 percent of users found the system easy to use, 92 percent found the tutorial helpful, 99 percent said they would use the system often or occasionally if it were available, and 66 percent felt the search was successful in finding the appropriate information.

POPULAR LITERATURE

Anonymous. "A Budding Mass Market for Data Bases." *Business Week* No. 2773 (January 17, 1983):128, 131.

The variety of uses for online databases is astronomical. The mass market for online services is just beginning to grow, with some three million personal computers in the U.S. Services such as Dow Jones, CompuServe, and The Source share the spotlight here, but DIALOG and BRS are among the databanks mentioned.

Bowen, Charles, and Peyton, David. *How to Get the Most Out of CompuServe*. New York: Bantam, 1984.

Recognizing the lack of good documentation for accessing CompuServe, the authors have put together a fun, "grass roots" approach which guides users through the various menus and services of CompuServe. From electronic mail to CB to shopping to special interest groups (SIGS) to games, the book takes a light-hearted look at what the end user can expect to get out of CompuServe. It is easy to see why this service is popular with computer buffs and the general public.

Cornish, Edward. "The Coming of an Information Society." *Futurist* 15 (April 1981):14-21.
The history of the information revolution is traced from the development of the human mind to the advent of computers. Electronic newspapers, electronic yellow pages, teleshopping, and networking are services provided through the advent of electronic information systems.

Dewey, Patrick R. "A Professional Librarian Looks at the Consumer Online Services . . . The Source, CompuServe, Apple Bulletin Board, et al." *Online* 7 (September 1983):36-41.
The consumer online services ("leisurely" services) are discussed for the librarian, who is more used to database searching. These are the "original" end user services. Everything from online shopping to electronic bulletin boards is provided.

Diodato, Virgil. "Popular Magazines Discuss Online Information Retrieval." *Online* 8 (May 1984):24-9.
There is an extensive and rapidly growing body of literature discussing online information retrieval in popular magazines. Diodato is legitimately concerned with the lack of mention of libraries as a source for expertise on these online sources. An extensive bibliography is appended.

Dolan, Donna R. "Offlines: Non-Technical Literature: Getting It Out of Databases. 1. BRS/AFTER DARK." *Database* 7 (August 1984):94-103.
Since the premise behind user-friendly systems is to provide access to information by users who are not familiar with searching, it may also be possible that end users may not know which databases are appropriate for their search. Databases vary in the level of information, so that the lay person may have difficulty in selecting a database which contains non-technical literature. Dolan discusses features which determine suitability for non-technical information: inclusion of abstracts, type of materials suitable, subsets, etc. Also, some databases are geared totally to the general public. Dolan applies these criteria in a table which presents all of the databases on BRS/AFTER DARK and outlines their suitability for the general public.

Falk, Howard. "The Source v. CompuServe." *Online Review* 8 (1984):214-24.

This is a good overview of the two information utilities for the professional searcher or for the individual who is deciding which of the utilities to join. The Source seems oriented toward "the user as an individual whose personal desires and tastes are to be catered for," whereas CompuServe is directed primarily "to organizational, professional and business needs," with the personal services being "added on." The detailed, comparative discussion covers communication services (e.g., electronic mail and bulletin boards), news and publications, business and financial features, education-related features, online publication and information, personal service features, travel offerings, and remote computer service. The article concludes with information on accessing the two services, including costs.

Glossbrenner, Alfred. "Personal Computers: Passport to the Electronic Universe." *Technology Review* 86 (May/June 1983):62-71.

Personal computers have literally opened up a universe of information sources. The basic mechanical aspects of going online are described along with the various online sources, from database vendors such as DIALOG to the information utilities such as The Source and CompuServe. Going online can be expensive, and numerous problems can occur with accessing these systems. This is a very general overview intended for the computer enthusiast.

Hecht, Jeff. "What You Can Get Online." *Computers and Electronics* 23 (February 1985):46-7, 50-3, 89-90.

Online database services are presented concisely and effectively as business and research tools. Concentration is on the "big four" (The Source, CompuServe, Dow Jones, and DIALOG). Examples of bibliographic databases are given, along with suggestions on how to search them; for example, it is pointed out that, just like searching printed indexes, the user must determine the appropriate index terms. A sample search from DIALOG is given. Full-text services, reference databases, and "job services" complete the article.

Kiechel, Walter. "Everything You Always Wanted to Know May Soon Be On-Line." *Fortune* 101 (May 5, 1980):226-8, 233, 236, 240.

The online information industry is crowded with companies wishing to enter the field or to increase their market share. This article views online information as a marketable commodity. Discussed are such vendors as the New York Times, LEXIS, DIALOG, and SDC. The pricing structure of DIALOG and SDC has been guided by libraries as their major clients. For the general public, in the future, emphasis must be placed on the development of software, with "search protocols that are easier for users to employ."

Leichtman, Kerry. "Making Online Databases Useful." *Computers and Electronics* 23 (February 1985):58-61.

The author contends that online searching is easy. The databanks or vendors (erroneously referred to in the article as "databases") provide excellent training and back-up services, and microcomputer software is making the systems more friendly. In-Search and SuperScout are examples of the new user-friendly software. *Online* and *Database* are listed as helpful sources of information, along with a variety of directories and guides to databases. Included in the article is a "Guide to Online Information Services," which lists addresses, costs, communications access, training availability, hours, and other features of online vendors.

Markoff, John. "The On-Line Society." *Computerworld* 17 (August 17, 1985):75-6.

Markoff overviews the online services available to individuals with a microcomputer and modem. In addition to the information utilities, DIALOG and BRS are billed as "offering subsets of their larger databases for evening and weekend use at greatly reduced rates." The market targeted for these two vendors is the office (business) and professional (e.g., physicians) user. Newsnet, Newsflash, and Dow Jones News/Retrieval also target the office market.

Miastkowski, Stan. "Information Unlimited; The Dialog Information Retrieval System." *Byte* 6 (June 1981):88, 90, 92, 94, 96, 98, 102, 106, 108.

Over 130 databases are accessible via DIALOG. This article provides an overview for the general public, discussing the history of DIALOG, popular databases, accessing and using DIALOG, and basic system commands. A typical search on MAGAZINE INDEX is illustrated.

Nicita, Mike, and Petrusha, Ron. "Guides to On-Line Information: From Beginners' Tutorials to Databases, You're Covered." *Popular Computing* 4 (March 1985):174-6.
    This is a group of reviews to books which are guides to, or directories of, databases and online services. These reviews are designed to make some sense out of the voluminous information available on databases.

Pearlman, Dara. "The Joy of Telecomputing: Everything You Need to Know About Going On-Line at Home." *Popular Computing* (July 1984):107-10, 152, 155-7.
    To access this new online world, "all you need is a personal computer, a modem, communications software, and a telephone line." The focus is on the information utilities (CompuServe, The Source, Dow Jones, and Delphi), with suggestions for use such as: sending electronic mail, conference calls via computer, "CB" communications, exchanging free software, playing computer games, online shopping and banking, and finding information (e.g., travel, weather, etc.). DIALOG's KNOWLEDGE INDEX and BRS/AFTER DARK are introduced, also, as providing access to a variety of databases.

Roberts, Steven K. "Online Information Retrieval; Promise and Problems." *BYTE* 6 (December 1981):452-61.
    This overview of online information retrieval has some good, solid advice for the computer buff. As an example of the utility of online searching, Roberts accessed DIALOG for information on bicycle odometers; searching several files, including MAGAZINE INDEX and CLAIMS, he retrieved relevant information. The historical development of the hardware and software necessary for online interaction is briefly described. Despite high database costs, online searching is portrayed as cost-effective when the searcher's time is taken into account. The development of user-friendly systems and better access modes are mentioned. Roberts suggests that everyone should have access to online databases. Briefly mentioned are database intermediaries, small firms which sell searching expertise; unfortunately, libraries are only mentioned in the context of being "avoided."

Seligman, Daniel. "Life Will be Different When We're All On-Line." *Fortune* 111 (February 4, 1985):68-72.

Online databases are heralded as changing the world. Online databases themselves are not new; what is new is their use by persons owning microcomputers. The article reviews online services for "endusers," from NewsNet to DIALOG. Also discussed are data entry into the databases, markets available for "data" databases, and a planned database from the Securities Exchange Commission (SEC) called EDGAR, which will contain financial disclosures online.

Siwolop, Sana. "Touching All the Data Bases." *Discover: The Newsmagazine of Science* 4 (March 1983):68-71.

This is another overview of online databases; however, database services of all levels are presented. Mentioned are AMA/NET, LEXIS and NEXIS, and vendors such as DIALOG, along with the more general information utilities. Equipment is only briefly dealt with, and little detail is provided about communications access.

Smith, Ralph Lee. "Plugging in to the New Technology." *Nation* 233 (October 3, 1981):313-5.

This is a general article about online technology, ranging from LEXIS, The Source, and CompuServe to teletext and videotex.

Tenopir, Carol. "Online Searching in the Popular Literature." *Library Journal* 109 (December 1984):2242-3.

Tenopir points out that the popular computer journals are advertising that online sources can be used to find everything. Even worse, online databases are advertised without mentioning libraries and search intermediaries. Much information provided in the popular literature is inaccurate. Tenopir discusses a group of articles which she recommends as providing an accurate and informative picture of online services.

Zarley, Craig. "Dialing into Data Bases." *Personal Computing* 7 (December 1983):135-7, 139, 234.

Online databases are heralded as giving users "unlimited access to all the libraries in the Western world from your home or office." The Source, CompuServe, and Dow Jones News/Retrieval Service (the so-called "information utilities") are mentioned, but the focus is on database services designed for professional researchers, such as DIALOG, ORBIT and BRS (incorrectly referred to in the article as "BSR"). Much information and sound advice is provided about the hardware necessary to connect to these online services; search formulations are presented haphazardly, building on one user's observations and "trial and error." Examples of users include a physician located in a remote area, the president of a professional research company (the focus on the article), and a professor of natural sciences at a university.

Glossary

Compiled by Bonnie Snow

The selection of terms included in this glossary was based on specialized terminology employed by one or more authors of articles in this volume. Definitions are included here both to explain the meanings of words perhaps less familiar to some readers, and to clarify editorial policy regarding usage, cross-referencing related terms mentioned by different authors and standardizing spelling. Terms related exclusively to MEDLINE database indexing features have been omitted. For definitions of "check tags," "data forms," etc., readers should refer to vendor-produced training materials previously cited. *Italicized words* in any entry indicate separate entries for these terms elsewhere in the glossary; ironically, it is often necessary to use jargon even when defining other jargon. No attempt has been made to produce a glossary sufficiently "user-friendly" for adoption in end user training materials.

ABSTRACT—a concise summary of ideas or concepts contained in a longer source document.

ACCESS POINTS—individual segments or elements (words, phrases, or numbers) which may be searched in an online *record*.

ACCESSION DATE—point in time when information is added to a *file*.

ACCESSION NUMBER—a unique, serial code assigned to a unit of information such as an online *record* when it is added or accessioned to a *database*.

AUTHORITY FILE—a listing of information which establishes a standard for terminology and format of items in a *database*. A *thesaurus* is an example of an authority file.

BASIC—*B*eginner's *A*ll-Purpose *S*ymbolic *I*nstruction *C*ode, a popular programming language designed for ease of use.

BAUD—a unit of communication speed equal to the number of separate signal events transmitted per second: e.g., 300 baud = 30-characters-per-second *(CPS)* transmission, 1200 baud = 120 cps. The number of characters per second is roughly equivalent to one-tenth the baud rate.

BIBLIOGRAPHIC DATABASE—a *file* which contains references or *citations* to source documents, rather than the full text of the source documents themselves.

BOOLEAN LOGIC—a logical system which uses the terms AND, OR, NOT (or AND NOT) to designate the relationship among search words or phrases. Named for George Boole, a British mathematician and philosopher, the three logical terms are known as "Boolean operators" or "connectors."

CAI—*C*omputer-*A*ssisted (or *A*ided) *I*nstruction.

CD ROM—*C*ompact *D*isk *R*ead *O*nly *M*emory. Circular plates on the surface of which information is permanently encoded in the form of digital symbols; cannot be altered or erased once "pressed" in the production process. Data stored can be randomly accessed via laser beams, eliminating wear and tear of physical contact via mechanical "heads" for reading data. CD ROM offers greater storage/memory capacity in less physical space than floppy or hard *disks* currently on the market, but requires longer time for data access than hard disk drives. See also *ROM*.

CITATION—a reference to a work from which a passage is quoted. Bibliographic references or citations in online databases generally include information to locate the source document, such as author(s), title, journal or book name, volume, pagination, publication date.

CLASSIFICATION—any systematic scheme for the arrangement of documents, usually according to subject.

COM—*C*omputer *O*utput *M*icroform.

COMMAND—an instruction in either words or symbols which directs the computer to take some specific action.

COMMAND DRIVEN—A term used to characterize *online* retrieval systems which require use of specific, predefined *commands* and syntax for user-computer interaction. Little or no online prompting is included. Command options are documented *offline*, generally in *hardcopy* format, rather than being displayed online via *menus*.

CONNECTOR—see *Boolean logic* or *proximity operator*.

CONTROLLED VOCABULARY—a standardized list of subject terms (*descriptors*) used in indexing *records* entered into a *database*. Also known as an *authority file* or a database *thesaurus*.

CPS—*C*haracters *P*er *S*econd. See *baud*.

CPU—*C*entral *P*rocessing *U*nit, that part of a computer system which controls the interpretation and execution of machine instructions.

CRT—*Cathode Ray Tube*, a terminal which displays on a screen. Synonym: *VDT*.

DATABASE—a collection of information in machine-readable form accessible by computer. Synonym: *file*.

DATABASE PRODUCER or SUPPLIER—an organization or company which collects and organizes information found in a *database*. Note that a *vendor* may be a totally separate organization.

DATABANK—Sometimes used as a synonym for *database*, but may refer to collections of numeric or factual data in machine-readable form, as distinct from *bibliographic* data files. For example, the National Library of Medicine's RTECS (Registry of Toxic Effects of Chemicals) database has been referred to as a databank. Recently, the term *databank* has been used as a synonym for *vendor*, referring to a company or institution which markets a group of databases accessible through a common command language.

DEDICATED LINE—a telephone line used solely for data transmission.

DEFAULT—term used to describe what happens automatically if no particular option is expressed by the user in a computer search.

DESCRIPTOR—a word or phrase added to an online *record* to describe the subject matter covered in the source document cited and to permit subsequent location and retrieval of that record.

DISK—storage hardware for machine-readable information, consisting of a circular plate with a magnetizable surface on which data can be recorded in tracks or sectors, enabling random access to data in a compact form.

DOWNLOADING—the process of copying in an electronic form results of an online query; usually done on *disk* storage devices.

END USER—the person who ultimately uses the information retrieved in an online search. This person may or may not perform the search.

FIELD—a section or portion of an online *record* designated for storage of specified information: e.g., the title field or the author field in a bibliographic citation. Synonyms are "paragraphs" (BRS), "data elements" or "record elements" (NLM).

FILE—an organized collection of information on a common theme, which can be searched as a unit. Sometimes used as a synonym for *database*.

FREE-TEXT—a mode of searching where all words in a *record* or citation online may be used as retrieval keywords. Used as a synonym for *natural language* searching.

FRONT END—a terminal or input device used to create or load data and/or instructions into a mainframe computer. Front-end software usually provides an *interface* or connection between the user and a host computer system; the interface translates user input into the host's *command* language. *Gateway* software is one form of front end software.

FULL-TEXT DATABASE—a *file* which contains complete documents rather than brief *citations* or bibliographic references.

GATEWAY—a computer system which provides access to other systems, usually directing a user to one or more online *vendors* on different computers.

GIGABYTE—one billion bytes. Each byte is a group (usually eight) of adjacent binary digits used to convey the coded representation of a character or symbol. Terms such as *megabyte* or gigabyte are used to describe storage capacities in the context of computer systems.

HARDCOPY—a document in book, journal, or manuscript form—as opposed to microform or magnetic tape.

HARDWARE—the actual physical equipment used in a computer system, as opposed to a computer program or *software*. May include *microcomputers*, printers, *terminals, disk* drives, etc.

HIERARCHICAL—arranged or classified in ranks or orders.

INTERFACE—a computer system which is used in front of, or between, the user and the target search service or *database*.

INTERMEDIARY—a searcher who performs online research on behalf of someone else (the *end user*).

ISSN—*I*nternational *S*tandard *S*erial *N*umber.

LAG TIME—the time period which elapses between the publication of source documents and their availability through indexing in online databases.

MAINFRAME—a large, full-scale computer, rather than a *mini-* or *microcomputer*.

MEGABYTE—one million bytes. See also *gigabyte*.

MENU-DRIVEN—a term used to describe a computer system which requires a user to select functions he or she wishes to perform from a menu or list of options displayed on a *terminal* or *microcomputer*.

MeSH—*Medical Subject Headings*, a *thesaurus* developed by the National Library of Medicine for use in indexing the MEDLINE database.

MICROCOMPUTER—a small (usually desktop) computer.

MINICOMPUTER—a computer of intermediate size, usually less powerful than a *mainframe* but more powerful than a *microcomputer*.

MNEMONICS—Codes which are used to identify segments of an online *record* in searching and are easily remembered due to their resemblance to the segment identified. For example, TI is a typical mnemonic for the title portion of a record.

MODEM—a device which transforms digital electronic signals from a computer into analog sound signals understandable for communication and phone line equipment. Acronym for *Mo*dulator-*Dem*odulator.

NATURAL LANGUAGE—ordinary spoken or written language. Natural language searching refers to accessing online databases with terms of the user's own choosing, versus *controlled vocabulary* searching, whereby a user adheres to a finite list of authorized terminology known to be used or preferred in indexing. Synonyms sometimes used are *free-text* or *text word* searching.

NLM—*N*ational *L*ibrary of *M*edicine (U.S.).

OFFLINE—processing after the searcher has given all instructions and is no longer connected with the computer.

ONLINE—interaction with a computer via a telecommunications system in which data is transmitted and processed immediately.

OPERATORS—see *Boolean logic* or *proximity operators.*

OPTICAL DISK—see *video disk.*

PARAGRAPH—see *field.*

PORT—an entry point in a *vendor's* computer system which allows searchers to connect via a *terminal* or *microcomputer.*

POST PROCESSING—manipulation of data obtained from an online system after a search has been completed. Usually refers to functions such as editing, word processing, or report generation performed *offline*, after the interactive connection with a computer system has been terminated.

PRODUCER—see *database producer.*

PROTOCOL—a set of conventions governing the format of messages to be exchanged within a communication or computer system.

PROXIMITY OPERATORS—connecting terms or symbols in *vendor* command languages used to express word adjacency or other specified positions for words in relation to one another. More precise than *Boolean logic*.

QUEUE—a set of jobs or specific pieces of work awaiting processing on a computer.

RAM—*R*andom *A*ccess *M*emory, a method of storing computerized data in which the locations or addresses of individual items may be calculated, thus allowing random access, and obviating the need to read a *file* sequentially to locate data.

RECORD—a unit of information in a *database*, such as a bibliographic *citation*, a directory entry, etc. A subset of a *file* or database, it may also be viewed as a collection of *fields*.

ROM—*R*ead *O*nly *M*emory. A type of information storage in which the contents cannot be changed after entry; permanently programmed at the time of manufacture. The antonym is RAM—*R*andom *A*ccess *M*emory, where content may be accessed and changed as desired. Information contained in RAM is lost when the power supply is turned off, but not in ROM. See also *CD ROM*.

SDI—*S*elective *D*issemination of *I*nformation, a method of alerting users to data of potential interest to them, instigated by a previously-defined search profile or strategy. Also known as "current awareness" searching.

SOFTWARE—control programs or instructions used to make a computer perform functions or tasks.

SORTING—the placing of items in a sequence. Refers to rearranging online search output in a specified order (e.g., alphabetically by author or journal name, or chronologically by publication date).

STOP WORDS—terms not directly searchable in an online system.

SUBSET—used in this context to refer to a predefined portion of a larger *database*; a subset is marketed, stored, and consequently searchable as a separate, independent *file*.

SUPPLIER—see *database supplier*.

TELECOMMUNICATIONS—the transmission and reception of data over telephone lines and other communication facilities (microwaves, satellite transmissions).

TERMINAL—a point in a computer system at which data can enter or leave. Usually refers to *hardware* (equipment) at such points, which is capable of sending and receiving information over a communication channel such as a phone line.

TEXT WORD—see *natural language*.

THESAURUS—a list of subject terms or phrases preferred in indexing a *database*; usually also includes cross references from *natural language* to preferred terminology and related terms. Synonym: *controlled vocabulary* or *authority file*.

TRUNCATION—literally "cutting off": removing a portion of a word for use as a search term to retrieve all words containing that portion or word root/stem.

USER-FRIENDLY—a marketing term used to describe a product easy to use and helpful when errors are made.

VDT—*V*ideo *D*isplay *T*erminal. See *CRT*.

VENDOR—a company or organization which provides *software* and/or *hardware* for searching one or more *databases*. A vendor may not have originally compiled the data to be searched, and thus should be distinguished from a *database producer* or *supplier*.

VIDEO DISK—a circular plate used to record visual and/or sound information, originally designed for playback on a television screen. Video disks can also be used to store information in digital form, enabling compact storage and random access of text, drawings, photographs, or other images.

WORD PROCESSING—the manipulation of words, sentences, paragraphs, and the like by a computer or other automated device.

REFERENCES

1. *Guide to DIALOG SEARCHING*. Palo Alto, CA: DIALOG Information Services, Inc., 1979.
2. Hartner, E.R. *An Introduction to Automated Literature Searching*. New York: Marcel Dekker, 1981.
3. Hawkins, D.T., and Levy, L.R. "Front End Software for Online Database Searching." *Online* 9 (November 1985): 30-37.
4. Herther, N.K. "CD ROM Technology: A New Era for Information Storage and Retrieval?" *Online* 9 (November 1985): 17-28.
5. Meadows, A.J.; Gordon, M.; and Singleton, A., eds. *The Random House Dictionary of New Information Technology*. New York: Vintage Books, 1982.
6. Pemberton, J. "Databank." *Online* 9 (May 1985): 95.
7. Reiss, L. *Computer Literacy*. Boston: PWS Publishers, 1984.
8. Williams, M.E. "Highlights of the Online Database Field—Gateways, Front Ends and Intermediary Systems." In: *Proceedings of the Sixth National Online Meeting, New York, April 30-May 2, 1985*. Medford, NJ: Learned Information, 1985, pp. 1-4.
9. Woods, L.A., and Pope, N.F. *The Librarian's Guide to Microcomputer Technology and Applications*. White Plains, NY: Knowledge Industry Publications, 1983.

Index

Abstract, defined 275
Access points, defined 275
Accession date, defined 275
Accession number, defined 275
Accreditation Council for Continuing
 Medical Education 28
AIM/TWX 5,9
AMA MINET 38,74
AMA/NET 55,74-75,210
American Library Association 92
American Medical Association 74,75
American Psychological Association 92
Annotated MeSH see Medical Subject
 Headings
Apple II 139,144
Area Health Education Centers 21
Arnold, Stephen 249-250
Auster, E.W. 261-262
Authority file, defined 275
Aversa, Elizabeth S. 263,264

BACS 86
Bader, Shelley 232
Baker, Carole A. 229
Barber, A. Stephanie 229
Barraclough, Elizabeth D. 229
Barriers 118-120
BASIC 199
 defined 275
Baud, defined 275
BCN *see* Business Computer Network
Becker, H.S. 259
Beckley, Robert F. 229
Berry, John 224
Beth Israel Hospital 72,152
 see also PaperChase
Bevan, Alice 237
BFU *see* Bibliographic File Utilities
Bibliographic database, defined 276
Bibliographic File Utilities 199-201
Bibliographic Retrieval Service *see* BRS

Bibliography 215-273
BIOSIS PREVIEWS 46,138,145,198
Bleich, Howard L. 229,230,234-235
Bodtke-Roberts, Alice 240
BOOKS IN PRINT 198
Boolean logic, defined 276
Bowen, Charles 267-268
Branden, Shirley 230
Broering, Naomi C. 230,231
BRS 5,37,39,55,66,68,71,76,78,80,81,
 86,128,138,164,190,191,202
BRS/AFTER DARK 37-38,56,66,67,68,
 86,87,88,114,137,139,140,141,142,
 144,145,146,152,163-178,198
BRS/BRKTHRU 68,87
BRS/PROMPT 80
BRS/Saunders Colleague 37,56,66,68-71,
 75,80,87,114,137,139,140,141,142,
 143,144,145,146,152,153,160
Bruce, Nancy G. 95-109
Budding Mass Market for Data Bases
 267
Burton, Hilary D. 217
Business Computer Network 202
Butler, Brett 217

CAI 23
 defined 276
Caputo, Anne S. 255
Caruso, Elaine 255-256
Caruso, Nicholas 255-256
CAS ONLINE *see* CHEMICAL
 ABSTRACTS
CD-ROM 92,93
 defined 276
CHEMICAL ABSTRACTS 46,145
CHEMLINE 121
Citation, defined 276
CITEHILL 114-115
CL/MEDLINE 93
Clancy, Stephen 231

283

Classification, defined 276
Clayton, Dennis 240
Cleverdon, Cyril 217-218
Cochrane, Pauline 218
Cole, Elliot 259
Colleague *see* BRS/Saunders Colleague
Collen, Morris F. 232
COM, defined 276
Command, defined 276
Command driven, defined 276
COMPENDEX 145
CompuServe 16,55,72,73
Computer-aided instruction *see* CAI
Computer literacy 54-55,207-208
CONIT 115
Connector *see* Boolean logic or Proximity Operator
Continuing education 25-28
Controlled vocabulary, defined 276
Copeland, Richard 240
Corcoran, Maureen 240
Cornish, Edward 268
Costs 124-125,155-156
 administration 124-125
 staff time 124
CPS, defined 276
CPU, defined 276-277
Crawford, R. G. 259
Crooks, James E. 240-241
CRT, defined 277
Crystal, Maurice I. 259
Curriculum
 online training 19-22
Curtis, Richard A. 241

D-SIRE 86
Dagoni, Ron 250
Dalrymple, Prudence W. 225
Databank, defined 277
Database, defined 277
Database producer, defined 277
Database supplier, defined 277
Davidson, Lloyd A. 241
DEC MicroVAX II 93
DEC PDP11 90
Dedert, Patricia L. 254
Dedicated line, defined 277
Default, defined 277
Des Chene, Dorice 218

Descriptor, defined 277
Dewey, Patrick R. 268
Diodato, Virgil 268
DIALOG 37,39,46,55,66,67,71,72,76,
 78,113-126,128,138,140,164,182,
 184,185,186,190,191,192,202
 see also KNOWLEDGE INDEX
DIALOG Seminar for Medical Professionals 183
Digital Equipment Corporation *see* DEC
Disk, defined 277
DISSERTATION ABSTRACTS 145
Dolan, Donna R. 218,268
Doszkocs, Tamas E. 232,260
Dowling, Karen 257-258
Downloading, defined 277
DRGs 205
Duckitt, Pauline 225

Eager, Virginia W. 260
EARS *see* Electronic Access to Reference Services
EARS (Epilepsy Abstracts Retrieval System) 9
Easynet 8
Educational materials 31-51
Educational role of librarian 15-30
Eisan, Andrew 238
Electronic Access to Reference Services 163-164
Electronic formats 61
Electronics Industry Association 55
Elias, Arthur W. 256
Elsevier 92
EMBASE 7,75,192
EMCLAS 7
Emerson, Susan V. 247
EMPIRES 75
EMTAGS 7
End User
 confessions 197-203
 defined 3,65,277
 online education for 15-30
 part of information transfer process 3,10-11
End user education 15-30,31-51,60,
 79,91-92,113-126,127-135,137-147,
 159-160,169-178
 administration 132-134

Index

BRS/AFTER DARK 137-147,169-178
BRS/Saunders Colleague 137-147
  content and structure 31-51
  costs 124-125
  database idiosyncrasies 40-42
  DIALOG 113-126
  educational materials 31-51
  follow-up 48-49
  goals 32-35
  in academic health sciences libraries 113-126,127-135,137-147,169-178
  in hospitals 159-160
  in the curriculum 19-22
  materials 42-48
  NLM (MEDLARS) 113-126,127-135
  PaperChase 159-160
  Search Strategy Outline 181-187
  software systems 37-40
  topic analysis/strategy formulation 36-37
End user environment 1-109
End user search systems
  evaluation 166-171
  implementation 154-156,191-192
  in academic health sciences libraries 113-126,127-135,137-147,163-178
  in hospitals 149-160,189-196,205-211
  marketing 156-159
  overview 65-83
  planning 151-153
  policies and procedures 165-166
  reference department use 78-80
  selection 190-191
  support services 159-160
  usage 192-195
  see also individual end user systems
End user searching
  education *see* End user education
  overview 3-14
  planning implications 53-64
  search systems *see* End user search systems
End user searching programs 111-178
End user training *see* End user education
End user's viewpoint 179-211
Ensor, Pat 241
Epson FX-80 139
Evans, Nancy 242
ERIC 92,138,145

Excerpta Medica 75,192
  see also EMBASE
External environment 54-58

Faibisoff, Sylvia G. 225
Falk, Howard 269
Fenichel, Carol Hansen 219
Field, defined 277
Files 97-99
  defined 277-278
  maintenance 106
Fisher, H. Leonard 261
Fjallbrand, Nancy 242
Flagle, Charles D. 232
Flexner report 21
Fogel, Laurence D. 250
Ford, William H. 260-261
Foreman, Gertrude 137-147
Free-text, defined 278
Freiburger, Gary A. 85-94
Friend, Linda 242-243
Front end 76-78
  defined 278
Full-text databases 56,72,75
  defined 278
Full-text searching 6-7,209-210
FYI 3000 96,108-109

Garman, Nancy J. 243
Gateway, defined 278
Georgetown University Medical Library 67,81
  see also Library Information System
  see also MiniMEDLINE
Gigabyte, defined 278
Girard, Anne 226
Givens, Mary King 233
Glasgow, Vicki 137-147
Glossary 275-281
Glossbrenner, Alfred 269
Gold standard citations 125
Goldstein, Charles M. 260-261
Goold, Karla Pearce 243
Graham, Deborah L. 223
Gray, W. Alexander 229
Griffiths, John 255
Grotophorst, Clyde W. 244
GTE's Medical Information Network 74

Haines, Judith S. 250-251
Halperin, Michael 244
Hampel, Viktor E. 261
Hansen, Carol 219
Harbert, Cathy 232
Hardcopy, defined 278
Hardware, defined 278
Hausele, Nancy 253
Hawkins, Donald T. 261
Hayes modem 139,202
Haynes, R. Bryan 233
HEALTH PLANNING AND
   ADMINISTRATION 138,145
Hecht, Jeff 269
Henderson, Brian 234
Hewett, Thomas T. 263,264
Hewison, Nancy S. 234
Hierarchical, defined 278
Hildenbrand, Suzanne 234
Hodge, Robert H. 181-187
Holloway, Clark 244
Horak, Ellen Brassil 15-30
Horowitz, Gary L. 234-235
Hospital Corporation of America 190
Hospital libraries 149-161,208-209
Hospitals 149-161,189-196,205-211
Howitt, Doran 219
Hull, Deborah M. 235
Hunt, Richard K. 261
Hunter, Janne A. 219-220
Hurd, Julie M. 241
Hurt, C.S. 245
Hurych, Jitka 225

IBM PC 92,144,201,202
Ifshin, Steven L. 235
ILIS see Integrated Library Information
   System
IMLAC 92
In-House search systems see Local
   databases
In-Search 67
Index Catalog of the Surgeon General 54
Index Medicus 19,54,61,117,190
Information Access Corporation 67
Information creators 3,6
   part of information transfer process 3,6
Information management 17
   see also Personal information
   management

Information transfer process 3-14
Institute for Scientific Information 76
Integrated Library Information System
   163
Interface, defined 278
Intermediary, defined 278
Internal environment 58-59
International Pharmaceutical Abstracts 71
INTERNIST 23
INTROMED 130,134
ISI see Institute for Scientific Information
ISSN, defined 278

Jackson, Angela R. Haygarth 226
Jackson, Jerome D. 230,235
Jakobson, Dr. Gabriel E. 259
Janke, Richard V. 245,246
Johnson, David L. 247

Kaiser Foundation 115
Kaplan, Robin 220
Kesselman, Martin 220
Kiechel, Walter 270
Kihlen Elisabeth 242
Kirby, Martha 236
Klausmeier, Jane A. 256
Kleiner, Jane P. 246
KNOWLEDGE INDEX 37,57,66,71-72,
   86,87,115,139,140,152,165
Kozak, Marlene Galante 251
Kravitz, Rhonda A. Rios 149-161

Lag time, defined 278
Lamb, M.R. 261-262
Lancaster, F. Wilfrid 236
Landsberg, M.K. 251-252
Lane Medical Library see Stanford
   University Medical Center
Lavin, M.A. 251-252
Leichtman, Kerry 270
Leipzig, Nancy 251
Lenon, Richard A. 113-126
Lescohier, R.S. 251-252
Lev, Yvonne 238
Levy, Louise R. 261,262
Library Information System 81
Library-placed obstacles 57-58
Linder, Gloria A. 113-126
Lingwood, David 256
Linton, Anne 232

LIS *see* Library Information System
LISA 92
Lister Hill National Center for
  Biomedical Communications 23
Local databases 80-81,85-94
  costs 90-91
  database content 88-89
  evaluation 92
  hardware 89-90
  service 91
  software 89
  staffing 90-91
  see also MiniMEDLINE
Lowry, Glenn R. 221
Lucia, Joseph 246
Lyon, Sally 221

McDonell, W. Ellen 53-64,233
McGowan, Anna Thérèse 95-109
McNabb, Corrine R. 205-211
Macy Conference on Basic Science
  Education 18
Mainframe, defined 278
MALIMET 7
Malmgren, Margareta 242
Mancall, Jacqueline C. 256
Marcinko, Thomas 266
Marcus, Richard S. 262-263
Marketing 55,115-118,140,156-159
  barriers 118-120
Markoff, John 270
Massachusetts General Hospital Health
  Sciences Libraries 149-161
Matheson report 4,16,18,114
Mead Data Central 55,75-76
Meadow, Charles T. 222,226,263,264
Meadows, Nolan R. 244
Medical Library Association 32,37,40,
  42,137
Medical Subject Headings 7,16,24,40,
  42,73,119,120,121,122,123,127,
  130,132,134,141,143,153,154,183
  defined 279
  see also Permuted MeSH
  see also Tree Structures
MEDIS 38,67,75-76,153,160
MEDLARS 5,7,37,113,114,128,130,
  131,134,164,190,195
  see also MEDLINE
  see also National Library of Medicine

MEDLARS Subset Policy 85,87
MEDLARS subsets 125
MEDLEARN 23,131
MEDLINE 7,8,9,10,11,12,19,20,23,28,
  39,40,42,57,61,67,70,72,73,75,
  81,85-94,88,90,91,93,114,115,116,
  118,120,127,128,130-134,138,141,
  145,151,153,164,166,182,183,189,
  192,193,198
  see also MEDLARS
  see also National Library of Medicine
MEDLINE subsets *see* MEDLARS
  subsets
  see also Local databases
MEDUSA 9
Megabyte, defined 278
Megatrends 53-54
Menu-driven, defined 278
MeSH see Medical Subject Headings
MGH *see* Massachusetts General Hospital
Miastkowski, Stan 270-271
Microcomputer, defined 279
Microcomputer software 96-97
  database management software 96
  file management software 96
Miller, Naomi 236
Minicomputer, defined 279
MiniMEDLINE 9,10,11,67,81,86
MML *see* Moody Medical Library
Mnemonics, defined 279
Modem, defined 279
Moghdam, Dineh 257
Moody Medical Library *see* University
  of Texas Medical Branch, Galveston
Mooers' Law 58
Mount, Ellis 221
Moureau, Magdeleine 226
MYCIN 23
Myers, Frederick J. 189-196

National Cancer Institute 74
National Library of Medicine 5,9,11,20,
  23,28,37,39,57,67,72,74,76,78,81,
  85,87,92-93,113-126,127,128,
  130,131,132,133,138,153,164,190
  defined 279
  see also MEDLARS
  see also MEDLINE
Natural language, defined 279
Neelameghan, A. 252

Neubauer, David N. 197-203
Newlin, Barbara B. 264
Nicita, Mike 271
Nielsen, Brian 227
NLM *see* National Library of Medicine
Nowacek, George 181-187

Occasional end users 181-187
Offline, defined 279
Ojala, Marydee 221,227
O'Leary, Mick 264-265
Olson, Paul E. 236-237
Online, defined 279
Online searching
  as a subject and a skill 22-25
Online training *see* End user education
Operators *see* Boolean logic or Proximity Operators
Optical disk *see* Video disk
O'Reilly, James C. 227
Osegueda, Laura M. 248-249
Ostrum, G. Kenneth 257

Pacific Southwest Regional Medical Library Service 118
Pagell, Ruth A. 244
PAIS 92
PaperChase 9,55,56,67,72-73,80,86,87, 114,115,149-161
Paragraph *see* Field
Pascua-Cruz, Ma. Davina 252
Pask, Judith M. 243
PDQ *see* Protocol Data Query
Pearlman, Dara 271
Peart, Peter A. 228
Permuted MeSH 130,134
Personal information management 95-109
  building files 97-99
  defined 95
  file maintenance 106
  indexing 103-106
  retrieval 99-103
  software 96-97
Petrusha, Ron 271
Peyton, David 267-268
PFS: File & Report 108-109
  PFS: File 103
Phillips, Linda L. 247
Physician allies 118

Physician searching 181-187,189-196, 197-203,205-211
Pisciotta, Henry 242
Pollett, A.S. 265
Port, defined 279
Post processing, defined 279
Primary publishers
  part of information transfer process 3,6-7
Pritcher, Pamela N. 252
Pro-Search 78,86
Problem-based learning 25-28
Producer *see* Database producer
Promotion *see* Marketing
Protocol, defined 279
Protocol Data Query 74
Proximity operators, defined 279-280
Pruitt, Ellen 257-258
PsycINFO 71,138,145,198

Quality control 56-57
Queens Borough Central Library Staff 258
Queue, defined 280

RAM, defined 280
Rapp, Barbara A. 232,260
Record, defined 280
Reintjes, J. Francis 262-263
Richardson, Robert J. 252-253
Roberts, Steven K. 271
ROM, defined 280
Rosenberg, Howard A. 230
Roysdon, Christine 246
Rudin, Joan 253

Saunders, W.B., Co. 68
Scharf, Davida 253
Schoolman, Harold M. 232
Schwartz, Ronald D. 251
Schwerzel, Sharon W. 247
Sci-Mate 67,76-77,86,96,108-109,152
Science Citation Index 76
SDC/ORBIT 76,128
SDI, defined 280
Search intermediary *see* Intermediary
Search Strategy Outline 181-187
SearchHelper 67
SEARCHWARE 78

Seligman, Daniel 272
Sewell, Winifred 3-14,237,239
Shedlock, James 65-83,222
Shelton, Anita L. 253
Shepherd, Michael A. 265
Shuman, Bruce A. 222
Simon, Marjorie 163-178
SIRE 86
Siwolop, Sana 272
Slingluff, Deborah 238
Smartcom II 202
Smith, Linda C. 265-266
Smith, Ralph Lee 272
Smith, Rita H. 247
Snow, Bonnie 31-51,238,275-281
Soben, Phyllis 239
Social Science Citation Index 76
SOCIAL SCISEARCH 198
Software, defined 280
Somerville, Arleen N. 228
Sonk, Joseph 253
Sorting, defined 280
Source 55
SSO *see* Search Strategy Outline
Stabler, Karen Chittick 228
Stanford University Medical Center 113-126
Stangl, Peter 113-126
Stewart, Concetta M. 254
Stollak, Jay 253
Stones River Hospital 189
Stop words, defined 280
Stout, Catheryne 266
Struminger, Leny 247-248
Su, Valerie 113-126
Subset, defined 280
SUMC *see* Stanford University Medical Center
Summit, Roger K. 222
SUNY 5,9,53
Supplier *see* Database supplier

Tatalias, Jean 254
Teitelbaum, Sandra 237,239
Telecommunications, defined 280
Tenopir, Carol 222-223,226,272
Terminal, defined 280
Texas Instruments 787 terminal 190,191

Text word *see* Natural language
Text word searching 121,127,130,131, 134
Thesaurus, defined 281
Thompson, Benna Brodsky 223
Tidball, Charles S. 239
Tousignant, Dwight R. 239
TOXLINE 121,138
Trauth, Eileen M. 259
Trautman, Rodes 223
Tree Structures 40,120,121,122,123, 130,134,153
 see also Medical Subject Headings
 see also Permuted MeSH
Truncation, defined 281
Trzebiatowski, Elaine 248

U-Search 137-147
University of Maryland Health Sciences Library 85,93,163-178
University of Maryland study 5,6,8,9, 10,11
University of Minnesota Bio-Medical Library 137-147
University of North Carolina Health Sciences Library 96
University of Texas Medical Branch, Galveston 127-135
Usenko, Lydia 254
User-friendly, defined 281

Vaupel, Nancy 256
VDT, defined 281
Vendor
 defined 281
 part of information transfer process 3,8-9
 see also individual vendors
Vickery, A. 266
Video disk, defined 281
Vigil, Peter J. 258

Walton, Kenneth R. 254
Ward, Sandra N. 248-249
Washington University *see* BACS
Watters, Carolyn 265
Wehmeyer, Jeffrey M. 230
Weinberger, Marvin I. 219
Weise, Frieda O. 85-94

Westel, E. R. 261-262
Westling, Ellen R. 149-161
Wible, Joseph G. 113-126,267
Wiggins, Gary 249
Williams, Martha E. 224
Williams, Phil 224,267
Wilson, John H., Jr. 249
Wood, M. Sandra 215-273
Word processing, defined 281

Wozny, Lucy Anne 258-259
Wygant, Alice C. 127-135
Wykoff, Leslie W. 228

Yoder, Diane K. 257

Zarley, Craig 272-273
Zigmund, Claire F. 250

For Product Safety Concerns and Information please contact our EU representative GPSR@taylorandfrancis.com
Taylor & Francis Verlag GmbH, Kaufingerstraße 24, 80331 München, Germany